Situational Mediation

Sensible Conflict Resolution

Oliver Ross, J.D., Ph.D.

A subsidiary of Idyll Arbor, Inc., PO Box 720, Ravensdale, WA 98051
www.Idyllarbor.com

Issues Press Editor: Kenneth A. Lucas

To the best of our knowledge, the information and recommendations of this book reflect currently accepted practice. Nevertheless, they cannot be considered absolute and universal. Recommendations for particular individuals must be considered in light of the individual's needs, situations, and location of residency. The authors and publisher disclaim responsibility for any adverse effects resulting directly or indirectly from the suggested procedures, from any undetected errors, or from the reader's misunderstanding of the text.

ISBN 1-930461-02-X

Library of Congress Cataloging-in-Publication Data
Ross, Oliver, 1942-
  Situational mediation : sensible conflict resolution / Oliver Ross.
    p. cm.
  ISBN 1-930461-02-X (alk. paper)
  1. Conflict management. 2. Divorce mediation. 3. Family mediation. 4. Labor disputes. 5. Anger in the workplace. 6. Mediation and conciliation, Industrial.
I. Title.
  HM1126.R67 2003
  303.6'9--dc21

                                                                    2003007823

For my loving wife, Jocelyn, and
wonderful children: Greg, Drew, Kim, and Jeff.

For my blessed teachers,
Florence Ross and Michael Shapiro.

And for those who labored over the manuscript:
Idyll Arbor's Kenneth Lucas,
my son Drew
and my administrative assistant, Rhonda DePesa.

Contents

Introduction

Mediation is the process of resolving conflict through a neutral intermediary who helps the parties in a dispute resolve their differences. Usually the mediation involves discussions and negotiations facilitated by the mediator. There are several types of mediation. In this book I discuss a concept I call situational mediation, which combines the most powerful features of evaluative, collaborative, transformative, and humanistic mediation, and present the reader with suggestions for when each type of mediation will be most effective.

My first goal in writing this book is to show how anyone who is involved in a dispute can resolve it through this situational approach to mediation. Professional mediators can use the concepts, techniques, and procedures detailed in this book to help resolve divorce and other family conflicts. They can also use this approach to resolve workplace conflicts. For professional mediators the techniques apply equally well to both situations and I believe they will see how the situational approach will improve their effectiveness in helping parties resolve disputes sensibly and in finding durable results.

Those primarily engaged in other professions — attorneys, psychologists, and counselors — can use the situational approach to mediation to enhance their conflict resolution skills. Business owners, human resource directors, workplace managers, and others can use this approach to solve work-related and contractual disputes.

Another of my goals in writing this book is to help potential participants prepare for mediation. Mediation is new to most people. This book gives potential participants the information and insight needed to make informed decisions when determining whether to mediate and with whom.

My hope is that this book will help transform how people perceive conflict. I look forward to the day when society no longer looks upon conflict as threatening or dangerous but rather as an opportunity to learn, collaborate, and create. In this way we will all be peacemakers — helping ourselves and others create mutually beneficial, relationship-enhancing, and inexpensive out-of-court solutions.

The situational approach to mediation came about not by design but rather as a result of my gradual awareness that something important was lacking in other mediation approaches I had learned and practiced. I first learned to mediate in 1993 using an *evaluative* or *directive* approach. This was the first of three approaches to mediation I would learn in the next few years. Patterned after court-based settlement conferences, the evaluative approach calls for the mediator to conduct a series of joint and separate meetings with the parties and/or their attorneys. During these sessions the mediator evaluates the strengths and weaknesses of each participant's position and strives to direct participants toward settlement by force of reason and persuasion. The goal is to achieve settlement in conformity with the legal standards involved. Although I was familiar with this model from my background in law, although I was adept at evaluating cases and quickly learned how to direct participants toward settlement, I was uncomfortable with its heavy reliance on persuasion by the mediator and its preoccupation with settlement.

In 1994 I was trained in the *collaborative* or *facilitative* approach to mediation. This approach calls for the mediator to create a process primarily aimed at facilitating interaction and cooperation between participants. Here the mediator facilitates settlement by helping participants communicate and negotiate effectively, clarify their respective interests, and solve problems. Rather than directing participants toward settlement, as in the evaluative approach, the mediator facilitates collaboration. Settlement is important under this approach, but it's not the end-all it is under the evaluative model. I was excited by this approach and over the next few years integrated it into my practice. Nevertheless, I sensed that something was missing and continued to search for a more complete approach.

In 1998 I was schooled in a third approach to mediation, the *transformative* approach. Here the mediator watches for opportunities to foster empowerment and recognition. Empowerment occurs when participants learn or become aware of something about themselves or the situation in which they are involved. Recognition is fostered when the mediator helps participants understand and acknowledge their mutual concerns, needs, feelings, perceptions, and interests. It is hoped that the empowerment and recognition achieved during transformative mediation better equips participants to handle current as well as future conflict. From the outset, I realized that this approach was too extreme for me. In direct opposition to the evaluative approach, transformative mediators take no part whatsoever in directing participants toward settlement. With this approach, any agreement reached by participants is incidental.

It was then that I realized that the evaluative, facilitative, and transformative approaches were useful, but incomplete. They were all deficient in the application of three essential elements that I historically used with my background in law and psychotherapy: empathy, humility, and compassion. Time and again I saw how my expression of these qualities: (1) lifted participants above their emotions; (2) fostered collaboration, empowerment, and recognition; and (3) created an atmosphere in which meaningful change occurred in the ways people felt, thought, and behaved. Based on this realization, for the next several years I identified my approach to mediation as *humanistic.*

It wasn't until I was in the process of writing this book that I discovered the work of Dr. Mark Umbreit[1] in which he too identified his approach to mediation as humanistic and emphasized the importance of empathy and compassion.

---

[1] *Mediating Interpersonal Conflicts: A Pathway to Peace* (CPI Publishing, 1995).

However, I also discovered significant differences in our approaches. For instance, whereas Dr. Umbeit's approach routinely involves separate pre-mediation sessions between the mediator and each participant, my approach routinely involves joint sessions between the mediator and all participants; whereas Dr. Umbreit's approach calls for the mediator to be uniformly nondirective and otherwise transformative, my approach calls for the mediator to be selectively evaluuative, facilitative, and transformative, depending on the nature of the dispute and the participants involved.

It was at this point, when I realized that the best style of mediation depended on the current state of the mediation process, that I decided that my approach to mediation was best described as *situational*.

As detailed in the chapters that follow, situational mediation is adaptive to the nature of the dispute and the parties involved. For example, when mediating interpersonal disputes between executives who aren't getting along, situational mediators are predominately transformative, and rarely directive. However, when dealing with issues concerning division of assets and allocation of debts during divorce mediation, situational mediators are typically facilitative, at times directive, but all the while humanistic in terms of empathy, humility, and compassion.

Empathy occurs when the mediator demonstrates the willingness to share in a participant's emotions, thoughts, or perceptions. Recognizing that empathic interactions with participants are likely to garner trust and promote an overall atmosphere of mutual respect, situational mediators are quick to engage in and model this kind of behavior.

Humility takes place when the mediator promotes equality and reveals his or her own shortcomings. It is for this reason that situational mediators look for opportunities to self-disclose instances when they themselves experienced uncontrolled anger or otherwise reacted inappropriately.

Compassion is an attitude (or state of mind) exhibited when mediators are sympathetic and caring in response to a participant's suffering. Situational mediators understand that compassion produces a climate of positive benevolence.

Situational mediators recognize that most interpersonal disputes entail the loss or potential loss of relationships and that many participants are in one stage or another of a *grief process* with varying degrees of anger, sadness, and other emotions. Contrary to many mediators, who as a result of their training (or personal discomfort) disregard, avoid, or eschew any display of emotion, situational mediators view emotional outbursts as fertile ground in which to further the mediation process.

It can be successfully argued, then, that the situational approach maximizes mediation. It is aimed at leading participants to settlement while fostering opportunities for transformation. It is a sensible, real-life approach for resolving disputes and teaching effective methods of conflict resolution. Nevertheless, situational mediators recognize their limits, know the difference between helping and enabling, and respect the need for everyone to go through conflict in his or her own way. Situational mediators are interested in outcome but focus on *process*, trusting that whatever occurs will ultimately be to everyone's benefit.

The first section of this book includes seven chapters devoted to the mediation of family disputes. Chapters 1 through 6 pertain to divorce (a frequently mediated family dispute) and feature dialogue and commentary that illustrate and explain the concepts, procedures, and techniques typically involved in situationally mediating the divorce of couples who have minor children. Chapter 7 discusses the mediation of other types of family disputes, including those between parents and adult children, siblings, and same-sex partners. It also shows how the concepts, procedures, and techniques involved in mediating divorce are easily transferable to the mediation of other family disputes.

The second section of this book includes five chapters devoted to workplace and contract mediation. Chapters 8 through 11 deal with the mediation of disputes between key personnel, while Chapter 12 pertains to the mediation of disputes between parties to contracts. Here, readers will see how the situational approach can be applied to any workplace or contractual dispute, either between partners and other co-owners of businesses, employees and employers, or those that arise within and between social groups, educational institutions, and religious organizations.

The third and final section of this book deals with the management of anger and other emotions that commonly occur during mediation. Chapter 13 explains the origins of anger and other emotions while Chapter 14 presents effective ways to manage these emotions.

I want readers to not only understand situational mediation but to get a feel for it. However, the capacity to feel something is based on experience with it, and most people haven't experienced mediation. On the other hand, most people have experienced air travel and are aware that both mediation and air travel involve journeys to places known and unknown, liked and disliked. For this reason the reader will periodically notice comments pointing out the similarities between the mediation process and travel by airplane. My hope is that by use of the airline metaphor the reader will be able to understand how the situational approach can be used to resolve any type of conflict. So fasten your seatbelt, and prepare for takeoff.

Section I: Family Mediation

Part A: Divorce

Chapter 1:
Pre-mediation Consultation (*Pre-flight*)

John and Mary Smith arrive at my office for a pre-mediation consultation. Mary had called to arrange for the consultation, informing my assistant of her intent to divorce John. Just as passengers preparing to travel by airplane select a particular airline, flight, and seat number, people preparing for mediation such as Mary and John select a particular mediator, setting, and meeting schedule.

After briefly reviewing the intake forms (Appendix, page 272) each of them completed, I escort Mary and John to a conference room and begin the consultation.

DIALOGUE
"Let me start out by saying that although I'm glad to meet you both, it's always kind of awkward for me in the beginning because I imagine that this is not the happiest of occasions."

"Uh huh," Mary replies.

"You got that right," John says, caustically.

"Okay then. I see from Mary's intake form that a counselor, Jane Jones, referred you. Is she *your* counselor, Mary, or did she see both of you?"

"Just me. He wouldn't go," Mary answers.

"Did Jane give you any written information about me or Out-of-Court Solutions?"

"Yes. She gave me your brochure and some other material."

"And did you have a chance to review it?"

"Yes," Mary replies.

"What about you, John? Did you have a chance to look at this information or perhaps visit our Website?"

"No," he curtly replies.

"Then let me give you one of our brochures along with a list of frequently asked questions. And would it be helpful if I were to start by briefly telling you about my background?"

"I guess so," John says, indifferently.

"Mary?"

"Sure," she answers.

"I'm 59 years old and have four children, two from my first marriage which ended in divorce, and two from my second. I practiced law in California for 19 years, starting in 1969. After my divorce I began to look inward and went back to school at night to study psychology. In 1987 I sold my interest in the law firm I founded (which by that time had grown to about 140 people), took over the management of a family-owned distribution company, and continued my studies in psychology. I first achieved a Master's degree in Clinical Psychology. Then in 1993 I earned a Ph.D. in Human Behavior Psychology, sold my interest in the family-owned business, and pondered my next move.

"It was then that I became aware of a continuing legal education class in mediation. You see, I've come to believe that nothing happens by coincidence. In fact, I've come to define coincidence as 'God's way of remaining anonymous' because within a few hours of starting this class in mediation, I sensed that this was the kind of work I was meant to do.

"Since moving to Arizona in 1994, I've been a full-time mediator, helping people such as yourselves work through all of the legal, financial, tax, and parenting aspects of divorce, while remaining attentive to what is known as the 'grief process.' By this I mean the stages of grief we all go through when dealing with the loss of a significant relationship. You see, unless we choose to self-medicate through alcohol, drugs, food, work and so on, we all go from *denial* (this isn't really happening to me), to *anger, frustration,* and *resentment,* to *bargaining* (if you do this I'll do that), to *sadness* and *depression,* and finally into *acceptance.* In this acceptance phase, we eventually accept that this is the way things are."

After pausing momentarily to let this information sink in, I continue:

"These stages of grief don't happen sequentially; one doesn't necessarily follow the other. In fact, I remember during my divorce that one day I was angry as hell and the next day I was crying. I see that you're nodding your head, Mary. Do you relate to this?"

"Yes, I certainly do," she emphatically replies.

"And what about you, John?"

"I don't know," he says.

"Well, I see from your intake form that you answered 'yes' to the question 'Interest in reconciliation' while Mary answered 'no.' I don't want to be presumptuous, but this may indicate that you and Mary are in different stages in the grief process. I want you to know that I'm not making a judgment about this; there's nothing good or bad about it."

"I don't want a divorce! She should try harder! I can't believe she thinks divorce is good for our kids!" John insists, raising his voice.

"I hear you. So you want Mary to try harder to stay in the marriage?"

"Yeah!" John snaps back.

"And what about you, Mary?"

After a moment's contemplation, Mary responds: "I tried for a long time. He wouldn't go to counseling and now he says I'm the one who hasn't worked on it. I can't live with him anymore — with his drinking and all. I never know when he's going to yell at me or the kids."

"Oh sure, Mary. What about your boyfriend?" John asks, angrily.

"He's not my boyfriend. He's just a friend," Mary counters.

At this point I intervene, saying: "Hold on folks. Since part of my job as a mediator is to provide information, perhaps it would be helpful for you to know that I neither encourage nor discourage divorce. This is your decision alone, and you can take whatever time you need to make it."

"No, I need to do this now!" Mary insists.

"I hear you. So perhaps I could mention that here in Arizona, as in most other states, if one person wants a divorce there's literally nothing the other person can do to stop it. But the other person does have a choice as to how it's carried out. They can enter the legal system with separate lawyers or they can mediate — unless of course they use a paralegal service or do it themselves."

"I don't want to get involved with lawyers," John protests.

"I hear you, John. But could I ask you another question?"

"What?" he replies sullenly.

"Mary mentioned your drinking; would you tell me about that?"

"Oh that's nothing. I just have a couple of drinks after work," he curtly responds.

"Okay. What's your take on this, Mary?"

"He drinks every night. But I wouldn't call him an alcoholic. I just can't stand how he yells and…"

Mary begins to answer until John interrupts, adamantly claiming: "I drink a few beers, that's all. I'm not a drunk!"

"I hear you," I reply. "But if you choose to mediate with me, it's my job to be as certain as I can that both of you make fully informed decisions about each and every issue involved in ending your marriage. I'll explain this in detail at the beginning of the first session but, above all, I want you to know that assisting you both in making informed decisions is the crux of my job. So if at any time during the mediation I sense that either of you aren't able to do this, for any reason including alcohol use, may I have your permission to check it out with you so I'm clear that your decisions are fully informed ones?"

"Sure," Mary answers.

"Absolutely," John says, cavalierly.

"Thank you. And John, I'd like to share something with you about my life. I'm going to take a bit of a risk here, Mary, because I don't want you to interpret this as my taking sides. But I want to share something about my experience after my first wife told me that our marriage was over. Is that okay?" I ask both of them.

"Yes," Mary replies, leaning forward with apparent interest.

"I guess," John says, hesitantly.

"Thanks. Looking back I can see that it took me a good year and a half to get into the acceptance stage of the grief process. And even then I would periodically slip back into anger and sadness. Then, although I wouldn't have believed it was possible in the first year or so, I began to see the blessings in disguise. I began to see some of the ways in which my divorce was actually for the good. For example, I could see how I was becoming more self-reliant and a better father. And with each year that went by, more and more blessings became apparent."

"I don't see that happening," John maintains.

"Well," I respond, "I guess there are no guarantees in life, but that's what happened to me."

John merely shrugs, and after a moment or two I continue:

"Mary, I also see from your intake form that you are a home-maker. Would you tell me more about that?"

Straightening up in her chair and smiling demurely, she replies:

"Sure. About six years ago John and I decided it would be best for me to stay at home with the kids. Our son Charlie was having some problems at school and I wanted to spend more time helping him study. Before that I was employed as a bookkeeper."

"How long were you a bookkeeper?"

"Oh, even before we were married."

"Are you planning to go back to work?"

Nervously glancing at John, Mary says: "I don't know… I'm really not sure, with Charlie and our daughter Sarah needing me to be home."

I then turn to John and inquire, "What do you think about

that?"

"She's gonna have to!" he loudly asserts.

"Do you have a time frame in mind?"

"The sooner the better," he replies.

"And what about your children?" I ask John.

Looking downward, John responds: "I'm not sure what to do with them."

"Okay, but let me ask you this: if Mary chose to stay home with them, are you open to talking about financial support for her?"

"Depends," John responds.

"On what?" I inquire.

"On how much."

"I see. And yet what I'm hearing is that you're open to discussing this issue, right?"

"Yeah. I guess so," he answers.

COMMENTARY

Even after seven years as a mediator, I still feel awkward every time I begin a divorce consultation. Yet I am very grateful for this feeling because it helps remind me to be humble, empathic, and compassionate while helping people make informed decisions about ending their marriage. After all, I'm a stranger entering into the lives of people who are going through difficult times. Some are embarrassed and ashamed, others are scared, hurt, angry, sad, or depressed. The awkwardness I feel serves as a recurrent and welcome reminder to respond compassionately to people who find themselves in these circumstances.

My overall goal at the beginning of a consultation is to give people the information they need to decide whether mediation, and my approach to it, is appropriate for them. At the same time I need to satisfy myself that each potential participant has the ability to make fully informed decisions. Thus, I made sure to give John the written material Mary had obtained from her counselor, and went into detail about my background, credentials, and approach to mediation. Also wanting to give potential participants a sense of how I go about doing my job as mediator, I disclosed appropriate personal information about my own divorce and provided legal information about how, in most states, one person cannot stop another from obtaining a divorce.

During the initial stages of a consultation, I also want to *normalize* the grief process. The grief process is one that takes us through the emotions and trepidations of healing from a loss, including the loss of a marital relationship. While we may be aware that a loss has taken place, or is about to take place, it isn't until we actually go through certain stages of grief that we can truly deal with that loss, and perhaps even learn and grow from it. Thus, during consultations I make it a point to introduce this process to potential participants, as I did with John and Mary when I said that in addition to helping them "work through all of the legal, financial, tax, and parenting aspects of divorce," I would also be attentive to their grief process. I want to make it clear from the beginning that painful and confusing emotions are normal during divorce and that part of my job as mediator is to help them transition through these feelings.

There have been numerous studies done on the emotions involved in suffering a loss. Sigmund Freud began with the concept of having to do "grief work." Later, others came up with their own versions of this process. In 1982, J.W. Worden wrote of the "four tasks of mourning."[2] These include accepting the reality of the loss, experiencing the pain, adjusting to a life without your loved one, and finally being able to invest your emotional energy into a new life.

Perhaps the best-known theory on the grief process is Elisabeth Kübler-Ross's "Five Stages of Grief."[3] Kübler-Ross defined these stages as Denial, Anger, Bargaining, Depression, and

---

[2] Worden, J.W. (1982) *Grief Counseling and Grief Therapy: A Handbook for the Mental Health Practitioner.* Springer Publishing Co., New York.

[3] Kübler-Ross, Elisabeth. (1997) *On Death & Dying: What the Dying Have to Teach Doctors, Nurses, Clergy, and Their Own Families.* Simon Shuster, New York.

Acceptance. In the first stage, Denial, people tend to deny that the loss has taken place and may withdraw from their usual social contacts. This stage may last a few moments, hours, days, or even longer. Anger is the second stage. Here the grieving person may become furious at the person who inflicted the hurt, or at the world for letting it happen, or he may be angry with himself for letting the event take place.

The third stage is Bargaining. Here the grieving person may make a bargain with herself or perhaps her Higher Power — "If I do this, will you take away the loss?" In the fourth stage people feel numb, although anger and sadness remain underneath. This is called Depression and is experienced to greater and lesser degrees. The final stage of the grief process is Acceptance. This is when the anger, sadness, and mourning have tapered off and the grieving person comes to terms with the reality of the loss.

Most researchers, including Worden and Kübler-Ross, agree that there are no absolute beginnings and endings in the grief process and that each person will experience his or her grief differently. While one person may spend a great deal of time and energy in depression, another may move quickly to acceptance. Also these stages can overlap and recur. A person may have gotten over most of the anger involved in their loss and then out of nowhere something can occur that will send them right back into the throes of the rage they first experienced. Most often, a person feels several of these emotions at the same time, perhaps in different degrees. The only certainty is that the grief process must take place for healing to occur.

In situations involving divorce and legal separation, the grief process is at the heart of situational mediation. Recognizing this, situational mediators are usually facilitative and humanistic in their approach; they foster communication and collaboration, and consistently respond to participants with empathy, humility, and compassion. On occasion they are also evaluative; for example, when participants stubbornly disregard plain facts or basic laws, situational mediators do not hesitate to set them straight — albeit with humility and compassion. Finally, situational mediators are also transformative in terms of fostering empowerment and recognition, but not to the extent that they are disinterested in settlement; participants in divorce and legal separation mediation expect to achieve final settlement and situational mediators respond accordingly.

In consultations, such as with John and Mary, I want participants to become aware of and expect the feelings that go along with the grief process. For as C.S. Lewis said: "In grief, nothing 'stays put.' One keeps on emerging from a phase, but it always recurs. Round and round. Everything repeats."[4]

I also want to *normalize* the grief process. This is why I disclose my personal experiences with it during my own divorce. Finally, I want to assure potential participants that as their mediator I will be attentive to their grief and respond to it with humility, empathy, and compassion.

Upon their arrival at my office, potential clients are asked to complete a "Confidential Client Intake Information" form (Appendix, page 272). Most readily comply, but occasionally some have refused. On one occasion, a husband initially refused to complete the form, proclaiming that he wasn't going to "help her get rid of me." He nonetheless agreed to participate in the consultation and shortly thereafter completed the form. Another time a wife wanted to retain her anonymity until such time as she was assured that we could accommodate her special need for privacy. In her position as a judge, she needed to remain completely anonymous, even to my staff.

Prior to a consultation, I briefly review each person's intake form as to the following:

Physical safety issue: Yes or No.
Mary and John both answered "no." Had either of them answered "yes" or not answered at all, I would have sought further information. For example, I might have asked, "I see that you marked 'yes' as to physical safety being an issue. Would you be

---

[4] Lewis, C.S. (1963) *A Grief Observed*. Seabury.

willing to tell me more about that?"

In mediation, each participant must be able to make decisions free of *physical* intimidation. I stress this to the extent that my staff is trained to decline consultations with couples that have a history of physical abuse or domestic violence. Although participants must also be able to make decisions without feeling *mentally* or *emotionally* intimidated, this kind of intimidation is usually more subtle and thus harder to detect — and on some level is likely to exist in any troubled marriage. Recognizing this, I respond to these situations by taking additional steps to foster informed decision-making.

For example, I would encourage any participant that I experience as being emotionally intimidated to employ an attorney, financial consultant, counselor, or someone else who could offer support and/or sound advice. In more extreme situations, I insist that they get this assistance.

When I have serious or lingering doubts about someone's capacity to make informed decisions on his or her own, I go so far as to condition my involvement upon the retention of legal counsel. The overall challenge here is for mediators to assess the capacity of each potential participant to make fully informed decisions, and when found lacking to take appropriate action to enhance it.

Court Actions that have been filed: Restraining Order? Order of Protection?
By their very nature, court orders prohibiting contact or other behaviors preclude mediation. My staff is on alert for these situations and will not arrange a consultation unless and until the parties and their attorneys agree to suspend or have the court vacate such orders.

Employer/Occupation:
Answers to this question such as "none" or as with Mary, "homemaker," usually indicate that spousal support will be an issue. Formerly known as alimony, spousal support can be a

highly charged and time-consuming issue. At the consultation stage I merely want to touch on this issue, probing lightly to ascertain the degree of emotional reactivity it evokes. This gives me some insight into this issue without having it boil over beyond the scope of the consultation. It also gives me the information I need to take this issue into account when estimating the time and cost of the mediation.

My questions to John were an attempt to gauge his level of reactivity about this issue. High reactivity usually results in additional time and cost. John's willingness to discuss support for Mary led me to believe that he was psychologically prepared to deal with it, a major hurdle for some participants. This being the case, I concluded that John would not be highly reactive when the time came to discuss spousal support for Mary.

Interest in Reconciliation: Yes or No.
Rather than answering "yes" as did John or "no" as did Mary, some people don't answer at all. Sometimes they merely overlook this portion of the form. Other times they aren't ready to make this decision and merely write in a question mark to denote their uncertainty. Whatever the reason for these non-answers, it would be less than compassionate to rush people into mediation, and thus situational mediators typically inquire further into the couple's willingness to seek marriage counseling.

Separated: Yes or No. If Yes, indicate date.
There is usually an inverse relationship between the length of time a couple has been separated and their level of emotional reactivity toward each other. When still living together, it's likely that one spouse (like John) is newer to the grief process and thus more likely than the other (Mary) to react emotionally. Conversely, the longer the separation, the greater the likelihood that both people have grieved to the stage of being less emotionally reactive to each other. Of course there are always exceptions; some couples remain highly reactive throughout mediation and beyond.

Information about your children: Date of Birth.

During mediation, parenting arrangements (including legal custody, time-sharing arrangements and child support) must be formulated for minor children. These issues, as with spousal support, are often emotionally charged. Thus at the consultation stage, I ask questions that help me get a basic sense of the couple's reactivity about these issues.

Child(ren) told about separation or divorce: Yes or No.

Often parents want to wait until they actually separate before telling their child(ren) that they intend to divorce. When people answer "no" to this question, I offer them written reference material on how to tell them. If they answer "yes," I usually defer any questions about offspring (how they are getting along in school, for instance) until the first mediation session.

How did you find out about Out-of-Court Solutions?

Most people find out about our mediation services from former clients, counselors (as Mary did), and the Out-of-Court Solutions' Website. Occasionally, people are referred by their attorneys — but usually not until they are financially and emotionally exhausted from protracted litigation.

In this consultation, John's drinking concerned me in terms of his ability to make informed decisions. As was mentioned, the ability of participants to make informed decisions is a prerequisite to mediation but all too often addiction precludes it. Recognizing the prevalence of addiction in our society, however, I do not automatically decline to mediate these situations. Rather, I focus on each participant's ability to make informed decisions, and continue to mediate as long as I perceive that both participants have this ability. If at any time I were to conclude that a participant's decision-making ability was materially impaired, I would insist that he or she obtain assistance from an attorney. In the absence of such assistance, I would terminate the mediation.

One additional comment about John's drinking. You will note that I asked permission to monitor my concern about it, asking both John and Mary's permission to "check it out" during the mediation. As I will explain further in Chapter 2, situational mediators consistently strive to be humble and thus always ask for permission to inquire about personal matters such as this—we never want to presume authority.

Finally, situational mediators also strive to be compassionate and therefore look for opportunities to instill hope. Thus, realizing that John was in the early stages of the grief process, I talked about the blessings in disguise that became clear following my divorce and grief. My divorce, as with several other events in my life, initially appeared catastrophic but turned out to be exactly what I needed at the time to progress toward becoming a more complete person.

DIALOGUE
I continue the consultation as follows:

"So folks, do you have any questions?"

"Yes, what does it cost?" John asks.

"Well, it might be helpful if I answered that question by explaining the major differences between mediation and using separate lawyers. Okay?"

"Alright," John says.

"Mary?"

"Sure," she replies.

Standing up and moving to a flipchart, I say:

"Since a picture is worth a thousand words, let me draw a picture of what it looks like to litigate using separate lawyers:

$$\Box_1$$

$$\Box_4 \quad \Box_2 \quad \Box_3 \quad \Box_5$$

"The judge is number 1. The attorneys are 2 and 3. And you folks are 4 and 5. Now who do you think is in control of decision-making in this process?"

"The judge?" Mary responds.

"Yes, ultimately, but here in Arizona it's likely to take seven to fifteen months for you to get a trial courtroom and see a judge. Who do you think is in control of decision-making during that time?"

"The attorneys," Mary replies.

"That's right. When I practiced law, I saw myself as an expert trained to make decisions for my clients. Sure, I would listen to them, but I was definitely in charge, making decisions as to how to fight for my client's rights."

Pausing momentarily, I continue:

"Now here's a picture of what mediation typically looks like:"

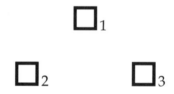

"Here, the mediator is number 1. And you folks are 2 and 3. Whom do you think is in control of decision-making in this process?"

"We are," Mary replies.

"Right," I confirm, adding, "It's not my job to make decisions for you or John. My job is to help each of you make fully informed decisions on your own. I do this by helping you communicate and negotiate effectively, by offering you different options and alternatives for resolving whatever issues there are between you. I also provide you with legal, financial, tax, and other information. But you will make all of the decisions. Any questions about this?"

"No," Mary answers.

"Nope," John replies.

"Okay, then as to cost. The difference between mediation and using separate lawyers can be described in this way. Whenever attorneys have anything to do with each other—telephone calls, letter writing, or legal work of any kind — they charge their clients for it. Additional charges result whenever attorneys call or write their clients, or engage in discovery procedures such as written questions, oral depositions, and so on. Clients are also charged for court conferences and hearings, as well as the time spent for the actual trial. So it's no secret that litigation is very expensive. All you have to do is to count the number of dollar signs in this diagram to see why."

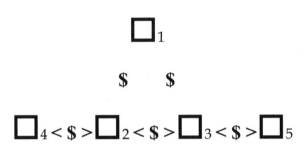

"If you haven't already done so I encourage each of you to call an attorney or two and see what they would charge."

"I already have," John counters.

"Good. What did he or she say?"

"He wanted a $2,500 retainer, and then would bill me from there."

"So together you would spend $5,000 right off the bat, correct?" I ask.

"Yep!" he replies, curtly.

"Did this attorney estimate what you would be likely to spend from start to finish?"

"About $7,500, but he said he couldn't be sure."

"And if Mary retained an attorney, she would spend about the same amount, right?"

"I guess so."

"So together you would spend about $15,000?"

"Yep, that's right!" John says.

"Okay. Let me now explain the costs involved in mediation:

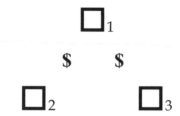

"There are two instances in which you will spend money here in mediation. The first is for the time I spend in meeting with both of you and in preparing a settlement agreement. I usually meet with people in a series of two-hour sessions. When children are involved it typically takes four or five sessions to cover everything—division of assets, allocation of debts, parenting, child and spousal support. Some people reach agreement quickly and spend less time; others take more. So the actual time we spend together depends entirely on you. So too is the frequency of our meetings. Some couples want to meet once a week, while others are more comfortable meeting once every two or three weeks.

"After we've worked through everything, I'll prepare a comprehensive settlement agreement covering everything you have decided about your assets and debts, parenting, child and spousal support. It typically takes me about five hours to prepare this agreement, and at the last session we will go over it line by line, page by page to make any final changes. However, as a matter of principle, I won't let you sign it at that time.

"The reason for this is twofold: first, not wanting you to feel any pressure to sign, I'll mail the revised version to each of you so you can review it carefully at your leisure; second, I want you to have a chance, if you choose, to have it reviewed by legal counsel. Having said that, the decision to do so is exclusively yours. Remember, in mediation you make all of the decisions. My job is to give you this kind of information so that you are making fully informed decisions.

"I might also add that this is only one way in which you may decide to use legal counsel; during the course of mediation you may want to consult with an attorney as to other issues. That's perfectly okay, and can be very helpful in some situations, as I'll explain in detail during the first session if you choose to mediate with me.

"The second instance in which you may spend money here is for the preparation of court documents. We can prepare all of the legal documents necessary to file and complete the divorce. During the first session I'll explain how the court process works, how long it takes, and how much it costs. Okay, any questions about any of this?"

"What do we bring with us?" Mary inquires.

"You won't need to bring anything for the first session. But after that I'll be giving you homework at the end of each session. I'll give each of you forms so that you can list all of your assets and debts, and other forms to budget your monthly expenses over the next year or so. This will help you prepare for each session, and usually saves a lot of time. Any other questions?"

"No," Mary replies.

"Not right now," John says.

"The last major difference between mediation and litigation is the effect on yourselves and your children. Having been a trial lawyer for 19 years I'm well aware that the adversarial process is likely to increase fear, tension, and hostility. When lawyers take control of a case, they typically discourage direct communication between clients. And when communication stops, fear increases. Remember that the legal system is adversarial and lawyers are trained to fight for their clients. Thus, tension and hostility are bound to increase. On the other hand, mediation is specifically intended to promote communication while reducing tension and hostility."

Pausing for a moment, I continue:

"I call the tension and hostility that result from the adversarial process 'nuclear fallout' because it not only falls on you, but also on your children. In fact, this is one of the primary reasons why I do this work. As a mediator I'm blessed with the opportunity to spare children from the 'fallout' that results from the adversarial process."

"I don't want to fight with you!" Mary asserts while plaintively looking at John.

"Look, Mary, do whatever the hell you want. You always do!" John exclaims.

"Wait a minute, John. Can I ask you a question?"

"What?"

"You make it sound like you don't have a choice. But you seem like a capable guy, and I'm wondering if you really feel like a victim—someone who is helpless?"

"No, but Mary's calling all the shots here," John replies.

"I hear you. But please remember that my job is to make certain as best I can that both you and Mary are making fully informed decisions. So I need to know if you are willing to do that."

"Oh, I'll make decisions all right. But Mary may not like them!" John asserts.

"So you're willing to participate, to be involved in making decisions?"

"Yep."

"And what about you, Mary? Do you think you can make fully informed decisions even if John doesn't agree with you, or gets angry?"

"That's what I've been working on in my counseling sessions," she responds.

COMMENTARY

As a trial lawyer I saw firsthand the destructiveness that is likely to result from litigation. I saw how it drains clients emotionally as well as financially, and how it affects children and other family members. I also saw this when I was the client in my own divorce. The truth is that ultimately most divorce cases settle, but usually not before months or years of expensive, energy-draining litigation. Sadly the adage that "in lawsuits no one wins except the lawyers" is most often true. This is one of the reasons why mediation is becoming increasingly popular.

Attorneys for participants can and often do take part in the mediation process, but as *consultants* rather than *combatants*. Indeed, I welcome the involvement of attorneys in this manner, and encourage clients to consult with them with respect to any doubts they may have during mediation and, certainly, before they sign a settlement agreement. During the consultation with Mary, I determined that she intended to rely on her counselor for support in making decisions. Nevertheless, I wouldn't hesitate to suggest that she, or John, consult with legal counsel should either of them have difficulty deciding any issue on their own.

It's not unusual for potential clients to act out their anger, as when John lashed out at Mary, telling her to "do whatever the hell you want!" Nor is it uncommon for other emotions to surface during a consultation, including resentment, remorse, sadness, and depression. As will be detailed in Chapter 14, there are many ways for mediators to help participants manage their emotions.

During the consultation with Mary and John, I helped John manage his anger by asking questions about his view of himself as a "victim." Knowing that people who perceive themselves as victims try to compensate for their feelings of helplessness by becoming angry and blaming others, I attempted to respond to John compassionately, while concurrently assessing his ability to make fully informed decisions.

DIALOGUE

I continue the consultation by providing both John and Mary with a copy the *Agreement to Mediate* (see Appendix, page 273). After giving them a few minutes to read the Agreement, I continue:

"As you see, the first paragraph says that you will arrive on time and give us at least 24 hour's advance notice if you have to postpone or cancel a session. The next paragraph deals with fees and costs. My fee is currently $220 per hour and I don't require a retainer. It's pay as you go except for a two-hour deposit that will be applied to the time it takes me to prepare your settlement agreement. The third paragraph states that both of you are responsible for the fees, but can agree to divide it in any way you choose.

"So if you were to spend a total of nine hours with me in session, and it took me another five hours to prepare your agreement, together you would spend $3,080 for mediation. It could be less or it could be more, depending on how quickly you reach agreement. Then, if you want me to prepare your court documents, you would spend another $500 (not including the filing fees charged by the court). So as you can see, although mediation isn't cheap, it's definitely inexpensive compared to using separate lawyers. In mediation you're likely to spend a fraction of the cost of litigation. In fact if you compare the diagram for using mediation to the diagram showing the use of separate lawyers, you can see how mediation typically costs no more (and sometimes a good deal less) than two-fifths or 40% of the cost of litigation. Okay so far?"

"Yep," John replies.

Mary merely nods her head, indicating "yes."

"The fourth paragraph deals with *confidentiality* and I'd like to explain this. Here in Arizona (as in many states) anything said or written during mediation is strictly confidential, meaning that if you were not able to reach full agreement through mediation, nothing that went on here could be used later on in court. Last year I mediated 58 divorces and only four didn't fully resolve. But let's say that you were one of the few that didn't reach full agreement and had to use separate lawyers. Nothing that went on here could be used in court. I couldn't be brought in to say 'John said this,' or 'Mary said that,' and a judge couldn't order me to produce my notes in court. So you have this wonderful safety net of confidentiality.

"So folks, where would you like to go from here? I could answer any other questions you have, or perhaps you would like me to leave the room so you can have time to talk about this?"

"No, that won't be necessary," Mary says, adding, "I want to do this, John!"

"Okay, whatever you say," John replies.

Chapter 2:
The Journey Begins (*Taking Off*)

Two weeks after their consultation, John and Mary arrived at my office for their first mediation session. They were about to begin their journey in mediation, which as with airline travel entails rules and procedures aimed at ensuring safety and reducing anxiety. For example, just as passengers on an airplane are instructed as to policies regarding seatbelts and emergency exits, participants in mediation are informed about the use of legal counsel, private sessions, etc.

DIALOGUE
After briefly reviewing their intake forms, I begin the session:
"I hope that you are both well, and unless you have something that you want to cover right away, I have an agenda in mind for today's session. I'd like to write it on the flipchart and then explain it to you. Okay?"

"Sure," Mary replies.

"Why not," John says.

Still standing, I write *Tentative Agenda* at the top of a flipchart page and continue:

"I'm going to call this a 'Tentative Agenda' because if it works for you we'll use it. If it doesn't, we'll figure out something else.

"The first thing I'd like to do involves the *Rules and Procedures* (Appendix, page 274) which govern mediation, at least the way I conduct mediation. We'll invest about 15 or 20 minutes going over each of them in detail. However, my experience is that doing this literally saves hours because it provides a map, if you will, for the mediation. Let me put it another way. Let's say that we all jump in a car to take a trip together, say to the East Coast. Wouldn't we want a map to get us there as quickly, inexpensively, and smoothly as possible in terms of stress and strain?"

"Uh huh," John murmurs.

Mary nods her head, indicating "yes."

"Well these *Rules and Procedures* provide that kind of map for the mediation. John, I remember from our consultation that you're interested in reconciliation, but I imagine that if that can't happen, you might still share in the goal of getting through this quickly, inexpensively, and smoothly. Is that right?"

"Yeah. She wants to do this, and I'm not going to fight her," John states, dejectedly.

Sitting down and facing John, I say: "Okay, but let me be clear about this. Are you saying that since Mary wants a divorce, you're going to participate in this process, getting the information you need to make fully informed decisions?"

"Yep. But Mary may not like what I decide," John replies.

"I hear you. But having decided to mediate, I take it that you want to get this done quickly and inexpensively, is that right?"

"Definitely!" John exclaims.

"Good. And what about you, Mary? Do you share in this goal?"

"Sure," she responds.

Standing up and moving to the flipchart, I begin to talk while writing the next agenda item:

"The next thing I'd like to do is what I call *Getting Current*."[5] While sitting down, I continue:

"At this point I'm going to ask each of you to tell me about your situation from your own perspective. My experience is that we all see things a little differently. We all have different points of view. What I would like each of you to do is to share with me, from your own perspective, what you may have already talked about, and perhaps decided. These decisions often serve as

---

[5] I learned this term during mediation training conducted by James C. Melamed, Esq. founder of the Mediation Center in Eugene, Oregon, and a world-class mediator.

building blocks for making other, even larger decisions. I'd also like to hear about what in your minds is still undecided; in other words, the issues as you see them. In addition, if you are willing, I'd like to hear about your concerns. Most people come into conflicts such as this with real concerns, if not worries and fears. I would like you to tell me what your concerns are, or perhaps what you are fearful of. Finally, I'd like to hear about your goals, for you and for your children. What would you like to see as results or outcomes of this mediation? So I'm going to ask each of you to share with me everything and anything you can to get me current with you. Okay?"

"I guess so... I'll try to remember everything," Mary says.

"I know it's a lot to remember. But don't worry. I'll prompt you by asking questions."

"Good," she says, appearing to relax a bit.

"Okay then. I have one more request. Would you let each other talk without interruption? I know that this can be hard. I remember situations when I was personally involved in a conflict, and someone said something that I experienced as hurtful or painful, or just not true. Before I knew it my old lawyer-self came back and I jumped right in, interrupting, wanting to 'set the record straight.' I'm asking you to do your best not to interrupt each other. Okay?"

"Yes, I'll try," Mary answers.

"Yep," John says.

"Great. Yet knowing that we're all human and can slip, may I have your permission to remind you of this if I hear either of you interrupting the other?"

"Yes," John and Mary reply, simultaneously.

"Thank you," I say.

Standing and moving to the flipchart, I resume:

"After the *Getting Current* portion I'm going to check in with you about any *Immediate Concerns*. These are the things that you feel are urgent and need immediate attention. My experience is that most people have a hard time concentrating on the other things that need to be handled if they have something urgent on their minds. Now I'll probably hear about anything urgent during the *Getting Current* portion, but I always want to list *Immediate Concerns* as an agenda item to make certain that we cover them first."

Continuing, I write the next four agenda items:

"The other items that need to be handled are: *Assets*, that is, how your marital assets will be divided. *Debts*, that is, how they will be allocated between you. *Parenting*, which includes everything from legal custody, to how you will spend time with your children (weekdays, weekends, holidays, and vacations) to child support. In fact, if I were to list them, there are probably no fewer than 100 parenting issues we will need to cover. The fourth large area we will be dealing with is *Spousal Support*. As I recall from our consultation, this is an issue for you folks, right?"

"Yes," Mary replies.

"Yep," John replies, contentiously.

Pausing for a moment, I go on:

"The only other thing I want to cover is the court process. I'll explain how it works in terms of the legal documents required, the time it takes, and the cost.

"Okay then. After the *Getting Current* portion, and addressing any of your immediate concerns, I'm not sure which area we'll cover next. In fact, you folks will decide what we cover next, whether it is *Assets*, *Debts*, *Parenting*, or *Spousal Support*. It's not for me to decide, for as I'll explain in just a few minutes, you will be making all of the decisions here, including the order in which we handle these items. So any questions about this?"

"No," Mary replies.

John merely shakes his head, indicating "no."

"So can we use this agenda as a way to start off?"

"Fine," John answers.

"Yes," Mary responds.

"Good. Here's a copy of the *Rules and Procedures* for each of you. Please take a few minutes to read them, and then I'll talk about each of them."

COMMENTARY

My experience is that most participants are relieved when I get down to business, promptly offering an agenda. Some people have waited months if not years to begin the process of divorce and are anxious to get started. Others are in no rush, preferring to slowly acclimate while I explain the *Rules and Procedures*. Similar to airline passengers who appreciate the pilot announcing anticipated weather conditions, arrival times, and the like, most participants in mediation are relieved to know what's in store for them.

For these reasons, situational mediators and most facilitative mediators regularly set an agenda. On the other hand, most evaluative and transformative mediators do not. Evaluative mediators are likely to introduce themselves and promptly proceed to separate sessions with each participant. Transformative mediators deem any type of agenda to be directive and thus inappropriate.

A flipchart is an important tool for a situational mediator. It is used to (1) organize a session, i.e., a *Tentative Agenda*; (2) highlight issues such as division of assets, allocation of debts, etc.; (3) explain such concepts as *informed decisions*; (4) focus everyone's attention on particular issues; and (5) intervene on emotional outbursts.

Often, all it takes to end an angry exchange between participants is for the mediator to stand up, move to the flipchart, and begin to write. Indeed, this is one of many instances in which mediators need to be conscious of the strategic importance of standing and sitting.

I always make it a point to sit down when explaining the *Getting Current* portion of the first session. When asking people to share their perspectives, especially their concerns, worries, and fears, I want to be humble, demonstrating as best I can that we are all very human, subject to error and emotion. My experience is that this can best be accomplished when I sit down, physically putting myself on an equal level with everyone else. This is why I sat down when John dejectedly answered one of my questions by saying, "She wants to do this, and I'm not going to fight her." I sensed that he had crossed a psychological threshold in terms of being willing to accept Mary's decision to divorce and participate in mediation.

Another way for mediators to demonstrate humility is to ask participants in advance for permission to say or do certain things. For example, having asked for permission to remind them about letting each other talk without interruption, I can respectfully intercede later on if, for example, one person were to repeatedly interrupt the other.

I also make it a point to always help participants establish shared goals, as I did with John and Mary when I asked if they both wanted to get through mediation quickly, inexpensively, and smoothly. This too can be used to intervene later on if participants repeatedly argue or otherwise veer off-track. This is a goal that is more or less shared by a majority of participants. Indeed, only once during the past seven years have I had a person disagree with it.

In mediation, time is money. Recognizing this, I always use the word *invest* when talking about the time it will take to explain the *Rules and Procedures*. I want participants to recognize that the money spent during this time is truly an investment in the future. Without this, the mediation is apt to stray off course and unnecessary time and expense could result.

As I mentioned in the introduction, my goal in writing this book is to help people understand the situational approach to mediation, not to explain the many different procedures and time requirements of courts in each state.[6] Thus, although I did go through this with Mary and John, I will not describe that part here or elsewhere in this book.

DIALOGUE
Noticing that John and Mary are finished reading the *Rules and*

---

[6] The American Bar Association provides information about divorce in all 50 states at www.abanet.org/family/familylaw.

Procedures, I continue:

"The first paragraph explains what I do and don't do as a mediator. My job as your mediator is broken up into several parts. One part helps you communicate and negotiate effectively. I know from personal experience that my emotions often get in the way of self-expression and hearing others clearly. It's difficult to communicate when in the midst of emotional turmoil. Knowing this, part of my job as your mediator is to help you deal with the emotions that are likely to surface during mediation, so that you communicate and negotiate as effectively as possible and stay on course toward your goals.

"Another part of my job is to offer you options and alternatives, different ways of resolving whatever issues there are between you. After all, with my background in law, business, and psychology, there's likely to be some options or alternatives I can offer for your consideration which will individually and then collectively make sense."

Pausing momentarily, I continue:

"Yet another part of my job as your mediator is to provide legal, financial, and tax information. However, I want you to clearly understand that I will provide you with legal *information* but I will not give you legal *advice*. When I practiced law, I would give legal advice such as, 'I think you should do this or you shouldn't do that.' If you were to hear me say something like that as your mediator, you would know that I had slipped into the role of attorney—which is not my role. Sure, I'll provide you with a lot of legal information based on my understanding of the law in certain areas. But I won't be providing you this information for the purpose of telling you what you should or shouldn't do. Rather, I'll provide it for the sole purpose of letting you compare it to what you think is fair.

"You see, laws in this country are supposed to be—if you can take politics out of them—nothing more than 'community standards of fairness.' And by that I mean what the local, state, or federal communities think is fair in various circumstances. Here in mediation, I'll give you written information and tell you about my understanding of the law as it pertains to divorce, but only for the purpose of making certain that you can compare it to what you're thinking is fair. In this way, you can make fully informed decisions. Okay? Any questions about this?"

"Nope," John answers.

"No," Mary replies.

Standing up and moving to the flipchart to write the words *Informed Decisions*, I continue:

"I can sum up everything I've just said in these two words: *Informed Decisions*. In fact, I always write these two words on the flipchart, as I've just done, and leave them in plain sight during the mediation because they will remind all of us of what my job is and isn't as your mediator. It's not my job to make any decisions for you. I am not here as an attorney or a judge. Nor am I here to say what you should or shouldn't do, who wins, who loses, who's right, or who's wrong. The essence of my job is to try as best as I can, using my head and my senses, to assist each of you in making fully informed decisions. Is that clear?"

"Yes," Mary responds.

"Yeah," John says.

"Good. So let me ask you a trick question that I always ask at this point: Do you think my job is to make sure that you make *fair* decisions?"

"I don't think so," Mary says, hesitantly.

"No," John replies.

"That's right. You folks will be deciding what's fair, not me. My job is to help you communicate and negotiate, explore different options and alternatives, and provide the information needed to make fully informed decisions on your own."

I then add that, "The last sentence of the first paragraph in the *Rules and Procedures* concerns how you might want to use legal counsel during mediation to make informed decisions. In fact, there are two instances in which I will encourage you to consult with legal counsel. The first is if you have any doubt at any time about a particular issue. Let's say that I've provided you with legal information about, say, division of assets. We've discussed it, and perhaps even explored various alternatives for resolving it. But after all is said and done, let's say that one or both of you remains ambivalent and unable to make a decision. At that time I might turn to that person and ask him or her if it would be a good idea to consult with legal counsel.

"I'm not suggesting that you must retain an attorney and pay the large retainer fees they typically require. All I would be encouraging you to do is consult with an attorney to get legal advice or more information. In fact, I maintain a list of attorneys for this purpose. I call the attorneys on this list 'mediation friendly attorneys,' and there are two qualifications for an attorney to be on my list. One is that they are experts in family law. The other is that their hearts are in the right place. In other words, they don't have a hidden agenda to stir you up and generate fees. If you go to them for an hour, you pay for an hour. Just like here. Okay?"

"I'd like to see that list," Mary states.

"What for?" John says, contentiously.

"I just want to...I don't know...I'm..." Mary stammers.

"Well," I interpose, "may I ask a few questions?"

"I told her I don't want lawyers involved in this!" John exclaims.

"Yes, I know, John. However, you do agree that Mary should have all of the information she needs to make informed decisions, don't you?"

"Yeah," John begrudgingly admits.

"And the same holds true for you, right?"

"Yeah, I guess so," John replies.

"So if either of you needs to consult with an attorney in order to get additional information, doing so wouldn't be a problem, is that right, John?"

"Yeah, alright. If she wants to spend the money, she can go right ahead," John responds.

"I didn't say I'm going to do it. I just wanted to see the list," Mary asserts.

"That's fine, Mary," I interject, "but I want to confirm that you and John both know that this kind of expert advice is available, and that I am encouraging you to use it whenever you feel the need for more legal information or advice from an attorney."

Pausing momentarily, I continue:

"And the second instance in which I will encourage you to seek legal advice is when we are finished with mediation and I've prepared a draft of your settlement agreement. At the last session we'll go over the draft line by line, page by page, making any final changes. However, I won't let you sign the agreement at that time. There are two reasons for this. First, I don't want either of you to feel any pressure to sign it. Second, I want each of you to have the time for review by legal counsel. Having said that, the decision of whether to have legal counsel review the agreement is entirely yours — just like every other decision to be made in mediation."

COMMENTARY

I go to great lengths to clearly delineate what I do and don't do as a mediator. Many people readily understand that mediators aren't judges, deciding who's right or wrong, or who wins or loses. Indeed, this is the very reason why many people choose mediation. They don't want to turn over control to some outside authority or "roll the dice" on a decision made by a stranger. However, the distinction between mediator and attorney can be harder for some people to grasp. Many people are accustomed to relying on so-called experts to tell them what to do, and no matter how much I explain my role as mediator, sooner or later they forget and either ask me what they should do or seek legal advice from me.

I'll admit that at times it's been hard for me to resist the temptation of taking on the role of judge or attorney. Some people present for mediation in need of so much help that it sometimes seems easier, even more compassionate, to just tell them what to do. It is on these occasions that the evaluative approach to mediation may be the most effective; this approach calls for the mediator to direct participants toward settlement. Yet knowing that I rarely know what's best or fair for someone else, and that it would be arrogant to suppose that I do, I usually resist this temptation and let participants find their own way toward fully informed decisions.

Writing the words "informed decisions" on a flipchart page and keeping it in plain sight during the mediation provides a readily accessible tool for dealing with participants who forget or confuse the mediator's role. Typically, all I need to do is point to these two words to remind that person of my role as mediator, and then begin a discussion about other options for getting additional information or advice, whether from legal counsel or some other expert.

Informed decision-making by participants is central to situational mediation and my role as mediator. If at any time during mediation I were to conclude that a person was unable or unwilling to participate in this way, I would terminate the mediation. In this first session with John and Mary, it appeared that Mary might be in need of additional support in making decisions, perhaps from legal counsel. It also appeared that John was opposed to this, exclaiming, "I told her I don't want lawyers involved in this!" It was unknown to me, and really didn't matter, whether John's opposition was based on concerns about money, antipathy toward lawyers, or the need to control Mary. What was important was to ensure that both Mary and John clearly understood their prerogative to obtain additional legal information or advice, and to confirm that neither would stand in the other's way. Having obtained John's acquiescence for Mary to see my list of "mediation friendly attorneys," and knowing that I could if necessary revisit this issue later on, I felt comfortable in proceeding to explain the second paragraph of the *Rules and Procedures*.

DIALOGUE

I then tell Mary and John that Paragraph Two explains joint sessions and private sessions:

"Right now all of us are together in joint session. However, there may come a time when I ask that we break into private sessions where I'll meet with each of you individually. Let me give you an example of when this may be needed. Let's say we have been talking about a particular issue for some time but we seem to just keep circling around it without resolution. At this point, recognizing that you may not be progressing as quickly as you want, I might ask that we break into private session. I would turn to one of you, say Mary, and ask if you would excuse John and me while we talk privately. Mary, you would then leave the room while John and I talk about whatever issue or issues were under discussion. Then, John, when we were done, you would leave the room, and Mary would come back and we would meet privately to discuss the same issue or issues. We would then get back together in joint session. Any questions so far?"

"No," Mary and John answer, simultaneously.

"Good. So I want you to know three more things about these private sessions. The first is that there is absolutely nothing about them that is intrinsically good or bad. It is simply a method that has proven effective to help move the mediation process forward. I've had situations where we have never met privately and others where we have met privately six, seven, even ten times.

"The second thing I want to say about private sessions is that I don't keep secrets. In other words, if you privately tell me something that I believe is important for the other to know, I feel at liberty to appropriately disclose it. I don't want the person who's outside the room to wonder what the other is telling the mediator. This creates fear and hinders the mediation. So I don't keep secrets. Alright?"

"Yeah," John replies.

"That's good," Mary says.

"The last thing I want to tell you about private sessions is that if either of you at any time thinks that it would be helpful to break into them, all you need do is say so; if you both agree, that's exactly what we'll do."

COMMENTARY

There has been a long-standing controversy among mediators as to the use of private sessions. For example, evaluative mediators usually adhere to a structure in which participants routinely meet in private session and rarely in joint session, whereas transformative mediators often refuse to ever meet privately. The situational approach calls for mediators to make selective use of joint and private sessions. I typically spend most of my time in joint session, but don't hesitate to meet privately with participants whenever I sense that doing so would provide greater opportunities for understanding and empowerment, or would otherwise help participants reach agreement.

Here are some of the situations in which I am apt to ask for private sessions. As in the example I gave John and Mary, I may ask to meet privately with participants when I sense that they are stuck on a particular issue. Perhaps they have spent hours discussing it; I've provided different options and alternatives, as well as legal information, but one or both participants are unable to make further progress. My experience is that, most often, this is because one participant hasn't fully disclosed all of the information needed for the other to make a fully informed decision.

In one situation, for example, the wife, prior to mediation, led the husband to believe that she was disinterested in his retirement benefits. I had no knowledge of this, but when the time came to discuss division of marital assets, the wife hemmed and hawed, made unusual demands, and was unwilling to make final decisions. At that point, I asked to meet privately where I soon learned that she had changed her mind and was worried about how to tell her husband that she wanted a portion of his retirement benefits.

Another instance in which I am likely to suggest private sessions is when I sense that one party may be attempting to dominate or intimidate the other. Let's say that as I progressed with John and Mary, I saw that John was increasingly hostile to the idea of Mary consulting with legal counsel about her rights concerning spousal support. At that point, I would ask to meet privately. I would want to make certain that John understood the importance of Mary having the freedom to make informed decisions by consulting with legal counsel. And I would want to know if Mary would be willing to consult with legal counsel, despite opposition from John.

Private sessions can also be useful to intervene on repeated or extreme outbursts of emotion. Sometimes one or both participants simply need a "time out." Other times, I want to offer a participant some of the anger management tools described in Chapter 13 without causing that person any undue embarrassment or discomfort.

DIALOGUE
I go on to explain the third paragraph of the *Rules and Procedures*:

"Paragraph Three addresses an attitude that I am going to request that you folks strive to maintain during mediation. I call it one of 'mutual respect.' So could we make it a rule that each of you will let the other talk without interruption?"

"Yes," Mary replies.

"Yeah," John says.

"Well, sometimes that's easier said than done, at least for me. As I've said before, emotions are very common in mediation. In fact, mediation is often like an airplane ride. You can be up there flying along in smooth air and all of a sudden out of the blue you hit turbulence and it gets bumpy. And then it's white-knuckle time because you're bouncing around all over the sky. Well, mediation can be very much like that. You folks might be going along smoothly, collaborating and dealing with one issue after another, and then, all of a sudden, some emotion triggers one or both of you and it gets bumpy. This is very common. In fact, sometimes people who never express any emotion worry me. I wonder what's really going on with them. So knowing that it's likely to get bumpy in here from time to time, I'm going to give you a guarantee. In fact, it's the only guarantee you'll ever get from me. If you stay in your seats during the bumpy weather (meaning that you stay with the mediation process) you will land safely. After all, the odds are with you. Last year, over 95% of the couples who mediated with me landed safely."

After pausing briefly to let this sink in, I continue:

"So knowing that you are likely to experience at least some bumpy weather, and that we're all human and slip and make mistakes, may I have your permission to remind you about letting each other talk without interruption if I hear either of you forget about this?"

"Yes," Mary answers.

"Uh huh," John murmurs.

"Thank you. Could we also have it that threats, intimidation and verbal aggressiveness are against the rules?"

"Sure," Mary responds.

"Fine," John says.

"Okay then. I have one more request in terms of maintaining an attitude of mutual respect. Would you be willing to do your best to call each other by your first names? Instead of using pronouns such as 'he, she, you,' or the like, would you use first names when talking about each other? I know this can be a little awkward at first, but my experience is that it helps maintain an atmosphere of mutual respect. And since I've already taken the liberty of calling you by your first names, I'm wondering if you would call me Oliver? Okay?"

"Yeah," John replies, looking annoyed.

"Okay," Mary answers.

"Thank you. And if I hear you slipping on this, may I have your permission to remind you that we are all going to be on a first name basis?"

"Sure," Mary answers.

Looking even more annoyed, John merely nods his head.

COMMENTARY

Using an airplane ride as a metaphor for the emotions that are likely to surface during mediation serves several purposes. First, it gives participants a common experience to which they can relate. I'm personally aware that such metaphors help allay my fears of the unknown, and I've noticed they help others as well. Second, the metaphor can be used later on to intervene on angry outbursts or other displays of emotion. Sometimes all that's needed for participants to put their anger aside is for the mediator to acknowledge that they appear to have encountered "bumpy weather." Finally, this metaphor serves to give participants hope that they too will "land safely."

Never wanting to presume authority, situational mediators ask permission to remind participants of a rule or procedure. This is one of the ways in which situational mediators express humility. Furthermore, having obtained permission, the mediator can respectfully intervene if, for example, someone were to later on threaten, become verbally abusive, or repeatedly interrupt. Thus, knowing the importance of getting this permission, I simply ignored John's apparent annoyance.

Two brief comments about asking participants to use first names. In ordinary conversation, use of pronouns such as "he" or "she" is usually innocuous. However, in situations of conflict, these pronouns are frequently used to indirectly communicate gender-biased, negative, or hostile messages. Participants may be unaware that they are sending these indirect messages, but they definitely detract from an attitude of mutual respect. Furthermore, asking that participants also refer to the mediator by first name is another way to give voice to the situational mediator's desire to approach participants humanisticly; empathy, humility, and compassion are most likely to occur when people are together as equals.

DIALOGUE

I continue by explaining the fourth paragraph of the *Rules and Procedures*:

"The next paragraph is the shortest one, but I'm wondering if it's as important to you as it is to me? You see, this paragraph says that each of you will put your children first when making decisions; that your children's interests will be given top priority. So let me ask if you are willing to do this?"

"Yes, certainly," Mary replies.

"I always have. That's why I don't want this divorce," John

exclaims.

"I hear you. But are you willing to do that now?"

"Yeah," John states.

"Okay. So knowing that emotions can get in the way, might I have your permission to remind you if I sense that either of you may be overlooking this?"

"Yes, my children are very important to me," Mary answers, assertively.

"Yeah," John replies.

COMMENTARY

One of the major blessings as a mediator is helping people avoid the hostility and destructiveness of the legal system. This is particularly true with regard to the children of divorcing couples. I feel good knowing that I can help save them from the additional pain and suffering that would have been likely if their parents had chosen to litigate instead of mediate.

I am aware that in asking parents for permission to point out instances when they may be overlooking the best interests of their children, I am actually asking for permission to evaluate their decisions. I am also aware that for situational mediators, this degree of evaluation is at the outer limits of directing instead of facilitating the couple's actions. Nevertheless, I feel strongly about the welfare of children and I routinely ask for this permission. After all, my life experiences, education, and lack of personal involvement frequently allow me to see things that participants don't. And remember, situational mediation is eclectic; it calls for the selective use of whatever mediation method is most effective for the circumstances—which in many instances involving significant parental indiscretion is the evaluative or directive approach.

DIALOGUE

I then elaborate on the next two paragraphs of the *Rules and Procedures*:

"Paragraph Five addresses how I might encourage one or both

of you to obtain additional information. On the same list with the 'mediation friendly' attorneys I told you about are other experts: tax accountants, real estate appraisers, psychologists, and others. I'm not saying that you must consult with any of them. All I'm saying is that they are available if and when you feel the need for additional information or advice. Okay?"

"Yes," Mary responds.

John merely nods his head, indicating his understanding.

"Okay then. Let's talk about Paragraph Six that deals with 'information and documents.' When I practiced law, part of my job was to make it as difficult, expensive, and time-consuming as I could for the other side to get information and documents. After all, litigation is an adversarial system; it's a fight and one way to fight is to financially wear the other side down. Here in mediation, it's the exact opposite. By cooperating with these *Rules and Procedures* you are agreeing to be open, honest, and fully disclosing of any and all information needed to make fully informed decisions (financial statements and tax returns, etc.). Are you both willing to do this?"

"She already has all that!" John exclaims.

"Okay, John, but if Mary were to need additional information, perhaps a financial statement, would you be willing to provide her with a copy?"

"Yeah, okay."

"Then let me ask both of you about how you handled financial matters. Was one of you primarily responsible for paying the bills, making investments, preparing tax returns and the like, or did you share the responsibility for those things?"

"Mary paid the bills, and our accountant did our taxes," John replies.

"Who would gather the information that would be given to your accountant?"

"I did," John answers.

"And who was responsible for investments?"

"You mean like my retirement account?"

"Yes, or any investments in stocks or property."

"I was," John says.

"Alright. So let me ask each of you another question. Mary, if you were to rate yourself on a scale of one to ten in terms of your familiarity with and ability to understand financial matters, (one being the lowest and ten being the highest), what number would you chose?"

"You mean our finances?" Mary asks.

"Yes," I respond.

"I'd say about three or four."

"And what about you, John?"

"Maybe six or seven," John says.

"So you are on different levels in terms of your familiarity with and ability to understand financial matters. Is that a fair statement?"

"Yeah!" John states, emphatically.

"I think so," Mary answers, hesitantly.

Noticing Mary's hesitancy, I add, "Well, part of my job is to make certain that you both understand the financial matters we will be discussing when, for example, we talk about your marital assets. So if I were to sense that one of you, perhaps you Mary, needed more information to completely understand what's involved with a particular asset, say John's retirement benefits, I would take extra time to elicit that information. Would that be okay with both of you?"

"Yes," Mary answers.

"Whatever!" John says, petulantly.

"Does that mean 'yes,' John?"

"Yeah," John begrudgingly replies.

COMMENTARY

As I've noted, referral of participants to "experts" can be an essential part of the mediation process. It is all too easy for mediators with expertise in certain areas, say taxation or real estate, to slip into the role of expert. But my experience says it's better to have a readily available list of trustworthy, impartial experts to whom I can refer participants who need reassurance or answers to complex questions.

When difficult or complex issues arise in litigated divorces, lawyers for each side typically want to employ one or more experts to support their position. For example, when the issue is spousal maintenance, lawyers for each side will usually want to employ an accountant and/or a career consultant. The stage is then set for the proverbial "battle of experts" which can be extremely costly and time-consuming. Participants in mediation typically hire one impartial expert, thereby avoiding substantial time and expense.

The willingness to provide all the information and documents needed by each participant to make fully informed decisions is an essential part of situational mediation. Let's say, for example, that the husband owns a business about which the wife knows little, if anything. The wife, perhaps during a mediation session, wants the husband's accountant to prepare current financial statements for the business and to explain them to her. Or, let's say that the wife wasn't involved in the preparation of the joint federal and state tax returns filed during the marriage, and wants copies of these returns to review. In the absence of these returns, the wife wouldn't have the information necessary to decide how to allocate responsibility for any subsequently assessed tax liability.

On occasion, a mediation participant has been reluctant to provide certain information or documents because of cost or time considerations. However, only once in seven years have I encountered a participant who refused to provide needed information, despite his prior agreement to abide by the sixth paragraph of the *Rules and Procedures*. In this one instance I had no choice but to terminate the mediation.

DIALOGUE

I continue with the next paragraph of the *Rules and Procedures*:

"Paragraph Seven is divided into three parts, all meant to do the same thing: maintain your assets in status quo pending completion of the mediation. The first part says that neither of you, without having agreed in advance, will 'transfer, encumber, nor otherwise dispose of any assets.' Can you both agree to that?"

"Yes," John and Mary respond, simultaneously.

"The next part says that neither of you will, unless you agree in advance, 'make any loans or extraordinary charges on any credit cards.' Can you both agree to that?"

"Yep," John answers.

"Okay," Mary says.

"Good. The last part of this paragraph essentially says that neither of you will file for divorce nor take any other actions once a petition for divorce is filed, without having agreed to do so in advance."

COMMENTARY

The overall purpose of Paragraph Seven is to give mediating couples protections similar to those commonly granted by courts upon the filing of an action for dissolution of marriage (i.e., divorce). Mediation protections are contractual rather than court ordered. Nonetheless, rarely have any of the people I have mediated with breached their agreement to abide by this rule. On the contrary, my experience is that once people make these kinds of agreements, they have no trouble committing to them.

I then finish explaining the last paragraph of the *Rules and Procedures*:

DIALOGUE

"I call this last paragraph my 'escape clause' because if someone were to continually violate one or more of these rules and procedures, I reserve the right to either suspend or terminate the mediation. Okay?"

"Yes," Mary answers.

"Yep," John replies.

COMMENTARY

Only twice in seven years have I had to invoke this paragraph. In one situation, the wife became so verbally abusive toward the husband that I initially suspended the mediation and eventually terminated it. In the other situation, I terminated the mediation after the husband repeatedly refused to provide the wife with information about his earnings from a part-time job. I explained that this information was easily obtainable through a subpoena should the wife retain an attorney, but the husband persisted in his refusal, clearly violating the provisions of Paragraph Six.

Once I finish explaining the *Rules and Procedures*, I ask both participants to sign an original. Then I sign it myself, and make a copy for each of them. This routine is intended to give the *Rules and Procedures* additional credence and importance in the minds of the participants.

Chapter 3:
Gaining Understanding *(Altitude)*

Following a short break, I continue the first session of mediation with John and Mary. As is typical with airline passengers who feel a wide range of emotions, from calm when flying conditions are smooth to fear when turbulence strikes, participants in mediation are likely to experience varied emotions in this, the *Getting Current* stage.

Before proceeding further, it should be noted that in this stage of mediation I begin to organize the information disclosed by participants into three categories: *What, Want,* and *Willing*.

These three categories provide a simple yet highly effective model for conducting any type of mediation, including divorce. I first strive to bring out each participant's perspective as to *what* is involved—in the past and in the present. These are the facts, circumstances, concerns, worries, fears, and issues as perceived and experienced by each participant. I have learned to take my time when eliciting this information. Not doing so greatly increases the likelihood that the mediation will sooner or later stall, deadlock, or otherwise run into trouble.

Next, I attempt to engage each participant in dialogue about what they *want*. Having had the opportunity to disclose their perspectives about the past and present, most participants are then willing to shift their attention to how they *want* things to be in the future.

Many of the things that participants *want* are obvious from the positions they take, the needs they express, and the demands they make. However, many of the other things that people *want* involve their emotional interests and are more difficult to discern. These are the things that subconsciously influence one's thinking and behavior, and include human needs for safety, security, acknowledgement, closeness, respect, honesty, fairness, trust, etc. Situational mediators endeavor to discover and then bring out these interests. This opens the way to collaborative problem solving.

Finally, I seek to elicit information about the things participants are *willing* to do to get what they *want*. These are the changes in position, modifications of demands, and adjustments of needs that each participant is *willing* to make to resolve the dispute.

DIALOGUE

"Okay, the next agenda item is *Getting Current*. As you will recall, this is the time in which each of you will let the other talk without interruption, sharing with me from your own perspectives: (1) what you believe has already been agreed upon; (2) what is still undecided; (3) your concerns, if not your worries and fears; and (4) what you would like to see as results or outcomes of this mediation. In other words, I'd like you to tell me anything and everything so that I can get current with you. So who would like to go first?"

"I don't know. Do you want to start?" Mary asks John.

"It's your show," John counters.

"Well, what do you want to know?" Mary asks me.

"Perhaps you might want to start with any concerns you have," I offer.

"Well I'm most concerned about our children, Charlie and Sarah. They have already been through so much, with John and me arguing about…"

John interrupts: "Don't blame me! You're the one who wants to do this!"

"Oh, right, John. You're perfect, aren't you?" Mary snaps back.

I intercede: "Hold on a minute, folks. I know it's really hard, but remember about letting each other talk without interruption?"

"Yeah, okay," John responds.

"Sorry," Mary says.

"No need to be sorry. We're all human, right? So Mary, what concerns you about Charlie and Sarah?"

"Well, I'm not blaming anyone, but I don't want to disrupt their lives more than necessary. That's why I want to stay in the home, at least until Sarah finishes sixth grade."

"What grade is she in now?" I inquire.

"Fifth," Mary replies.

"So what I'm hearing is that for about the next 18 months you want to live where you are now. Yes?"

"Yes."

"Have you talked to John about that?"

"Kind of. But he just gets mad and storms off. And now that he's moved, we don't talk at all."

"Moved?"

"Yes, last week."

"Where is he living?"

"He took an apartment. At least that's what he said."

"Okay. I'll ask him more about that when it's his turn. Do any other concerns come to mind?"

"Well sure. I'm worried about getting a job. I haven't worked for a long time. I had a good job as a bookkeeper, but that was over six years ago. I don't know what kind of job I can get now. I'm not very good with computers."

"I hear you. What's your educational background?"

"I have about a year of community college."

"Okay. And what about your work background?"

"After high school, I worked for a public accountant for two years. Then I worked for a CPA firm until I had Charlie."

"For how many years?"

"About four."

"And what was your annual salary at the time you left?"

"About $20,000."

"Have you thought about taking computer classes?"

"Yes, but you know, with everything that's going on I haven't gotten around to it."

"Well, let me ask if you are you willing to start exploring the kinds of classes available, how long they will take, and how much they will cost?"

"Sure," Mary replies, leaning forward in her chair, appearing interested.

"Would you bring whatever information you obtain to our next session?"

"Sure."

"Thank you. Have you and John talked about the timing of when you might go back to work?"

"We tried."

John then interrupts loudly: "What do you expect? You lay this on me, and want me to act like nothing happened. I can't believe you. You…"

I intervene: "Excuse me, John. I understand that some of these things can be really difficult to hear, and that anger is very normal in these circumstances. I know it was hard for me in my own divorce. But remember, you agreed to let Mary talk without interruption. Right?"

"Yeah, but she acts so high and mighty!"

"I hear you. Yet would you try not to interrupt? It's important in terms of maintaining an atmosphere of mutual respect. Okay?"

"Yeah, I guess," John says, dejectedly.

Turning back toward Mary, I continue: "What else, Mary?"

"I don't know. What else do you want to know?"

"Perhaps you could tell me about Sarah and Charlie, and how they're doing."

"Sure. Sarah is a good girl, but lately she seems kind of sad. I know she misses her dad. He's not home much."

"Did John often spend time with Sarah?"

"Well, he had to work, and then there are those cars of his. But Sarah likes to hang around him, even when he's working on a car."

"What about his relationship with Charlie? Does John spend much time with him?"

"Sure. Charlie helps him with the cars."

"Well, let me ask if you view John as a good dad?"

"Overall, I would have to say that he is. He loves his children."

"So you trust that he would take good care of them?"

"Yes."

"Okay. Perhaps you could tell me a little about John's cars."

"He collects old cars. He always has two or three that he's working on. But eventually he sells them."

"So he restores old cars?"

"Yes, he…"

Interrupting, John says: "It's just a hobby."

Turning toward John, I ask: "Would it be alright if you and I talk about this when it's your turn to get me current? That way Mary won't be interrupted. Okay?"

"Yeah, okay," John responds.

"Thank you."

Turning back to Mary, I continue: "How are Charlie and Sarah doing in school?"

"Well, like I said, Sarah seems a little sad and her teacher asked me about it. I told her that John and I are having problems so she's going to keep an eye on it."

"Have you thought about counseling for Sarah?"

"No. I don't think it's gotten that far."

"Would counseling be an option if it were to get that far?"

"Yes, certainly."

"Have you talked to John about counseling for Sarah?"

"No."

Quickly glancing at John and satisfying myself that he seemed calmly attentive, I continue with Mary:

"How about Charlie? I remember from our consultation that you stopped work because he was having some problems and you wanted to be home with him. Right?"

"Yes, that's right. But he's much older now and doing fine. Though I still think I should be there when he gets home from school."

"So are you envisioning part-time work?"

"Well, maybe. Sarah's still too young to be left alone, even if

Charlie's there."

"Have you talked to John about the possibility of working part-time?"

Looking angrily at John, Mary says: "You don't want to talk about anything, do you John! You just want to work on those cars of yours. You never want to…"

John cuts in: "What do you mean? What's there to talk about? You've already made up your mind about everything!"

"Right, John. You're always right, aren't you! You're perfect, aren't you! You never do anything wrong, do you!" Mary lashes out.

John angrily replies: "Well let me tell you something! This whole thing is your idea; so don't make it seem like I don't care about my kids. I want to be with them as much as you do!"

Mary begins to cry. John remains silent, glaring at her.

After a couple of seconds, I say: "I imagine this is very difficult and frustrating for both of you, and I also imagine that you have been down this road many times before, arguing with each other like this. Is that right?"

"Many times," Mary says.

"That's an understatement!" John exclaims.

"Well, then let me ask if it's gotten you where you want to be?"

"No." Mary responds.

John merely shakes his head from side to side, indicating "no."

"Well, I guess that's why you are here. So let me ask you another question: After all these years of being together, do you really expect that either of you is going to all of a sudden change?"

"No," Mary answers.

John doesn't respond, so I ask him: "What about you, John? At this point in time, do you expect Mary to change?"

"No, not really."

"Okay, so would both of you agree that the only thing that can change is yourselves; that is, how you behave toward each other?"

"Yes," Mary says.

John merely nods his head, indicating "yes."

"Okay then, Mary. Knowing this, do you think it's helpful to lash out at John when he says or does something that aggravates you?"

"No. But I can still get angry!"

"Absolutely, and I'm not suggesting that you shouldn't. All I'm asking is whether you want to keep reacting as you have in the past?"

"Oh, I see. No. Certainly not. I want to live my own life."

"And what about you, John?"

"I'm done with her! I just want to get this over with," he replies.

"Okay. So if I were to see either of you slipping back, going down that old road again, could I bring that to your attention?"

"Yep," John answers.

"Okay," Mary replies.

Facing Mary, I continue: "Do you know how much your home is worth?"

"No."

"Are you familiar with what real estate professionals call 'comps'?"

"No."

"Comps are the prices that comparable homes in your neighborhood have sold for in the last six months or so. I wonder if you would be willing to ask a real estate person to run comps on your home?"

"Sure. I'll ask my friend Betty."

"Good. That would be helpful. And I'll be asking John to do the same. So other than your home, what other assets do you and John own?"

"You mean like cars and furniture and things like that?"

"Yes. Or stock investments or anything else of substantial value."

"Let's see, we have an investment account at Schwab and John's work pension."

"Okay. Anything else of substantial value?"

"Not that I know of," Mary replies.

"That's fine. I'll be giving each of you an 'Assets and Liabilities' form (Appendix, page 275). You can complete them together, or separately, whichever way works best. We'll use these when we go into detail about your assets. Okay?"

"Sure," Mary responds.

"What about liabilities, Mary? Do you and John have significant debt?"

"No. Besides the mortgage we only have two credit cards with small balances."

"Good. Let's switch back to Charlie and Sarah. How much time do you envision that John will spend with them?"

"Well, they would live with me. But he can have them as much as he wants…as long as he's not drinking."

John angrily cuts in: "Damn it! I don't have to sit here and listen to this. I have a few beers, that's all!"

I intercede, leaning toward John and saying: "Okay, John, we can talk about that. But one of your goals is to get through this quickly and inexpensively. Right?"

"Yeah."

"Well, does interrupting help you reach that goal?"

"No, but I don't want to hear that crap about drinking!" John counters.

"I hear you, John. But remember, you don't expect Mary to all of a sudden change, do you?"

"No."

"And you want to get through this quickly and inexpensively, right?"

"Yeah."

"So what if I were to remind you of this goal by, say, holding my hand up a little? That would be our signal that you are getting off track in terms of this? Do you think that would help?"

"Fine," John answers.

"Good. Let's try it, okay?"

"Yeah. Go ahead."

Turning toward Mary, I continue: "So what I heard you say is that you envision Charlie and Sarah living primarily with you but

John spending as much time as he wants with them, if he doesn't drink when he has them. Is that right?"

"Yes."

"Do you have a particular schedule in mind; for example, certain days of the week that they will be with John?"

"No, not exactly."

"Okay, that's not a problem. In fact, I'll be giving you and John a handout that illustrates five or six different weekly time-sharing arrangements."

"Good," Mary responds.

"One last thing, Mary. During our consultation, you mentioned needing financial help from John. Would you tell me more about that?"

"I still want to be with Charlie when he gets home from school and Sarah needs me to be there."

"What time does Sarah get home from school?"

"Around 3:30 p.m. Same as Charlie."

Mary then adds: "And another thing; I put my own career on hold long enough. I want John to help me get started."

"Okay. What kind of help do you have in mind?"

"I don't know for sure. But I gave up a lot, and I don't want to work for minimum wage. So he has to help me, at least for a while."

"So what I hear you saying is that you have certain goals in mind in terms of returning to work—to be with Charlie and Sarah when they come home from school and to earn more than minimum wage. I also hear that you would like John's help in reaching those goals. Right?"

"Yes. I think that's only fair."

"I hear you. And I'll be asking John about this when he gets me current. Just one more thing: In general, how is your health?"

"It's good."

"I ask this only because it's relevant to the issue of spousal support."

"Sure," Mary answers, hesitantly.

"Is there anything else you want to share?"

"No. I think that's all."

"Alright, thank you, Mary. This has been very helpful. And you should know that there will be plenty of opportunity to talk about anything else that comes up as we go along."

COMMENTARY

The *Getting Current* stage is an essential part of the situational approach to mediation. Early on it creates an environment in which participants can safely talk about their situation and be heard. Participants are asked to allow each other to talk without interruption, and to share anything and everything that might be helpful to bring the mediator up to speed. They are encouraged to give voice to their concerns, worries, and fears, those feelings which might otherwise be difficult or unsafe to express. The act of talking is curative, as Sigmund Freud knew when he initially called psychoanalysis "the talking cure."

Being heard is also curative. The *Getting Current* stage is structured so that conversation occurs between one participant and the mediator, while the other participant listens. This structure affords the silent participant an opportunity to listen, perhaps as never before, without having to plan a response. Similar to many divorcing couples, it's likely that John and Mary rarely heard each other. The *Getting Current* format provides them with this opportunity.

Situational mediators perform three essential communication tasks: They (1) *listen actively* (this includes letting participants know that they are heard); they (2) *reflect* what they hear ("I imagine that this is very difficult and frustrating for both of you"); and they (3) *summarize* ("So what I'm hearing from you Mary is that for the next 18 months you want to live where you are now.") In these ways situational mediators foster the empowerment and recognition primary to the transformative approach to mediation, and inspire the empathy, humility, and compassion essential to the humanistic and situational approaches.

Getting Current in this way sets the stage for later sessions. Except for occasional private sessions, mediation participants talk to each other about their situation. They are able to hear one another, experience each other's emotions, and simultaneously get the information needed to make fully informed decisions.

The *Getting Current* stage is important in other ways. It lets the mediator get an overall understanding of the participants' situation and helps to identify points of agreement and disagreement concerning assets, debts, parenting, and spousal support. It helps the mediator understand each participant's concerns and goals—Mary returning to work, for example. It also serves to reveal sensitive or unusual issues such as John's drinking or, as will be discussed later, the value of his antique cars.

During this stage the mediator can also identify and request that one or both participants procure material and/or data that may be useful in making fully informed decisions. In other words, the mediator can give the participants "homework" that is likely to facilitate their decision-making in subsequent sessions. For example, in Mary and John's case it's likely that information pertaining to computer classes would facilitate later agreement as to when Mary will return to work. Likewise, information as to real estate "comps" would probably be useful in deciding the fair market value of their home.

The *Getting Current* stage also helps the mediator begin to understand each participant's "interests," that is, their needs for safety, security, acknowledgment, respect, and the like. These are the interests that typically cause people, perhaps subconsciously, to do what they do and say what they say. For example, one of Mary's interests was to provide stability for her children. This was evidenced by her desire to remain in the home "at least until Sarah finishes sixth grade." Another of Mary's interests was for John to acknowledge the role she played in raising their children, putting her career on hold to be home with them. However, as with many participants in mediation, Mary was unable to express these interests directly. She could only lash out, complaining, "Oh, right John. You're perfect, aren't you!" while meaning just the opposite. As I will explain in Chapter 13, such forms of indirect communication are sarcastic, albeit common.

It should be noted at this point that during the *Getting Current* stage situational mediators primarily rely on certain aspects of the transformational and humanistic approaches. They strive to foster recognition and empowerment, and relate to participants with empathy, humility, and compassion. They know that these approaches are the most effective in helping participants express themselves genuinely and uncovering underlying interests.

When children are involved, I typically ask each parent during the *Getting Current* stage about their view of the other parent as a father or mother. In this case, I asked Mary: "In your view, is John a good dad?" The answer to this question often provides useful information. It can help gauge whether parents are truly willing to put their children's interests first (as they agreed to do under the fourth paragraph of the *Rules and Procedures*). If one parent answered by portraying herself as all good and the other parent as all bad, I would be concerned about this type of dualistic thinking and dig deeper into the situation. However, Mary's answer ("I would have to say that he is. He loves his kids.") suggested a willingness to rise above her anger and acknowledge that John's role as a father was beneficial. The answer to this question also opens the door for each parent to acknowledge the other in positive terms. My experience is that most participants see their spouse as a good parent, and hearing this often goes a long way towards counteracting their usually negative judgments of each other.

I also ask about counseling when children are involved. At this point my intent is to get a preliminary reading on each parent's willingness to consider counseling should it become apparent that their child(ren) would benefit from it. In this case, Mary was willing to consider counseling for Sarah and as you will soon see, John was too. Had this not been the case, I would have pursued the subject further. Indeed, when it's obvious that a child is greatly in need of counseling, I can become quite directive.

During the *Getting Current* stage, participants are likely to display varying degrees of emotion: *Anger* about being forced to consider the prospect of dividing assets, allocating debts (or as with John the divorce itself); and *sadness* about having to live apart from their children and be a single parent. These and the other matters discussed during this stage are likely to trigger the emotions involved in the grief process discussed in Chapter 1.

It is at these times that the situational approach to mediation helps participants rise above their emotions. Thus, when John and Mary first began to argue I emphatically said: "I know it's really hard, but don't forget to let each other talk without interruption." And when Mary apologized, my intent was to be humble: "No need to be sorry. We're all human." Then, when John continually became angry and interrupted, wanting to be compassionate I said: "Excuse me, John. I understand that some of these things can be really difficult to hear, and that anger is very normal in these circumstances. I know it was hard for me in my own divorce. But remember, you agreed to let Mary talk without interruption. Right?"

Finally, when both Mary and John again became angry, I sat quietly while they argued back and forth, Mary accusing John of not wanting to talk about anything with John protesting, "What do you mean? What's there to talk about?" and so forth. On this occasion, I sensed that humility would be best demonstrated by my remaining silent for a while.

DIALOGUE

I continue the *Getting Current* portion of the first session by turning toward John and asking: "Where would you like to start?"

"Well, she makes me out to be the bad guy. She makes it seem like I neglected the kids, and she was the good one. That's not the way it was!"

"I hear you, John, and I want to hear more about your perspective. However, we all agreed to be on a first name basis, and I'm wondering if you could remember to call Mary by her first name?"

"Yeah, alright."

"So tell me about your view that Mary is making you out to be the bad guy."

"I spent plenty of time with the kids. I can't help it if they like to work on antique cars with me."

"Okay. Did you do other things with them?"

"Sure. I went to Charlie's Little League games. I took Sarah for ice cream. And, you know, that kind of…"

Mary interrupts: "You only went to one or two games, and even then…"

Turning toward Mary, I intercede: "I know it's hard to just sit and listen. But it's John's turn. Right?"

"I'm sorry," Mary replies.

Turning back toward John, I continue: "I heard Mary say that she stopped work to be home with Charlie. Is that right?"

"Yeah. Pretty much."

"And how would you rate Mary as a mom?"

"I'd say pretty good."

"Okay. And how would you rate your overall relationships with Charlie and Sarah?"

"Good. No matter what she, I mean Mary, says."

"Have you noticed anything unusual about either of them lately?"

"Not really."

"What about Sarah's teacher saying that she seems sad?"

"This is the first I heard of it."

"Mary didn't tell you?"

"Nope."

"I see. Do you think Sarah's sad?"

"I guess. A little."

"Do you think counseling might help her?"

"Couldn't hurt."

"So you would be willing to have Sarah see a counselor?"

"Sure."

"What about paying for it?"

"We have insurance through my work. But I'm not sure how much it covers."

"Would you be willing to check the coverage and perhaps

converse with Mary about it? In any event, would you bring that information to our next session?"

"Yeah, okay."

"Alright then. I heard Mary say that she wants the children to live most of the time with her, but that you could be with them whenever you want. What do you think about that?"

"I've got just as much right to be with them as she does. Maybe they should split their time with us, especially with her boyfriend coming over so much."

"What's that about?" I inquire.

"What do you think? Mary already has this other guy, and I hardly think that's best for Charlie and Sarah."

"How often does he come to the home?"

"A lot."

Mary interrupts: "That's not true! He's only been there twice. I needed a ride to the gym. If you had fixed my car on time, I wouldn't have had to ask him!"

John argues back: "Oh yeah, right, Mary!"

Mary counters: "You don't know anything. And anyway, you never cared before. You…"

John shouts: "What about you!"

I intervene assertively: "Just a minute, folks. I can see how angry you both are, and as I said before, that's very common in mediation. But remember about your goal of getting through this quickly and inexpensively. Do you think that this is helping?"

Mary replies close to tears: "I don't like it when he says that. He's just a friend, and I resent that kind of accusation. At least he listens to me."

"I hear you, Mary. But I wonder if arguing like this is helpful. You do share in the goal of getting through this quickly, inexpensively, and with as little emotional stress and strain as possible, right?"

"Yes, but I wish he would stop bringing Ted into this."

"Ted?"

"He's the one who took me to the gym."

"I see. But could you try not to interrupt while John is getting me current? In fact, remember what I told John about holding my hand up as a reminder about getting off track? You think my doing that for you might be helpful?"

"I'll try, but he can be so nasty sometimes."

"You mean John?"

"Yes. I'm sorry."

"I know this can be hard, Mary. Especially when things are said that seem hurtful and your emotions come up. But let's let John have his turn, okay?"

"Okay," Mary replies while sitting back in her chair.

Turning to John, I say: "And I imagine that this is hard for you too, John?"

"I'm used to it!" John replies.

"Okay. Do you want to go on?"

"Yeah, sure. What's next?"

"Well, I remember you mentioned something about the children 'splitting their time.' Do you mean that they would live half of the time with you and half of the time with Mary?"

"Yeah, something like that."

"What about someone being with them after school?"

"Charlie's old enough to be there alone, but I'm not sure about Sarah."

"How might you get information about what's in their best interests?"

"I guess that I could ask the Employee Assistance guy at work."

"Okay. That's one option. At our next session would you share whatever you learn?"

"Alright."

"Another option might be to talk to a counselor, right?"

"Yeah."

"Do you think you and Mary could discuss this after you get information about the insurance coverage through your work?"

"We could try."

"If you can't or it causes an argument, we can discuss it here. Okay?"

"Yeah. I guess so."

"By the way, John. You mentioned Sarah, and I'm wondering what you think about Mary wanting to stay in the home until Sarah finishes the sixth grade?"

"I'm not sure."

"Okay. Would you be willing to discuss this with the Employee Assistance person at work and perhaps with a counselor to determine Sarah's and Charlie's best interests?"

"Yeah. I guess."

"Good enough. So would you tell me how much time you are currently spending with Charlie and with Sarah?"

"We used to be together a lot more, but lately it's been hard."

"How's that?"

"Well, you know, with Mary and me arguing, and this guy she's involved with, I just don't want to be around."

"I imagine that you miss being with them as much as you were."

"Yes, I do."

"So perhaps I could share something with you from my personal life. And I know Mary's listening, so I would be sharing it with her at the same time. Would that be alright?"

"I guess."

"If someone were to have asked me, say, ten years ago, how to define 'love,' I would have answered by saying that it's like how I feel about my wife, or my children. In other words, I would have *described* not defined it. However, about seven years ago I finally learned how to define love. For me, love is the giving of time and attention without expecting anything in return. Isn't that what we all want — time and attention from our family and friends?"

"Yeah."

"So what I heard you saying is that you were giving Charlie and Sarah your time and attention — working on cars, at Little League games, buying ice cream — without expecting anything in return from them. Right?"

"Yeah, I guess so."

"In other words, you were giving them your 'love.' Right?"

"Yeah, that's true."

"So despite your anger with Mary, might you be willing to again give them your love in these ways?"

"That's what I want. But I just moved into this crummy apartment and it's too small for them."

"Did you lease the apartment, or are you month-to-month?"

"Month-to-month."

"Do you see yourself moving to a larger place, perhaps a house?"

"For sure! The sooner the better."

"And would Charlie and Sarah have their own rooms?"

"Sarah would for sure, she being a girl and all."

"Okay. And I take it that you could work on your cars there?"

"Yep."

"Okay then. Would you be willing to start looking for another house now? In this way you can get an idea of what it might cost, for rent, or the mortgage if you buy, and for utilities and things like that. We will be using this information when we get into budgeting expenses. Okay?"

"Okay."

"One more question pertaining to Charlie and Sarah. Okay, John?"

"What?"

"I'm wondering how having 'a few beers' fits into being with them?"

"It doesn't!"

"Not even if you must drive in the car with them?"

"I don't do that."

"But let's say that you are alone with them at your new house, and something unexpected comes up that requires you to drive with them. What would you do?"

"I could still drive. I don't get drunk."

"But I need you to know that this is something that a judge would probably be interested in to help determine what's in the best interests of your children."

"Yeah, so?"

"Well, I want you and Mary to know this in terms of making fully informed decisions about time-sharing arrangements for Sarah and Charlie."

"So I just won't drink when they're with me."

"Okay. But you still might want to check this out with independent legal counsel."

"Why?"

"Because I want to make sure that you are fully informed on this issue. Are you willing to consider seeing independent counsel?"

"I'll have to think about it."

"Okay. Would you let me know what you decide?"

"Yep."

"Thanks."

Glancing at Mary and observing that she seems attentive, I continue with John: "Perhaps we could talk about other financial matters. Would you tell me about your financial assets?"

"Well, like Mary said, we have our home, my 401(k) retirement account, our Schwab account, bank accounts, Mary's car, and my truck. That's about it."

"Are you presently restoring any cars?"

"Yeah. Two."

"Do you count them as assets?"

"I never really thought about it that way."

"I imagine they have value. Right?"

"Sure."

"And how would you go about determining their value?"

"I'm not really sure. There are magazines that list collector's cars, and I could check them."

"That might be helpful. How else might you go about determining their value?"

"I know a guy who manages antique car shows. I could ask him."

"Okay. Why don't you do what you can to determine their value, and bring whatever information you obtain to our next session? Okay?"

"Uh huh."

"With respect to your home, roughly how much equity is there?"

"Probably around $90,000."

"How do you come to that amount?"

"I figure it's worth about $170,000, and we owe about $80,000."

"Have you thought about costs of sale, such as real estate commissions, title insurance, escrow fees, and the like?"

"No."

"We will go into that when we get into detail about your assets, but in the meantime would you be willing to get comps on the home?"

"I thought Mary was going to get them."

"Yes, but you can too."

"No, that's okay. They come right off a computer."

"So you want Mary to get them?"

"Yep. I know Betty. She'll be straight."

"Mary also mentioned that there was little or no debt, except for the mortgage on the home. Would you agree?"

"Yep."

"Okay then. Could we talk about support for the children and for Mary?"

"Like what?"

"Well, let's start with the children. Do you anticipate paying child support?"

"Depends on where they are living, doesn't it?"

"Yes. To some extent it does depend on where they live and how much time they spend with each of you. But it also depends on how much money each of you makes, and the standard of living you want for your children. So I encourage people to approach this issue from two separate points of view.

"One view is based on 'expenses.' I'll be giving both of you *Income and Expense* forms (Appendix, page 281) to complete. This will let each of you budget your monthly expenses over the next year or so. We'll go over them, and list the expenses item by item

on the flipchart, and you and Mary can discuss any of them you
have questions about. In this way each of you will be able to see
how much it will cost to support yourselves and your children in
separate households. After you have that information, we'll look
at child support from another viewpoint, namely, gross annual
income, that is, the amount of money you make a year. That's the
way the courts calculate a so-called Guideline amount of child
support.

"You see, the courts calculate a preliminary or Guideline
amount of child support by using each parent's annual gross
income in conjunction with certain charts devised by economists.
Here in mediation, you will have the advantage of being able to
compare this Guideline amount to the total amount you budgeted
for yourselves and your children, and then decide what amount
both of you agree is needed to raise your children. Does that make
sense?"

"Yeah. All the more reason for Mary to get a job."

"Okay, I hear you. Yet would you agree that Mary would
probably get a higher paying job after taking some computer
classes?"

"Yeah. Probably."

"So in the long run this would also benefit you. Right?"

"Yeah."

"So would you be willing to help Mary financially during the
time it takes to complete these classes?"

"Depends on how many classes and how long they take."

"But you are willing to talk about a temporary support
arrangement for Mary?"

"We already have one. I'm paying the mortgage and all the
household bills. Isn't that enough?"

"Well, that's not for me to say. Perhaps it's an *Immediate
Concern* that should be discussed next, after you finish getting me
current."

Mary interrupts: "Yes, it should be next! I need to know how
much money I'll have while we work this out."

Standing and moving toward the flipchart, I take a break from

Getting Current with John and ask:

"Would it be alright with both of you if I list 'temporary support arrangements' as an *Immediate Concern* on the Agenda?"

"Fine," he says.

Mary nods her head, indicating "yes."

"Okay then. Since temporary support arrangements are closely related to longer-term financial support, perhaps I could give you legal information about spousal support. Would that be okay?"

"I guess," John replies.

"Sure," Mary answers.

"I want to start out by saying that this issue can be emotionally charged, and I'll be giving you information about it in small doses—by the spoonful rather than the shovel. To begin with, unlike child support for which there have been Guidelines for many years, there were no spousal support guidelines here in Arizona until very recently. Each court was basically left to decide this issue on its own, relying on criteria developed from appellate court decisions. As a result, there was a great deal of inconsistency in the awards that were made. There was little, if any, predictability. You could walk into five different courtrooms and get five different results.

"In an attempt to lend some certainty to this issue, about a year and a half ago Guidelines were published, including a formula for calculating, at least preliminarily, spousal support. We will go over these and use the formula to calculate a Guideline amount in your case. However, as stated in the Guidelines themselves, the amount derived from the formula is only intended as a starting place for 'discussion, negotiation, and decision-making.' In other words, it is not a determinative or final amount. It's a preliminary amount. In fact, some courts give it little, if any, weight and continue to make decisions as before using the criteria developed by case law.

"So folks, there is a formula for calculating a Guideline amount of spousal support, but many courts will do what they think is correct regardless. Here in mediation, you will again have the advantage of being able to compare the Guideline amount of spousal support to the expenses you budgeted. You also will be able to talk about Mary's career goals and see how you might agree to support these goals so that over time Mary will become financially independent. Does that sound like it might be helpful?"

"I guess so" John replies.

"Yes," Mary answers.

"Okay. Just a few more questions concerning financial matters. Okay, John?"

"Okay."

"What was your annual income last year?"

"About $80,000."

"Do you usually get a bonus?"

"No."

"And what about income from the cars you sell?"

"That's a hobby!"

"I hear you. However, I understood Mary to say that you regularly sell your cars."

"Yeah, so what?"

"Well, do you make a profit on the ones you sell?"

"Most of the time."

"So wouldn't that be income?"

"Technically, I guess. But in some years I didn't sell any."

"Would your tax returns show the income from the cars you did sell?"

"I don't think so."

"Would you be willing to bring in the last three years' federal income tax returns, so we can all see?"

"It just a hobby!"

"I hear you, John. But you did agree to disclose any and all information needed by Mary to make fully informed decisions. Right?"

"Yeah, but this shouldn't count as income."

"I'm not saying it should, or it shouldn't. That will be for you and Mary to decide, as with all other decisions to be made. I'm merely requesting that you provide the information. Okay?"

"Yeah. I guess so."

"Is there anything else you want to talk about? Perhaps any concerns that you haven't mentioned?"

"Well, Mary's not the only one with money problems. I'm worried about money too. I want a decent place to live."

"I hear you. So you have your own worries about financial security. Right?"

"You bet. And my health isn't the greatest. I have high blood pressure and take medication for it."

"So I imagine that this adds to your concern about supporting Mary and the children. Is that right?"

"It sure does. I can do it, but I don't know for how long."

"I hear you, John. Anything else?"

"No."

"Well, thank you. And as I told Mary, there will be plenty of time to share anything else you think of later on."

COMMENTARY

Here with John, and before in my dialogue with Mary, you see the importance of having asked for permission to remind participants of certain rules and procedures. To wait until after they interrupted each other would have severely diminished my ability to intercede humanisticly. In terms of my air travel metaphor, by that time the plane would have already left the gate, making it very difficult to bring it back without taking control or assuming authority, an approach contrary to that of a situational mediator. On the other hand, having asked for permission, it was relatively easy to empathically remind John to call Mary by her first name and to humbly remind Mary: "I know it's hard to just sit and listen. But it's John's turn." I cannot overemphasize the importance of laying the groundwork for interventions such as these early in the mediation, preferably while explaining the *Rules and Procedures*.

Obtaining permission in advance is equally important when intervening on participants who constantly argue back and forth.

Most participants are relatively calm while discussing the *Rules and Procedures*. However, emotional reactivity tends to increase during the *Getting Current* stage and later stages of mediation, as does the difficulty of respectful intervention. For instance, securing advanced permission allowed me to intervene assertively and yet humanisticly when Mary and John argued about Mary's "boyfriend." Having obtained their permission in advance, I could compassionately remind Mary and John of their shared goal of getting through the mediation quickly and inexpensively.

You also see from this dialogue how the *Getting Current* stage is used to identify and clarify points of agreement and disagreement. It was clear from talking with John that he agreed that Sarah would see a counselor should she need it. It was equally clear that John and Mary disagreed about how much time Charlie and Sarah would spend with each of them. Mary envisioned Charlie and Sarah living primarily with her, while John thought "they should split their time." Issues pertaining to child and spousal support were also identified, with Mary asserting that "he has to help me, at least for a while," and John contending that any financial help from him would depend on how many classes Mary would need to take.

It should be noted that most divorcing couples have poor communication skills, especially when dealing with each other. The reasons for this are varied and complex, but often include emotional immaturity, anger, and mistrust. For instance, there was apparently little if any conversation between Mary and John about Sarah's sadness or Mary's talk with Sarah's teacher. The *Getting Current* stage facilitates communication about children while providing participants with a neutral forum for discussing family, financial, and logistical matters.

The *Getting Current* stage also provides a platform from which the mediator can set in motion the gathering of information by participants. For example, having suggested that Charlie and Sarah spend half their time with him, John agreed to gather information about what may be in the children's best interests by talking to the Employee Assistance person at work. Mary also agreed to gather information, including "what kind of computer classes are available, how long they will take, and how much they will cost."

A platform is also provided in the *Getting Current* stage for the mediator to offer the option of using "experts" to obtain specialized information. As you will recall, the fifth paragraph of the *Rules and Procedures* provides for the use of counselors, appraisers, and other experts when particular information or advice is required for one or both participants to make a fully informed decision. John was offered the option of seeking advice from a counselor concerning the issue of Charlie and Sarah spending half their time with him, and to talk with the person who manages antique car shows about the value of his cars.

The *Getting Current* stage also serves to facilitate the mediation process in several other ways. It permits the mediator to gradually introduce legal concepts that at times may be complex, such as those pertaining to spousal support. It also allows the mediator to probe each participant's willingness to discuss certain topics, obtain specific information, or provide particular documents. John was willing to discuss the issue of spousal support, albeit without committing to anything definite. Mary was willing to obtain comps, whereas John saw no need to get his own. Although somewhat reluctant, John was willing to provide federal tax returns, which would shed light on his income from the sale of antique cars.

Finally, my dialogue with John brought out two other important matters. First, when the mediator suspects that a participant is engaging in potentially harmful behavior, such as John's drinking "a few beers," I believe he has the responsibility to ask questions and otherwise probe such behavior. Although mediators ultimately have no control over participants, they are in a position to raise awareness and perhaps influence a participant's behavior.

And second, should the opportunity arise, the mediator should not hesitate to assume the role of teacher. As will be discussed in the next chapter, situational mediators teach in *beneficent* rather than *intellectual* ways, limiting their instruction to subjects about which they can speak from personal experience. Thus, recognizing that John had let his anger with Mary affect the amount of time he was spending with Charlie and Sarah, and wanting to spare them from more suffering, I shared what I had learned in my life about "love."

DIALOGUE

Addressing both Mary and John, I conclude the first session:

"Well folks, I'm mindful that it's time to stop for today, and I want to give you some homework. As you will recall, there are four major areas we will be dealing with over the course of the mediation: division of assets, allocation of debts, parenting (which includes child support), and, finally, spousal support. In light of the fact that we decided to write "spousal support" under the heading *Immediate Concern*, do you want to start with budgeting expenses?"

"Yes," Mary replies.

"I guess," John answers.

"Okay, then. Here's an *Income and Expense* form for each of you, and what I'd like you to do is budget your monthly expenses over the next 12 to 18 months. The Income form is rather self-explanatory. Mary, I suggest that you complete it after you find out what computer classes you'll need to take to get a good job. Would that be alright?"

"Sure," Mary responds.

Noticing that John remained silent, I ask him: "Is that alright with you, John?"

"Yeah, okay."

Again addressing both Mary and John, I continue: "You'll notice that the Expense form has columns for yourself and for the children, and I would like you to divide the amount you spend for each item between yourself and the children. You'll also notice that some of the first expenses deal with mortgage payments, utilities, and the like. These can be more difficult to divide than other expenses such as groceries. So here's a suggestion: figure if you were living someplace without the children, and divide the expenses accordingly. For example, how much do you pay for rent each month, John?"

"$800."

"Do you have any idea how much your mortgage payment would be when you buy a house that will be big enough for Charlie and Sarah?"

"Probably around $1,200."

"And when do you anticipate buying a house?"

"As I said before, the sooner the better!"

"In the next three or four months?"

"Yeah."

"So you might want to allocate two-thirds of the mortgage payments, utilities, and the like to yourself, and one-third to the kids. Right?"

"Yeah. I see."

"And you can apply the same logic, Mary. If you weren't living in the house, you might be spending about $800 per month for rent or a smaller house, right?"

"Right."

"So you can divide your current mortgage payments, a third to the children and two-thirds to you. Unless you have any questions, I'll see you next session."

Chapter 4:
Increasing Communication and
Collaboration *(Acceleration)*

Having gained altitude by establishing the *Rules and Procedures* and the process called *Getting Current*, situational mediators, at this stage of divorce mediation, will rely heavily on the facilitative approach to mediation to help participants communicate, collaborate, and gather the information necessary for them to make fully informed decisions. Situational mediators will also look for opportunities in this stage to express the empathy, humility, and compassion involved in the humanistic approach. They know that these qualities increase and accelerate effective communication and problem solving.

One week after our last meeting, I begin John and Mary's second mediation session:

DIALOGUE
"Could we start out by each of you bringing me up to speed, keeping me current, as to what happened between our last session and now?"

Mary replies: "I obtained some information on the house."

"Did you get comps?"

"Yes."

"Would it be alright if I make copies for John and for my file?"

"Okay."

I leave the room to make copies. Upon my return, I give the original comps to Mary, a copy to John, and keep a copy for myself. I then continue:

"Looks like Mary's comps show that your home is worth

$195,000, right?"

Mary asserts: "Yes! That's a lot more than John said it was worth!"

John argues: "That's not what my comps show! We don't have a pool and our street…"

Mary protests: "You said you weren't going to get comps!"

John counters: "Well I did! So what?"

I intercede: "I'm wondering if this exchange isn't adding more heat than light. In other words, is it generating more anger than shedding light on the value of your home? The comps show what they show, right? Remember that nothing is final in mediation until you sign a settlement agreement. It may turn out that both of you will change your minds several times during the course of the mediation, as it seems John did in this instance. Right?"

John replies: "Yep."

Mary complains: "That's just like him!"

I respond to Mary: "So what I'm hearing is that when John changes his mind you become frustrated."

"Yes, I can't trust him. He always says he will do one thing and then does another!"

"Alright, I hear you. My experience is that trust is a very common issue in mediation, especially during divorce. And a certain amount of mistrust can help you remain alert when making decisions. But would you agree that John should get whatever information he needs to be fully informed about the home?"

"Yes, but he doesn't have to lie!"

"Well, are you open to the possibility that he didn't lie? That he just changed his mind?"

"Yes, but I doubt it."

"Okay, fair enough. And are you also open to the possibility that arguing back and forth may be hindering your goal of agreement on the value of the home?"

"Yes. I'm sorry."

"No need to be sorry. We just hit some bumpy weather, that's all."

Turning to John, I ask: "What do your comps show?"

"About $180,000."

"Do your comps show the average comparable sales price per square foot?"

"Yeah, $72."

"How many square feet are there in your home?"

"2,500."

"So if I were to multiply $72 per square foot times 2,500 square feet, the value of your home would be $180,000. Right?"

"Yep."

"Okay, John. Perhaps we could take a few minutes to compare your comps to Mary's." I silently review my copy of the comps Mary provided, compare them to John's, and continue by asking Mary:

"Looks like some of the houses which were included in your comps have pools. Do you see that?"

"Now I do," she responds.

"That's new information for you?"

"Yes, I'm surprised. Betty was in a hurry. So we didn't have a chance to talk about it."

"Okay. I see."

Turning to John, I ask: "Your comps don't include any houses with pools, is that right?"

"That's right!" he asserts.

Turning back to Mary, I ask: "Most real estate professionals can estimate how much a pool is worth. So would you be willing to talk to Betty about how much of a difference in value there is between houses with and without pools?"

"Alright," she responds.

"Thank you. And will you let us know what you find out?"

"Yes."

"John, do you want to get this information too?"

"Yeah, fine," he replies.

"Okay. Could we go on to another subject?"

Mary and John both nod their heads, indicating "yes."

"Mary, my notes show that you were going to get information

about computer classes. Were you able to do that?"

"I talked to one person at the community college and it looks like they have some classes. But I want to check with some other schools."

"Alright. Did you find out how many classes would be involved?"

"Yes, three or four."

"And how long would they take to complete?"

"Well, first you must take a beginning class. Then you can take the others. So I figure two semesters."

"Okay. Perhaps you can get more information about this and bring it next time."

"Alright, I will."

Turning to John, I say: "My notes also reflect that you were going to talk to the Employee Assistance person at work about Charlie and Sarah spending half their time with you. Right?"

"Yeah, but he just told me about an outside counselor."

"I see. Are you going to see one?"

"I don't know. I talked to my brother and he doesn't think it would be good for the kids to...you know, with so much going on, to...you know, make a major change at this time."

"So are you rethinking whether Charlie and Sarah should spend half of their time with you?"

"I want them with me, but I just don't know if right now is the best time."

"I hear you. Perhaps it might be helpful if I were to give you some legal information concerning this. Anything you decide now about your children is always what the courts call *modifiable,* meaning that it is always changeable based on a material change of circumstances. In other words, nothing is permanent when it comes to the decisions made about children. After all, as children grow older their needs change, as might yours and Mary's. So nothing you and Mary decide now about Charlie and Sarah is written in stone, including whatever time-sharing arrangement you agree on."

John then asks: "So if I decided to have them with me less than half the time, I could get that changed later on?"

I reply: "The court would want to know what circumstances had changed. However, the children's age is certainly a circumstance that a court would consider in determining what's in their best interests. And if they were, say, a year or two older, that might be sufficient for a change. But I doubt that you and Mary would need court consent to change the time that Charlie and Sarah spend with each of you. This is because most of the settlement agreements I prepare include a provision for handling future conflicts, including how much time children spend with each parent.

"This provision sets forth a 'Future Conflict Resolution' procedure for resolving these kinds of conflicts, or any other disputes that may arise. If you and Mary agree to include this provision in your agreement, you would be obligated, before either of you were to take court action, to attempt to resolve any conflict by going through three steps. First, you would be obligated to make a good faith effort to talk about it; second, you would need to make a good faith effort to seek help from an impartial friend or advisor, such as a counselor, minister, or someone else whom you both trust; and third, you would be obligated to make a good faith effort to return to mediation, not necessarily with me but with any mutually acceptable professional mediator.

"Should one of you not act in good faith in following this procedure—if one of you intentionally disregards one or more of the steps—then that person agrees to pay the other person's attorney fees. This puts some teeth in the provision."

John remains silent, so I ask him: "Does that help you make a decision about Charlie and Sarah being with you half time?"

"Yeah, I guess."

"Do you want to think about it some more?"

"Yeah."

Turning to Mary, I ask: "Where are you in terms of how much time Charlie and Sarah spend with John?"

"I want them to be with him. But I really think they need to spend most of their time, especially school days, with me. I could see them spending a lot of weekends and holidays with John. In fact, I guess they would wind up spending at least a third of their time with him."

John breaks in: "As long as I can be with them like that, I'm fine."

I ask John: "So if you and Mary can work out a schedule for weekends, holidays, and vacations in which Charlie and Sarah are with you about a third of the time, you could live with that for now?"

"Yep."

"Good. So about your cars; were you able to get any information?"

"No, I didn't have time."

"Do you think you will have time before our next session?"

"Yeah, I suppose."

"That would be helpful because we will probably be ready to discuss all of your assets and debts at that time."

"Okay, I'll do what I can."

COMMENTARY

After the first mediation session, I typically open each subsequent one by asking participants to bring me up to speed, to get me current again as to anything of import that may have happened between sessions. This ensures a smooth bridge from one session to another. Then I usually follow up on my notes from the last session, in this case asking Mary whether she obtained information about computer classes and whether John had talked with the Employee Assistance person at work. Tracking and helping participants remember the information they agreed to obtain for each other expedites mediation.

Providing legal, financial, and tax information is a key role of the situational mediator. Sometimes the information provided is legal in nature, such as that I provided Mary and John about the temporary or "modifiable" nature of all decisions concerning children. Other times the information provided is based on documents obtained by participants, such as the value of John and Mary's residence as calculated by the average comparable sales price per square foot.

This dialogue also illustrates that it is not unusual for participants to change their minds, as John did about getting his own comps. The reasons participants change their minds vary drastically. However, my observation is that such changes are most likely to occur when participants have shifted from one stage of the grief process to another. Perhaps they have transitioned from anger to acceptance, or have obtained new information. Whatever the reason, the point is that changes of mind are to be expected during the course of mediation. As I told John and Mary, nothing is final until a settlement agreement is signed. Knowing this, situational mediators respond empathically to changes of mind, acknowledging, for example, that "It may turn out that both of you will change your minds several times during the course of the mediation."

As you may see, this block of dialogue is primarily about *trust*, one of the most frequently encountered issues in mediation. Conflict breeds mistrust. Indeed, when marital discord is severe, trust may be the deciding factor with those who choose to litigate rather than mediate. However, distrust is most often localized to specific matters or behaviors, such as Mary's mistrust that John "always says he will do one thing, and then does another!" However, as we saw in Chapter 3, Mary trusted that John would take good care of Charlie and Sarah.

Mediators strive to normalize trust issues. And they certainly don't discount them. Thus, I was normalizing when I told Mary, "My experience is that trust is a very common issue in mediation, especially during divorce. And a certain amount of mistrust can actually help you stay alert when making decisions." I wanted her to know about the frequency of this issue while encouraging her to be on guard when she felt mistrustful of John.

DIALOGUE
I resume the second session by asking Mary and John: "At the end

of our last session you decided that we would work on child and spousal support first. Remember that we will be approaching these areas from two points of view. The first is based on expenses and we will be using the forms I gave you last week to project your expenses over the next year or so. Did each of you have a chance to complete the *Income and Expense* forms?"

Mary answers: "Yes, but I'm not sure I did the Expense form right."

I reply: "That's okay. You will have plenty of time to make changes as we list each expense on the flipchart. John, did you have a chance to complete your Expense form?"

"Yeah, kind of. It was hard figuring out how much I would spend for Charlie and Sarah," John answers.

I respond: "No problem. We can discuss any questionable items and you may ask each other questions about your expenses."

Standing up and moving to the flipchart, I write the following across the top:

Item	Mary	Children	John	Children

COMMENTARY

At this point, the task is to elicit information from the participants about how much it will cost (on average each month) to support themselves and their children in separate households for the next year or so. Using the Expense form as a guide, I first ask about the amounts each participant budgeted under the category of "Home."

Anticipating that he would purchase a house within the next three to four months, as set forth below, John estimated the amount he would pay for monthly mortgage payments (including property taxes and insurance). Furthermore, both he and Mary divided their mortgage payments between themselves and their children, assigning 70% to themselves and 30% to Charlie and Sarah. Consistent with their mortgage payments, both Mary and John also assigned 30% of the following expenses to Charlie and

Sarah: Electricity, Water, Trash, Sewer, Yard Maintenance, Association Fees, Maintenance, and Repairs. I then proceeded, item by item, to get information about all of the monthly expenses Mary and John anticipated under the categories for "Transportation, Insurance, Uninsured Medical, Household, Children, Personal, and Miscellaneous." After obtaining this information, the flipchart looked like this:

Item	Mary	Children	John	Children
HOME				
Mortgage	$770	$330	$700	$300
Electricity	63	17	42	18
Telephone	45	0	60	0
Water, Trash, Sewer	77	36	63	27
Yard Maintenance	21	9	21	9
Association Fees	15	7	0	0
Other	35	15	28	12
	$1,026	$414	$914	$366
TRANSPORTATION				
Car Payment	$304	$0	$0	$0
Insurance	90	0	100	0
Gas	60	20	80	10
License/Tax	41	0	33	0
Maintenance and Repairs	45	0	20	0
	$540	$20	$233	$10
INSURANCE				
Health	$80	$0	$42	$18
UNINSURED MEDICAL				
Doctors	$10	$15	$5	$0
Dental	6	12	4	0
Orthodontia	0	50	0	50

Medicine	8	12	5	0
	$24	$89	$14	$50

HOUSEHOLD

Groceries	$175	$250	$200	$ 90
Restaurants	25	35	60	60
Lunches	0	40	50	0
Laundry, Dry Cleaning	8	0	10	0
Cable TV	0	35	30	10
Newspapers, Magazines	7	3	7	0
Internet Service	0	18	0	0
	$215	$381	$357	$160

CHILDREN

School Supplies	$0	$40	$0	$0
Allowance	0	20	0	20
Recreation	0	15	0	15
Summer Camp	0	25	0	25
	$0	$100	$0	$60

PERSONAL

Entertainment	$25	$20	$25	$20
Hair Care	15	22	10	0
Clothing	35	100	25	0
	$75	$142	$60	$20

MISCELLANEOUS

Vacation	$35	$70	$50	$40
Gifts	32	20	10	0
Donations	30	0	10	0
Pets	0	15	0	0
	$97	$105	$70	$40

I then summarized this information about expenses, as follows:

EXPENSE RECAP

	Mary	Children	John	Children
HOME	$1,026	$414	$914	$366
TRANSPORTATION	540	20	233	10
INSURANCE	80	0	42	18
UNINSURED MEDICAL	24	89	14	50
HOUSEHOLD	215	381	357	160
CHILDREN	0	100	0	60
PERSONAL	75	142	60	20
MISCELLANEOUS	97	105	70	40
	$2,057	$1,253	$1,690	$724

MARY + CHILDREN = $3,310
JOHN + CHILDREN = $2,414
TOTAL (BOTH HOUSEHOLDS) = $5,724

The next step was to get information about income. John's salary was easily determined from his payroll records that showed a gross monthly income of $6,700. After deduction of federal and state income taxes, Social Security, and Medicare, his net or take-home income was $5,092. Review of John and Mary's federal income tax returns showed that they had not declared any income from John's "hobby" of restoring antique cars. However, after discussion, they both agreed that on average he made about $10,000 a year (or $833 a month) from this activity. Thus, John's total monthly net income was $5,925.

At first glance it appeared that John produced enough monthly income to cover the expenses of both his and Mary's separate households. However, this did not take into account John's monthly 401(k) contribution of $425. So after deducting this contribution, the cash available each month was reduced to

$5,500, leaving a monthly shortfall of $224. As I will now recount, it was the discussion of this shortfall that lead to an agreement between John and Mary as to when Mary would return to work.

DIALOGUE

I continue the session by providing information as to 401(k) contributions:

"The reason I didn't initially account for John's monthly 401(k) contributions is because these contributions are *discretionary*, not mandatory. Furthermore, they aren't really an expense but an investment in a tax deferred savings account."

John asserts: "I need to make them. I can't work forever!"

I reply: "I hear you, John. What do you think, Mary?"

"I want him to have a retirement."

"Then let me give you both some information. There are only four ways in which to make up a shortfall: reduce expenses, increase income, dip into some asset (such as an investment or a savings account), or borrow."

"I don't want to use savings or borrow," John protests.

"Neither do I," Mary concurs.

"Well then, that leaves two options: decrease expenses or increase income. Right?"

"I can't reduce expenses any more than I have," Mary says.

"Neither can I. And we can't really count on that income from my cars," John asserts.

"Let's face it, John," Mary states, appearing close to tears. "You just want me to go back to work right now, don't you?"

I intercede: "I know that these can be difficult decisions, and I see that our two hours are almost up. Perhaps you could use the time until our next session to review what you've budgeted for expenses and to consider Mary's work situation in light of what each of you think would be in Charlie and Sarah's best interests. Alright?"

"Yeah," John responds.

Mary merely nods her head slightly, indicating "yes."

"At our next session we can go over your expenses again—if

there are any you want to revisit. We will also calculate child support from the point of view of income. Remember that courts use your gross monthly incomes to calculate what's called a Guideline amount of child support.

"So unless there are any questions, let me prepare you for our next session by giving each of you *Assets and Liabilities* forms (Appendix, page 275). Please complete them and bring whatever documentation you have — your latest bank and investment account statements. Alright, I'll see you next time."

COMMENTARY

Budgeting expenses, as I did with John and Mary, usually takes about an hour or so to complete, depending on the extent to which a couple discusses or argues about each item. However, this is a worthwhile investment of time because it provides couples with detailed information about how much it will cost to live in separate households. In the absence of this information, couples would have to rely solely on court-determined Guidelines that are based on gross income and generalized economic data.

Many couples discover that budgeting expenses is often an eye-opening experience. It's usually the first time they clearly realize the economic consequences of divorce. They now understand that choices must be made as to certain discretionary expenses, such as entertainment or travel. They may also encounter hard choices regarding income, as when Mary pondered her eventual return to work. Recognizing this, I responded empathically, suggesting that they use the time between this session and the next to review their expenses and to consider Mary's work situation vis-à-vis Charlie and Sarah's best interests.

Chapter 5:
Continuing Onward (Cruising)

After reaching cruising altitude airline passengers are likely to have become comfortable with their surroundings. So too with participants in mediation: having become accustomed to the mediation process, they are usually ready to move forward toward negotiation and decision-making. However, turbulence may still occur (as you will soon see!) with situational mediators standing ready to help participants rise above their emotions.

I begin the third mediation session as follows:

DIALOGUE
"Well folks, have you had time to consider what we talked about at our last session concerning spousal support?"

Mary replies: "Well, I guess I could work part-time while the children are in school."

"How many hours are you thinking about?" I inquire.

"I don't know. Maybe 15 or 20 a week?"

"What about taking computer classes?"

"Oh, yes. I guess 15 would be tops."

"Do you have a specific kind of job in mind?"

"No."

"How much do you think you'll make?"

"A couple of dollars above minimum wage. Probably around $10 an hour."

"So if you were to work 15 hours a week at say $10 per hour, you would earn about $645 a month. And after taxes you might bring home around $525 a month. This would bring yours and John's total monthly cash intake up to $6,025 — $5,500 from you, John, and $525 from you, Mary. Right?"

"Yes, I think so," Mary answers.

"What do you think about that, John?"

"It's okay, but only until Sarah finishes sixth grade."

"I hear you. But remember that everything you decide concerning Charlie and Sarah is modifiable, including child support. If Mary works more hours, or gets a full-time job after Sarah finishes sixth grade, and her income goes up, say, 15%, you could request a change in the amount of child support you pay. Is that clear?"

"Yeah."

"And the same would be true if either of your incomes were to decrease, or yours was to increase. Shall we go on to see how the courts determine a Guideline amount for child support?"

"Yes," Mary responds.

"Fine," John answers.

COMMENTARY

The purpose of having Guidelines for child support is to provide consistency—a uniform starting place for discussion and negotiation concerning child support. Such Guidelines are derived from periodic economic studies that determine the amount of money typically spent by families with differing numbers of children and income levels; they specify both parents' "total support obligation." For example, based on their combined gross monthly incomes of $7,345 ($6,700 from John and $645 from Mary, excluding, as a court might do, the income from John's antique cars), John and Mary's total support obligation for their two children is $1,334, under Arizona's current Guidelines (available at superiorcourt.maricopa.gov/ssc).

In many states, including Arizona, each parent's share of the total support obligation is based on a percentage of their combined gross income.[7] In John and Mary's case, John's gross monthly income is 91.2% of their combined gross income ($6,700

---

[7] The American Bar Association provides tables summarizing child support guidelines in all 50 states at www.abanet.org/family/familylaw.

divided by $7,345). Accordingly, John would be responsible for $1,217 of the total support obligation for Charlie and Sarah while Mary would be responsible for 8.8% ($645 divided by $7,345) or $117.

The parent obligated to pay child support is entitled to adjust downward his or her share of the total support obligation by the amount they pay for their children's medical insurance, child-care, extra education, and special needs. This parent is also entitled to a downward adjustment for the number of days the children are primarily with them. Since John agreed to pay for Charlie and Sarah's medical insurance, and will have them with him about 120 days a year, he would be entitled to a downward adjustment of $90 per month for medical insurance and $226 per month (19.5% of $1,334) for the days Charlie and Sarah will be with him.

DIALOGUE

I resume the session:

"Now you can compare this Guideline amount to the total amount you budgeted for Charlie and Sarah. In this way you can decide what you both think is a fair amount for child support."

John asks: "What about the amount I must pay Mary?"

"You mean for spousal support?"

"Yeah."

"Good question, John. Whatever amount you agree to pay Mary for spousal support will be deducted from your income and added to Mary's to calculate child support."

"So you mean that if I were to pay her, say, $1,000 per month, that would be deducted from my income?"

"Yes. If you were to pay Mary $1,000 per month, your income would be reduced to $5,700 per month and Mary's would be increased to $1,645 per month. That would reduce your percentage from 91.2% to 77.6%, and increase Mary's from 8.8% to 22.4%. You see?"

Addressing both Mary and John, I inquire: "Would it be helpful if we discussed spousal support at this point? In Arizona the first question to be answered in terms of spousal support is whether either spouse is *entitled* to it. There are several grounds for entitlement to spousal support, including: (1) the length of the marriage; (2) the likelihood that the person claiming it could obtain employment that would generate sufficient income to adequately support himself or herself; and (3) whether the person claiming support has sufficient income producing property, such as real estate, stocks, or other investments that could reasonably provide for their needs. You've been married for 18 years, right?"

"Eighteen and a half," Mary replies.

"Okay. What does each of you think about Mary's current prospects of obtaining employment to adequately support herself?"

Appearing agitated, John blurts out: "Damn it! This isn't my idea! She's the one who wants a divorce, and now I have to pay."

Mary counters: "I was the one who stayed home with the children! You paid more attention to those cars than anything else!"

"There you go again! If I was such a lousy husband, why didn't you leave a long time ago? I'll tell you why, because it's not true. What about all those times I wanted to be with you? You always had an excuse…"

Mary interrupts: "I had good reason and I don't see how that…"

John cuts in: "Well now you have your boyfriend. I'm sick and tired of you making it seem like this is entirely my fault. You never wanted to be alone with me. You started sleeping in the other room right after we had Charlie. And after Sarah, you wouldn't do anything but bitch and complain. Now it's all my fault and you want me to pay, and…"

John's face becomes flushed and his voice constricted. Lowering his head, he appears to be on the verge of tears.

I wait a moment or two and then intercede by asking:

"Remember when I told both of you that sometimes it's helpful to meet in private sessions? Where I'd like to be alone with each of you?"

"Yes," Mary answers.

Without looking up, John nods his head.

I continue: "Well, I'm wondering if we could do that now, perhaps starting with John?"

"That's fine," Mary responds.

John remains silent.

"Mary, would you excuse John and me for a while? I'll come get you when we're done."

"Alright," Mary responds.

Mary leaves the room. After a few moments when John appears ready to talk, I ask: "How are you doing?"

"Okay, I guess."

"It's really hard sometimes, isn't it?"

"Yeah. It's just that…"

John turns away from me and begins to cry. I wait silently, going within to seek Guidance while giving John time and space. Minutes pass. John reaches for a tissue, wipes his eyes and nose, and turns back toward me.

I ask: "Is it okay for you to be emotional like that?"

"Not really. But I'm not myself lately."

"Remember John, this is part of the grief process. When I was going through my divorce, one day I felt fine but the next I was totally depressed and crying. It was really hard."

"It sure is, especially with Mary thinking she's so high and mighty."

"I hear you. And I can tell you that it turned out to be a really good thing for me. I got to work through all kinds of emotional stuff including a lot of pent-up anger. And, as I already told you, many blessings came from it."

"Yeah, I guess. The truth is that Mary and I haven't been together, you know, *physically* together for a long time. I need that, you know?"

"I do and I hope you get what you want. But my job is to help you get through this mediation as quickly and smoothly as possible, right?"

"Yeah."

"And I take it that you want Mary to become financially

independent as quickly as possible, right?"

"Yeah."

"And she needs computer training to get a better paying job, right?"

"I guess so."

"So wouldn't you benefit by paying Mary support, at least during the time it takes her to complete this training?"

"Yeah, I guess it would. But she expects me to support her in grand style."

"When did she say that?"

"Well, she didn't say that exactly. I don't know what she really wants. We can't seem to talk without arguing."

"Okay, perhaps when she and I meet privately I could ask what she's looking for in terms of support. Would that be okay? And one more thing: remember the hand signal we talked about before? With your permission I'm going to start using it if you appear to be letting your emotions get in the way of resolving this issue."

"Sure," John replies.

COMMENTARY

Arizona's spousal support Guidelines were devised to eliminate inconsistencies between different judges as to the amount of spousal support ordered in similar cases.[8] However, they are relatively new and how they are used varies from court to court.

Expressly intended as a point of departure for "discussion, negotiation, and decision-making" in mediation, Guidelines for spousal support also serve as a platform from which to discuss and negotiate *goals*. Mary has two goals: (1) being with Sarah when she arrives home from school and (2) becoming financially independent as quickly as possible. My experience is that focusing on goals, rather than win-lose adversarial legal tactics, greatly enhances the likelihood of agreement when the highly charged

---

[8] The American Bar Association's tables summarizing alimony/spousal support factors in all 50 states are at www.abanet.org/family/familylaw.

issue of spousal support is discussed.

When John blurted out, "Damn it! This isn't my idea" and then argued with Mary at length, I remained silent for a while because there are times when I simply don't know what to do. These are the times when I find it best to go inside myself, trusting that Spiritual Guidance will provide the next step, as it did in this instance when I asked to meet in private sessions. It was then that John was able to disclose the bitterness he felt toward Mary for her withdrawal of intimacy. As is often the case, private sessions provide the additional comfort and safety needed for participants to disclose uncomfortable or embarrassing information.

John's crying touched me. He was finally able to release his pent-up anger. Realizing how hard this must have been for him, I responded with humility and empathy, sharing about my own divorce and the blessings that followed it. My experience is that emotional releases such as John's hasten transition through the various stages of grief, and I am honored to take part in them.

Before ending my private session with John, I took him through Arizona's Guidelines for spousal support. The key variables under these Guidelines are each spouse's gross income and the length of the marriage. In John and Mary's case the Guidelines suggested $1,635 per month as the starting place for discussion and negotiation, and that this amount be paid for a minimum of one-third to a maximum of one-half the length of their marriage (for 6 to 9 years).

DIALOGUE

Following my private session with John, I begin a private session with Mary: "How are you doing, Mary?"

"Oh, I don't know. This is all so hard for me."

"Yeah, I imagine it is."

"I want to do what's right. I'm not out to hurt John, but I really need some help for a while."

"I hear you. What do you have in mind?"

"Well, something that would be enough for us to get by every month—at least until Sarah completes sixth grade and I get a full-time job."

"You mean something like the amount you budgeted for yourself and the children?"

"Yes, around $3,300 a month."

"Do you want me to talk to John about that?"

"Not now. Let me think about it."

"That's fine. In fact, you may want to discuss it with legal counsel."

"Yes. I might want to do that."

"Good. Is there anything else you want me to talk to John about?"

"Well, I would like him to be more consistent. During our first session he was willing to discuss spousal support, but then today he blew up over it!"

"Yeah, that must be frustrating for you."

"Yes, it really is."

"But is this something new? Has John been consistent in the past?"

"No. No way!"

"So do you expect him to all of a sudden change?"

"No."

"So what's the only thing that can change?"

"I don't know. Me, I guess."

"Yes, that's my experience," I say. "I've learned that I have no control over what anyone else says, does, or thinks. And for me to expect them to change would mean that I am under an illusion. Would you agree?"

"Yes, I would."

"So from now on, may I bring it to your attention if I see that you have slipped into the illusion of control and get angry because you expect John to suddenly change?"

"Yes, I guess so."

"Remember, Mary, we all slip into this illusion from time to time. I know that I do. It's very human. Do you remember when I mentioned that your argument with John may be adding 'more heat than light?' Well, this adage might help remind you about the illusion of control. When I notice you getting angry, I'll mention something about more heat than light being generated. What do you think?"

"We could try it."

"Good. Let's see what happens. Is there anything else that you want to discuss before we get back together with John?"

"No, not that I can think of."

COMMENTARY

Once agreed upon, tools such as the hand signal with John and the "more heat than light" reminder with Mary often serve to quickly end arguments. In this case, these tools (1) helped John remember that paying for Mary's computer classes furthers his goal of Mary becoming financially independent; and (2) helped Mary remember that she can't change John.

After these private sessions, John, Mary, and I reconvened in joint session. It was then that I encouraged them to take time between this session and the next to think about the information they now had about Arizona's Guidelines for child and spousal support. I also encouraged them to consider this information in light of their respective goals. John's goal was to live in a house large enough to accommodate Charlie and Sarah as well as his cars. Mary's goal was to take computer classes and work part-time until Sarah finished sixth grade. I also encouraged them to consider this information in light of the expenses they had budgeted: $3,310 per month for Mary and the children; $2,414 per month for John and the children.

The remainder of this third session dealt with assets and liabilities. John and Mary had completed the *Asset and Liability* forms I gave them, and I used the flipchart to organize and promote discussion about each of their assets and debts. By the end of the session, John and Mary decided to divide their assets and debts as shown on the next page.

Some couples strive for an equal division of community assets and debts, as did Mary and John. Others do not. Either way is perfectly acceptable—to me the mediator and to the court—as

ASSETS (DEBTS)			
Item	Value	To Mary	To John
Assets:			
Bank savings account	$ 5,600	$2,800	$2,800
1999 Buick automobile	16,000	16,000	
1997 Ford Truck	12,000		12,000
1938 Ford automobile	38,000		38,000
1942 Dodge automobile	23,000		23,000
Schwab Investment account	78,400	39,200	39,200
Marital house:			
Fair Market Value	$188,000		
Less: Mortgage	(80,000)	108,000	108,000
General Corp. 401(k)	233,000	100,000	133,000
Automotive tools & equipment	18,000		18,000
	$532,000	$266,000	$266,000
Debts:			
Visa Card	(1,200)	(600)	(600)
Total	$531,400	$265,400	$265,400

long as both parties have made fully informed decisions.

As the flipchart shows, Mary is to become sole owner of their home. John agreed to this in exchange for him becoming sole owner of the antique cars, the automotive tools and equipment, and a greater share of the General Corp. 401(k) retirement account. It should also be noted that a court order (Qualified Domestic Relations Order) must be obtained to accomplish the division of John's 401(k).

Having divided all of their assets and debts, and discussed all matters pertaining to parenting and support, I ended the session by explaining that the next step was for me to draft a settlement agreement. I wasn't concerned that Mary and John had not yet agreed on the exact amounts of child and spousal support. These amounts could easily be included in the draft during the review of it at the next session.

Chapter 6:
Finalizing Settlement *(Landing)*

John and Mary arrived at my office to review a draft of their settlement agreement. The overall purpose of this session is to enable participants to finalize any pending matters (in John and Mary's case, the amounts of child and spousal support to be paid), and to make certain that the final agreement conforms to all decisions made during mediation.

Providing both John and Mary with copies of the draft agreement, I begin the session:

DIALOGUE
"Before we review the draft of your agreement, could we pick up where we left off last time with child and spousal support?"

John replies: "We already talked about it."

Mary adds: "That's true. We agreed on it."

"Good. What exactly did you agree upon?"

John answers: "I'll pay Mary $2,410 a month for 18 months and then $1,300 for 48 more months. Until Sarah graduates sixth grade, I'll pay $900 for child support."

Turning to Mary, I ask: "Is that right?"

"Yes," Mary responds.

"I want to support both of you in all of your decisions, including these, but I also want to make sure that you have made fully informed decisions. So let me ask if you are aware that the amount of spousal support you agreed on is below the Guideline amount that we talked about last session?"

Mary answers: "I know it is. But it's fair."

"Good enough," I respond, and then add, "Now I need you and John to make one more decision concerning spousal support:

is the agreement you reached modifiable, that is, changeable, or is it nonmodifiable, meaning that it can never be changed?"

"We didn't discuss that."

"Well let me give both of you some additional information. *Modifiable* means that either of you can request that it be increased or decreased if there is a material change in circumstances. Such as if you, John, were to suffer a big pay cut, lose your job, or become sick or disabled. Or, let's say Mary got a high paying job. John could then request a downward modification of spousal support. The same would be true for you, Mary. If John were to get a big increase in salary, you could request an upward adjustment in spousal support."

Mary says: "I don't think that's fair to either of us."

John adds: "Neither do I."

I respond: "That's fine. Then I'll put in a provision for *non-modifiability*. In fact, let's start reviewing the draft agreement and I'll point out where this provision will be included. The goal today is to put the agreement into final form. My experience is that it's best if you each read the agreement page by page, trying to stay close to the same page. As you read, you can ask questions or point out anything that needs to change. Alright?"

"Yes," Mary and John reply, simultaneously.

"One more thing before you begin; remember that you won't be signing the agreement today. Before you actually sign it, I want you to have the opportunity to read it again and think about having it reviewed by legal counsel."

"I'm going to do that," Mary says.

"Why?" John asks.

"I'd just feel more comfortable, that's all."

"Okay, if you have to. But you're going to pay for it yourself."

"I know," Mary answers.

I inquire: "What about you, John? Don't you want to have an attorney review the agreement?"

"No. I already talked to one when we were dealing with the kids. I already found out what I needed to know."

"Okay, it's your decision," I reply.

COMMENTARY
Mary and John's agreement was typical of most that I prepare for divorcing parents with children. It was entitled "Mediated Marital Settlement Agreement" and began with "Recitals" setting forth basic information such as John and Mary's full legal names, the date and location of their marriage, and the names and birth dates of their children. It also stated that they intend to end their marriage because of "irreconcilable differences" as is customary in no-fault divorces and that the Agreement was a complete and final disposition of all matters.

John and Mary's final Agreement specified the following with respect to spousal support:

John represents that he has sufficient means for supporting himself and waives any right to spousal support from Mary. Mary represents that she currently has insufficient means for supporting herself, and requires assistance from John for her support and maintenance. For these reasons, commencing November 1, 2001 and continuing for eighteen (18) calendar months until April 1, 2003, on the first day of every calendar month John hereby agrees to pay Mary spousal maintenance in the amount of $2,410 per month; commencing May 1, 2003 and continuing for forty-eight (48) calendar months until April 1, 2007, on the first day of every calendar month John hereby agrees to pay Mary spousal maintenance in the amount of $1,300 per month.

The final Agreement also provided for termination of spousal support upon Mary's remarriage or death, and the following concerning modifiability:

Mary and John agree that these maintenance terms shall not be modifiable, and that any court having jurisdiction in this matter shall not have jurisdiction over the issue of spousal maintenance.

The provisions concerning division of John and Mary's marital property was prefaced with general language concerning: (1) their intent to effect an "equitable" division, with each of them receiving approximately one-half the net value (that is, after deduction of any loans) of all of their marital property; (2) that all taxes due upon a subsequent sale or exchange of any of the property divided under the Agreement would be the sole responsibility of the party receiving the property; (3) that the division of property was final, irrevocable, and complete; (4) that both John and Mary made full disclosure to each other of any interest they had in any and all property, whether held in one of their names alone, in trust for another, or jointly with a third party; and (5) that any property in existence prior to but discovered after the date of the agreement would be divided equally.

This general language was followed by provisions detailing how Mary and John agreed to divide their marital assets, as summarized on the flipchart page set forth previously. For example, Mary decided to trade a substantial portion of her interest in John's 401(k) for John's share of the equity in their home. In this way, Mary was able to stay in the home without having to pay John a large amount of cash.

Provisions concerning credit cards, income tax returns, and liability for tax audits were also included. Finally, John and Mary agreed to sign any additional documents that may be necessary to accomplish the intentions of the Agreement, and to abide by the following *Future Conflict Resolution Process:*

Should any disagreement arise concerning either compliance by John or Mary with this Agreement, or should any dispute arise concerning an alleged breach of this Agreement, Mary and John agree to the following Dispute Resolution Procedure:

STEP ONE. They shall first attempt to meet face-to-face to resolve the matter in good faith, after first having set forth in writing to each other the details of their disagreement, dispute, or proposed amendment.

STEP TWO. Should they be unable to reach agreement after such face-to-face meeting, they agree to consult such experts as may provide information that may help them in their decision, such as family counselors or financial consultants.

STEP THREE. If they are still unable to reach agreement, they agree to seek the assistance of a professional mediator, and attempt in good faith thereby to reach agreement.

A. John and Mary agree that all decisions reached through this procedure shall be committed to writing, signed, notarized, and dated by both of them, and shall become thereafter binding on them to the same extent as the provisions of this original Agreement.

B. Mary and John agree that they shall <u>not</u> file any court action concerning such dispute, alleged breach, or proposed amendment until they have first made a reasonable effort to follow the aforementioned dispute resolution procedure. The person violating this provision shall be liable for the responding person's legal fees and costs.

John and Mary's *Parenting Plan* came next in the Agreement. They agreed to: (1) joint legal custody of Charlie and Sarah; (2) a flexible and cooperative time-sharing arrangement under which Charlie and Sarah would reside primarily with Mary but freely spend time with John, and; (3) the specific days, weekdays, weekends, holidays, and vacations that Charlie and Sarah would be with John if he and Mary couldn't agree about a certain day.

The *Parenting Plan* also included provisions for child support payments by John to Mary, as well as the sharing of certain costs relating to Charlie and Sarah, including uninsured medical services (co-payments, orthodontia, etc.) and extracurricular activities (sports, social clubs, etc.). Agreements concerning parental cooperation (communication, courtesy, etc.), substitute child-care providers, and joint access to school and medical records were also included. Other agreements that were included involved decisions made about insurance on John's life for Mary, dependent deductions for state and federal income taxes, and "Review":

John and Mary shall review these parenting arrangements for possible change and improvement as follows:

1. *Annually, during December, beginning 2003.*
2. *Upon a change in either parent's employment, which conflicts with this time-sharing plan.*
3. *Upon either parent's salary changing by 15% or more for three consecutive months.*
4. *Upon Charlie and Sarah exhibiting signs of stress, which may be related to these parenting arrangements.*
5. *Upon Charlie and/or Sarah's repeated sincere request for a change in the parenting arrangements described herein.*
6. *In the event John or Mary intends to move more than 100 miles from Phoenix, Arizona they each agree to provide the other the greatest written notice reasonably possible, in no event less than 60 days' notice of the intended move, and Mary and John shall meet within 10 days of receipt of such notice for the review. Mary and John hereby agree that it would be in the best interest of their children, now and for three full years following the date this Agreement is signed, that they reside in close proximity to both of their parents, in the State of Arizona.*
7. *In the case of a serious illness or accident to either parent.*
8. *In case of a family emergency, which greatly impedes upon either parent's time or resources.*
9. *Upon remarriage or the cohabitation of John or Mary with an intimate partner or housemate for a period of 30 days or more.*

In so reviewing their parenting arrangements, Mary and John do not necessarily acknowledge these circumstances of agreed-upon review to be a "substantial change in circumstances" justifying court modification. At either party's request, any such review shall be with the assistance of a mutually acceptable mediator as outlined in the "Future Conflict Resolution Process" provision, above.

Having reviewed the entire agreement, and noted a few last-minute additions and changes, I bring the mediation to a close:

DIALOGUE

"Well folks, it seems that you have landed safely."

"Yes, it does," Mary responds.

"Yeah, I guess so," John says.

"I'll put the agreement in final form and mail it to each of you. This will give you an opportunity to read it again and, if you choose to, have it reviewed by legal counsel. In any event, please mail it back to me after it's signed and notarized. Any questions?"

"I don't think so," Mary replies.

"No," John answers.

"Okay then. Thank you for letting me be your mediator, and I wish you both many blessings."

CLOSING COMMENTARY

Most of the time I feel good after completing mediation and often get positive feedback from the participants. Moreover, I know that the mediation process has made a difference in their lives. Divorcing couples, their children, and other loved ones have been spared the increased hostility and tension that is endemic to the legal system. Many have made substantial progress in the grief process. They have also been exposed to new ways of relating to one another and dealing with conflict. Mediation is truly an antidote to the legal system, and I am blessed to take part in it.

Part B: Family Mediation — Other Disputes

Chapter 7:
Other Family Disputes

The situational approach to mediation can effectively resolve any type of family dispute. The concepts, procedures, techniques, and the forms presented with respect to divorce in Chapters 1 through 6 are easily transferable to the mediation of disputes involving parents and children, siblings, same-sex partners, and other family members.

The following is an example of a parent/adult child dispute. Patrick Jones called my office wanting me to mediate between himself and his two adult children, Andrea and Bart. Patrick told me that he had been estranged from Andrea and Bart since their mother's (his wife's) death five years earlier. Here are the steps I took:

Step One: *Pre-mediation Consultation (Pre-flight)*
I directed the conversation with Patrick away from the details of his family dispute and toward the convening of a pre-mediation consultation for the purpose of answering questions and providing information about mediation. I explained that it wouldn't be helpful for him to give me further details about his situation because the less information I have from any participant

111

prior to the actual mediation, the better it is for all concerned in terms of my ability to be impartial. I also explained that mediation is most likely to succeed when everyone is together with the mediator and simultaneously hears what each has to say.

Thus as a situational mediator, I believe it's preferable to consult face to face with all participants. With divorce (Chapter 1), I never agree to consult with one spouse alone. However, when logistics such as long distance travel or circumstances such as estrangement, as in Patrick's case, preclude joint consultation, I arrange a series of separate pre-mediation consultations and most often begin with the person who originally called. Remember, situational mediation is adaptive to the nature and people involved in a dispute, and the situational mediator is free to use whatever mediation approach is likely to be most effective. This includes, as I used here, the evaluative and humanistic approaches that typically call for the mediation to begin with the mediator meeting privately with each participant.

During our initial conversation (consultation), Patrick informed me that he had already visited Out-of-Court Solutions' Website and that he was favorably inclined to mediate but didn't know how to get Andrea and Bart involved. This is when I suggested an "introductory letter" in which I would: (1) explain to Andrea and Bart that Patrick had called to request family mediation; (2) provide them with Out-of-Court Solutions' *Family Mediation* brochure; and (3) invite each of them to call me to discuss whether they would be willing to participate.

Most people who receive an introductory letter respond by calling me, if for no other reason than to say that they are not interested in mediation. Others want more information about how mediation works before deciding whether or not to participate. However, many look upon mediation as an opportunity to clear the air and resolve lingering conflicts, and thus are quite willing to participate.

Later on in this consultation, I answered several of Patrick's questions concerning the number and length of mediation sessions he could expect. I also explained the provisions of the

Agreement to Mediate (Appendix, page 286) pertaining to family disputes (which Patrick agreed to sign). Finally, Patrick authorized me to send an introductory letter to Andrea and Bart.

Bart was the first to respond to my letter. He called me, said that he was quite willing to participate in mediation, and was glad that his father had taken the initiative to arrange it. I responded by acknowledging his willingness to mediate and, wanting to expand this conversation into a consultation, asked if he had any questions about mediation — either in general or as to his situation.

Bart asked and I answered several questions about what went on in mediation, including whether we would all meet together or separately, and if Patrick had agreed to pay for the cost of mediation (which he had). My consultation with Bart concluded after he agreed to sign an *Agreement to Mediate* which would be sent to him in advance of the mediation and under which he would have no responsibility for my fee.

About a week later, Andrea responded to my introductory letter. She said that despite serious reservations about her father's motives, she would "give mediation a try but for no more than four hours." I acknowledged her concerns and explained that her decision about a time limit was, like all other decisions to be made during mediation, solely hers to make.

As with Bart, I asked Andrea if she had any questions about mediation. Andrea's reply was definitive: "Your *Family Mediation* brochure was more than sufficient." I thus explained the provisions of the *Agreement to Mediate*, mentioned that Patrick had agreed to pay the full cost of mediation, and obtained Andrea's permission to send it to her for signature.

COMMENTARY

Unlike this situation with Patrick, many who call my office to initiate family mediation ask numerous questions and want a good deal of information before finally deciding whether or not to mediate. The same is true of many of the people who receive introductory letters; often they ask many questions, raise significant concerns, and express deep emotions. Consistent with the principles of the humanistic aspects of situational mediation, I make it a point to spend as much time as is necessary to help potential participants make fully informed decisions about whether or not to mediate.

Step Two: *The Journey Begins (Taking Off)*
When Patrick, Andrea, and Bart arrived at my office, they were welcomed, asked to complete a brief *Confidential Client Intake* sheet (Appendix, page 285), and were escorted to a conference room.

Patrick's intake information revealed that he was 67, a widower, and unemployed ("retired"). Andrea's sheet showed that she was 41, divorced with one child (age seven), and was employed as a bookkeeper. Bart's sheet showed that he was 36, married with three children (ages 14, 11, and 8), and was employed as a high school history teacher.

Upon entering the conference room, I introduced myself to the participants by briefly recounting my educational and professional backgrounds as well as certain aspects of my personal life (my divorce, remarriage, and four children). Situational mediators look for opportunities to disclose information about their personal lives that participants can relate to. This is because the humility and empathy demonstrated by such disclosure helps participants begin to trust the mediator as well as the mediation process.

Next, I offered an agenda, labeling it *Tentative Agenda* to make it clear that the participants (not the mediator) would have the final say as to whether or not to follow it. It included the following items:

(1) *Rules and Procedures.* I proposed that we invest 15 minutes while I explained each of the rules and each of the procedures that pertain to family mediation. I also explained that this investment of time was likely to save many hours because the *Rules and Procedures* serve as a map for the mediation that helps participants reach their goals quickly, inexpensively, and smoothly.

(2) *Getting Current*. I explained that the *Getting Current* stage gives each participant an opportunity to talk, and the mediator to learn, about the issues involved in the dispute as well as each participant's concerns and goals. I also explained that this stage of the mediation lets everyone involved hear and experience each other's perspectives first hand.

(3) *Immediate Concerns*. I explained that this agenda item is intended to give priority to urgent issues, such as health or money concerns. I also said that I imagined that it would be difficult for them, as it usually is for me, to concentrate on other matters unless and until their immediate concerns were addressed.

(4) *Issues*. I suggested that it's often helpful to define and clarify whatever issues are raised in the *Getting Current* and *Immediate Concerns* stages before attempting to resolve them. I also explained that I never really know the direction the mediation will take after the first three stages — the participants will decide this for themselves.

COMMENTARY

At this point I want to digress to point out two items. First, although the issues involved in divorce mediation fall into discrete categories (assets, debts, parenting, etc.), they are far less defined in most other types of family mediation. It is for this reason that the fourth agenda item in family mediation (*Issues*) is the final item, whereas in divorce mediation five additional discrete categories (assets, debts, etc.) are included in the *Tentative Agenda* and explained.

Second, as you may have already noticed, the titles of the first two steps in family mediation are exactly the same as the titles for Chapters 1 and 2: *Pre-mediation Consultation (Pre-flight)*, and *The Journey Begins (Taking Off)*. This duplication is intended to emphasize that these steps, as well as the ones that follow, can be used when mediating any type of dispute. The same is true for the airplane metaphors (*Pre-flight, Taking Off*); they serve to give participants in any type of mediation a visceral understanding of what's in store for them.

After getting their approval to proceed in accordance with the *Tentative Agenda*, I gave Patrick, Andrea, and Bart copies of the *Rules and Procedures* and then proceeded to elaborate on each rule and each procedure. Because the *Rules and Procedures* for family mediation are essentially the same as in divorce mediation, I refer you to Chapter 2 for in-depth dialogue and commentary.

Step Three: *Gaining Understanding (Altitude)*
This step involves the Getting Current stage of situational mediation. I typically begin this step, as I did with Patrick, Andrea, and Bart, by reminding the participants that this is the time in which they would each have an opportunity to talk without interruption and tell me from their own perspective: (1) the facts and circumstances involved in the dispute; (2) the issues in need of resolution; (3) their concerns, worries, and fears; and (4) their goals and objectives for the mediation.

The *Getting Current* stage is an integral part of the situational approach to mediation, and Chapter 3 features extensive dialogue and commentary about it. I encourage you to read (or re-read) this material before proceeding further in this chapter.

The substance of Patrick's disclosures during the *Getting Current* stage was that: (1) he had recently been diagnosed with stage-three lung cancer; (2) he wanted to see and get to know his grandchildren; and (3) he hoped that Andrea and Bart would "let bygones be bygones."

COMMENTARY
I actively listened while Patrick was *Getting Current*. I asked clarifying questions, occasionally summarized what I heard Patrick say, and reflected back the emotions underlying his words. I also provided Patrick with information about expectations and

encouraged him to consider the possibility that Andrea and Bart might be disinclined to "let bygones be bygones" until he first gained their trust. Finally, consistent with the situational approach to mediation, I was at all times humble, empathic, and compassionate.

Andrea was the next to get current. The main points that she disclosed were: (1) that Patrick was never around during her childhood, and didn't "give a damn" about her; (2) that Patrick's drinking and abuse were to blame for her mother's fatal heart attack; (3) that Patrick still didn't care about her, or Bart, and only wanted to see his grandchildren so he could pretend to be Mr. Nice Guy; and (4) that she mistrusted Patrick and wasn't about to let him "pour salt on old wounds." Again I listened empathically, and was humble and compassionate.

During Bart's time to get current, he made two major disclosures: (1) that while he wasn't particularly angry with Patrick, he didn't want to disrupt his family (his wife and children) to be with him; and (2) that he would do whatever Andrea decided because "she was the one who was always there for me."

As with Patrick, I asked Andrea and Bart questions, reflected back their emotions, and summarized what I heard them say. I also provided them with information about anger, resentment, control, judgment, and blame, all of which are discussed in both Chapter 3 and Section III.

Step Four: *Increasing Communication and Collaboration (Altitude and Acceleration)*

Here mediators help participants define, clarify, prioritize, and otherwise sort out their disagreements, concerns, and goals. They also help participants better understand one another by fostering effective communication. Situational mediators also look for opportunities to demonstrate empathy, humility, and compassion; they know that these are the qualities that increase and accelerate healthy, human interaction.

Up to this point in the mediation, Patrick's manner was reserved. His speech was hesitant and he never made eye contact with Andrea. For the most part, Bart was quiet and I wasn't certain whether he was aloof or detached. Andrea, on the other hand, was unmistakably caustic and hostile toward Patrick. She spewed anger and resentment at him during the entire first session (which lasted about five hours) and continued to do so in the second session. Despite her stated time limit of four hours, Andrea agreed, as did Patrick and Bart, to return for a second session. It was during the second hour of this session that the following exchange took place between Andrea and Patrick:

DIALOGUE

"You didn't give a damn about me or mom! When you weren't at work you were out drinking. Mom couldn't do anything without asking your permission, and she never did anything right as far as you were concerned. You blamed her or Bart or me for everything, anyone except yourself, when most of the time it was your own damn fault! Why do you think I should give a crap about you now?" Andrea angrily castigates Patrick.

"I don't know what to say," Patrick meekly replies.

"Of course you don't! Because it's true, every bit of it! You were a lousy dad, a drunk, and now that you're sick you want everyone to forget all about it and let you pretend to be a loving grandfather. Well, I can't pretend. You made your bed, and now you must lie in it!"

I intervene: "Would it be alright if I ask Patrick a question?"

"I guess so," Patrick responds.

"Why not?" Andrea answers sardonically.

"Okay then. Patrick, do you identify yourself as an alcoholic?"

Andrea breaks in: "He'll never admit that. He's so…My mom had to put up with his drinking, not to mention all the abuse and everything else he put her through. He beat her down, physically and emotionally, until she just didn't want to live anymore. But no, he won't admit to being an alcoholic; he's so damn self-righteous it makes me sick!"

"I hear you, Andrea. It sounds like your father's drinking really hurt you, and your mom?"

"That's an understatement," Andrea replies caustically.

"Yet I'm wondering whether Patrick really knows how much you were hurt?"

Andrea counters: "I don't think he gives a damn! And anyway, it won't change anything."

Patrick speaks up tremulously: "Okay, I drank a lot...yeah, and I guess most people would say that I'm an alcoholic. But I want...I mean...I didn't want to hurt her."

I ask Patrick: "But are you open to the possibility that your alcoholism deeply hurt your family?"

"I didn't want it to."

Nodding my head to confirm that I hear him, I answer: "I hear you, Patrick. Yet alcoholism is called a *family* disease because it's an illness that affects everyone in a family; everyone gets hurt."

Patrick replies: "I know it now. A few years back I went to some AA meetings. I didn't like them. I didn't think I fit in because I went to work every day and never got into trouble, you know, arrested or anything like that. But I knew, you know, underneath, that I had a problem. I was just too ashamed to admit it, you know, to admit that I was weak."

"Yes," I respond, "Denial can be very powerful. I know that from my own experience. You see, I identify as a workaholic, and I've been going to Workaholics Anonymous meetings for many years. However, I was the last one to know that I was addicted to work. This is how denial affects us; we don't know that we don't know. To most other people, especially our wives, children, and friends, it's obvious that we have a problem—an addiction. But we can't see it unless and until we get into enough trouble or have enough problems or experience enough pain that we can no longer ignore it. Does that make sense?"

"Yeah."

After a few moments Patrick continues: "I really thought that my drinking wasn't so bad. Hell, compared to my old man I was a model citizen; you know what I mean? He could never hold a job. My mom had to work her butt off to support us. He would sit at home, drink, and get mean—*really* mean! Give him any excuse and he would beat the hell out of you. The only good thing was that he died early, when I was 14."

I respond: "So alcoholism was in your family of origin and it's likely that you were affected, perhaps deeply hurt by it. Right?"

"Seems so."

"Well Patrick, that's the nature of addictions. They are intergenerational — passed on from one generation to the next."

"Guess so."

I reply: "That's what the research shows. And it doesn't have to be the same addiction. Adult children of alcoholics don't necessarily use alcohol to cover up the emotional pain they would otherwise feel; they often turn to other substances such as drugs or food, or they compulsively engage in activities such as gambling, sex, or work to numb themselves against the pain."

"Yeah," Patrick interjects, "My youngest brother was pretty heavy into drugs."

While nodding my head, I continue: "Well, it seems that we all have our 'drugs of choice,' such as alcohol, sex, or other people (codependency). And each drug distorts our thinking and our behavior becomes destructive. For example, when your father drank, he became violently angry. Does that make sense?"

Appearing pensive, Patrick merely nods his head.

Noticing that Andrea has remained quiet during this dialogue with Patrick, and that Bart has leaned forward and appears interested, I suggest that we take a short break so that they can reflect on this information.

COMMENTARY

Whether addicted to a *substance* (the ingestion and dependency on alcohol and other drugs) or a *process* (one that involves the way in which we do things such as work and gambling), all addictions: (1) are *family* illnesses that originate in childhood; (2) are unwittingly passed on from one generation to the next; (3) function to disconnect us from our feelings (numb the pain we feel from our impoverished self-esteem); and (4) cause distorted thinking and destructive behavior.

Many authorities believe that addictions permeate our families and societies,[9] and my experience is that most family mediations involve one or more addictions. In this mediation, Patrick's alcoholism was quick to surface as a major source of dysfunction and conflict. It would appear to have taken terminal cancer to break through Patrick's *denial* (his blindness to that which was plain to most others) about the effects of his drinking. Until then he seemed to have completely denied and/or minimized his alcoholism by favorably comparing himself to his father ("compared to my old man, I was a model citizen"). Indeed, it appeared that Patrick was still in partial denial. In the foregoing dialogue he was willing to admit only that "most people would say I'm an alcoholic."

Based on Patrick's disclosures about his childhood, including his father's alcoholism and abusive behavior, perhaps his self-esteem was impoverished and he subconsciously used alcohol to cover up his pain. For example, according to Andrea, Patrick blamed others for his problems, an indication of his unwillingness to accept responsibility. That's characteristic of people who have low self-esteem as a result of alcoholism and other family diseases. It's also likely that Patrick's thinking was highly distorted. According to Andrea, "Mom couldn't do anything without asking your permission," indicating that Patrick mistakenly thought that he could control others. And when Andrea said that "[Mom] never did anything right as far as you were concerned," it pointed to the hypercritical and judgmental thinking that are characteristics of people with entrenched addictions. Finally, it's likely that Patrick's destructive behavior (beating his wife down "physically and emotionally") derived from his addiction to a mind-altering chemical.

Much of Andrea's behavior during this mediation was also

---

[9] Bradshaw, J. (1987) *The Family*. Deerfield Beach: Health Communications, Inc.
Schaef, A.W. (1987) *When Society Becomes an Addict*. San Francisco: Harper & Row.

indicative of the extent to which addictions permeate families. She was noticeably overweight and during every break rushed outside to smoke a cigarette. The compulsive use of nicotine and/or food (which many authorities consider a powerful drug) is characteristic of people who are covering up or medicating painful feelings, including the fear of *abandonment*. It's likely that Andrea experienced childhood abandonment issues as a result of Patrick's physical absence and emotional unavailability. In the foregoing dialogue, Andrea castigated Patrick: "You didn't give a damn about me or mom! When you weren't at work you were out drinking." These types of experiences can leave deep wounds and a profound fear of being abandoned again.[10] Indeed, it seemed to me that Andrea was constantly on guard against such abandonment, as evidenced by her repeated condemnation of Patrick.

Although he remained silent during the foregoing dialogue, Bart appeared interested in the information I provided about family diseases. Thus it occurred to me that he might be *codependent*, another form of addiction. Most codependents are caretakers. They compulsively and repeatedly sacrifice their own needs for those of another person while being secretly resentful of having to do so. In this way they use others as their drug of choice, disconnecting from the painful feelings they would feel if they were to surrender control. Spouses of alcoholics (Patrick's wife, for example) are frequently codependent and one could speculate that Bart took over this role upon his mother's death. While Getting Current he claimed that he wasn't "particularly angry with Patrick"; however, it's hard to imagine that Bart would fail to be extremely angry with Patrick if Bart weren't, in fact, codependent. Bart also appeared to be *caretaking* Andrea, as indicated by his statement that any relationship he may develop with Patrick depended on "whatever Andrea decided."

At this point I want to make it clear that while noticing addictive thinking and behavior during mediation, it is not my

---

[10] Woititz, J.G. (1985) *Struggle for Intimacy.* Deerfield Beach: Health Communications, Inc.

intent to analyze or engage the participants in addiction therapy. As a situational mediator, I seek only to provide information that may help participants understand one another better, communicate more effectively, and make fully informed decisions.

Finally, I want mention the self-disclosure of my workaholism. Situational mediators go out of their way to appropriately disclose this kind of personal information as such demonstrations of humility are apt to promote like behavior from participants.

DIALOGUE

After a ten-minute break, we reconvene in joint session:

"So Patrick, might it be that your alcoholism originated from some of your childhood experiences, and that you use alcohol to avoid painful feelings that come from those experiences?"

"Yeah, I guess."

"Might it also be that your use of alcohol caused your thinking to become distorted and your behavior to be hurtful—especially to your family members?"

"Probably, but what good is it now? I'm dying. Everything's so messed up that...I don't know...the bottom line is that Andrea's right; I made my bed...my deathbed...and now I must lie in it."

Visibly shaken and pale, Patrick seems unable to say anything more. Then after a few seconds he lowers his head to the table, cradling it in his hands, and begins to sob.

Everyone remains silent for a minute or two, whereupon I say: "You know, Patrick, I find that my tears can be cleansing. How about you?"

Without lifting his head, Patrick replies: "I'm not sure...I'm not sure of anything any more. She's right, though. I was a lousy father...and husband."

"I hear you, Patrick. Yet I'm wondering if you can think of anything you could do to change the past? I don't know about you, but I've found it impossible to un-ring a bell?"

After a few moments, appearing to have composed himself, Patrick raises his head and answers: "I can't do anything to change what I did, even though I wish I could."

"Yes, it's the same with me," I empathize. "All I can do is make amends for the harm I did in the past, and then change what I do now and in the future. Would you agree?"

"Yeah," Patrick replies. He then turns to Andrea and for the first time makes eye contact with her and, after a few more seconds, says: "I want to do that right now! I'm very sorry, Andrea, for being a lousy father to you — and a lousy husband to your mother. And to you too, Bart."

Again pausing momentarily, and appearing to gain strength, Patrick continues: "I'm sorrier than you can imagine. I've known it for a long time, but I didn't have the courage to admit it to you. No matter what happens, I want you both to know how sorry I am. I'll take my guilt to the grave and I really can't expect anything from you. So I'm sorry that I brought you into this, and I won't blame you if you leave right now and never see me again. Don't worry; I won't bother you any more."

Andrea breaks eye contact with Patrick and appearing conflicted gazes out the window. Bart appears bewildered and remains silent.

Looking toward Andrea, Patrick continues: "I'm really sorry, and I hope you believe me. I want you to believe me; I really need you to believe me."

Andrea does not respond, nor does Bart. Indeed, everyone remains silent.

I sense that this silence is uncomfortable; nonetheless, trusting that Spiritual Guidance will be provided, I let it continue.

Two or three minute later, sounding emotionally drained, Patrick speaks resignedly: "Oh hell, it's all so helpless. I'm a sad case. I can't...I can't even find a way to tell you...to tell you...I love you."

Patrick begins to cry openly, more softly this time but seemingly more freely.

Looking toward Andrea, I notice that she too has begun to well up. I also noticed that Bart has leaned forward and covered his face with his hands.

COMMENTARY

Profound mental and emotional shifts often occur as a result of these types of interactions between participants, opening the way for empathy and compassion as well as problem solving. Indeed, exchanges like this can be transformational, as turned out to be the case for Patrick, Andrea, and Bart.

So too with *amends.* Once again a genuine apology was instrumental in helping to heal injuries from the past. It's no coincidence that two of the Twelve Steps of Alcoholics Anonymous (and most other Twelve Step recovery programs) involve the making of amends.

For me, exchanges like these are peak experiences for which I am very grateful. As the mediator, I am privileged to witness families heal in this way.

Step Five: *Continuing Onward (Cruising)*

This step typically involves the mediator helping participants discuss, negotiate, and make fully informed decisions about their situation. Having established what is involved in their situation and how they want things to be in the future, it is at this point that participants begin to discuss, negotiate, and decide what it is that they are willing to do to get what they want.

In Patrick's situation, I helped the participants discuss, negotiate, and make decisions about their relationships. During these discussions and negotiations it was obvious that Andrea had moved out of the past and into the present. It was as if she had broken through the sound barrier. She spoke civilly to Patrick, at times even warmly, and was willing to explore different options for normalizing their relationship and reintroducing him to his grandchildren. Bart followed suit, offering to arrange a family get-together at his home.

Step Six: *Finalizing Settlement (Landing)*

Unless they involve divorce, most family mediations end without any type of written agreement. However, Patrick, Andrea, and

Bart wanted to memorialize their understandings.

Here is the substance of the provisions that were included in the "Memorandum of Understanding" I prepared for them: (1) Patrick's visits with his grandchildren would be supervised by at least one of their parents (Andrea, Bart, or Bart's wife) unless and until the parents agreed otherwise; (2) Patrick would refrain from using alcohol for at least 12 hours before visiting his grandchildren; (3) Andrea would refrain from making any derogatory or negative remarks about Patrick; (4) Bart would encourage his wife to be respectful of Patrick; and (5) the participants would return to mediation should they be unable to resolve any future disagreements.

CLOSING COMMENTARY
It should be noted that the numbered steps presented above are intended only as guidelines from which a situational mediator can transition back and forth. They are not a set formula or sequentially ordered measures. After all, the practice of mediation is an art as opposed to a science, and the process of mediation is more circular than linear in nature. It is for these reasons that situational mediators are flexible in their practice, and never apply these steps by rote.

For example, should participants have great difficulty discussing, negotiating, or making decisions about a certain issue (Step Five), the mediator will facilitate a transition back to the *Getting Current* stage (Step Three) for the purpose of helping participants ferret out additional information. Likewise, should anger surface during Step Five, the problem-solving step, the mediator will return to Step Four and attempt to enhance communication and understanding between the participants before proceeding with additional problem solving.

This flexibility is essential to the situational approach to mediation. Situational mediators respond to the vicissitudes of human behavior by using the most effective aspects of the evaluative, facilitative, transformative, and humanistic approaches to mediation.

Section II: Workplace and Contract Mediation

Section Two of this book deals with the mediation of workplace and contractual disputes. As you will see, the first two steps for mediating a divorce, reviewing *Rules and Procedures*, and each participant *Getting Current*, are equally effective for workplace and contractual conflicts. Indeed, they are the first two steps for situationally mediating any type of dispute.

Part A: Disputes in the Workplace

Chapter 8:
Pre-mediation Consultation (*Pre-flight*)

In the material that follows I will delineate the mediation of a dispute between two key employees of a large company. However, please keep in mind that all of the concepts, techniques, and procedures illustrated and discussed in this and the following three chapters apply equally to the mediation of conflicts between business partners, members of professional practices, officers of corporations, managers of any enterprise or organization, and any other co-workers.

In this example, my office assistant buzzes me and tells me there's a caller on the line whose name I do not know. He introduces himself as Peter Jones, president of Medical Doctors Insurance Company (MDI), a large medical malpractice insurance company. He explains that a colleague in Los Angeles, for whom I had recently mediated a dispute, referred him to me.

DIALOGUE
Mr. Jones volunteers that MDI is headquartered in Chicago but has a branch in Phoenix that is responsible for the western United States. He then begins to tell me about an ongoing conflict between two senior people in Phoenix, claims manager Cynthia

129

Sanders and claims analyst Kent Stone.

I politely interrupt:

"Excuse me, Peter. Before you go any further, please understand that it wouldn't be helpful for you to tell me the details of what's going on. If I am to be the mediator, it's important that I don't form any preconceived notions about the situation. I want to hear about it directly from the people who are involved."

"I understand," he replies.

"Thank you. Perhaps it would be helpful if I were to explain how I work?"

"Yes, please do."

"I usually meet in a series of sessions with the people involved. The first session typically lasts from three to five hours. During this session, I explain the *Rules and Procedures* that apply to mediating workplace disputes. Then I ask the participants to tell me about the situation from their own perspectives: what's gone on in the past, the issues as they see them, any concerns they may have and their goals."

"I see."

"From then on I meet with them in three hour-long sessions."

"How many sessions in total?"

"It varies. But my experience is that most situations are resolved in 12 to 15 hours. I typically send the client a contract that allows for up to 15 hours of my time."

"That's fine. What is your fee?"

"$260 an hour."

"Alright. How do we get started?"

"Well, first let me explain a few more things. First, you need to know that I don't report to anyone. That would include you. Everything that goes on in mediation is strictly confidential unless the participants decide otherwise. Is that okay with you?"

"I never thought about it before, but it makes sense. So I can live with it."

"Good. Second, all of the sessions need to take place outside of your company's offices."

"That's not a problem. We can arrange for a conference room."

"That would be okay, but I would prefer if they came to my office."

"Alright. Good."

"May I ask if Cynthia and Kent know that you are talking with me?"

"They know that I'm concerned and that I've mentioned the idea of a mediator."

"How did they respond to that?"

"I think they're aware that something must be done."

"Okay. Perhaps you could give them our Website: www.outofcourtsolutions.com. They can read my biography and the information pertaining to workplace mediation. This will give them a feel for what I do."

"Sure. I'll take a look at it, too."

"Great. Would you also tell them that they can call my assistant if they have questions or particular concerns?"

"Sure."

"Good. Should I send you a contract?"

"Yes."

"And will you arrange for Cynthia and Kent to call for an appointment?"

"Sure."

"They can ask for my assistant."

"Very well. I'll get them going."

COMMENTARY

My involvement in workplace disputes between key personnel usually begins with a call from a senior corporate executive (as it did with Peter Jones) or from a government official when a municipal, state, or federal agency is involved. It can also begin with a call from their legal counsel, as is typical in situations involving employee grievances or workplace discrimination claims. In other situations (a disagreement between partners or co-owners of a business, etc.), my involvement might begin with a call from one of them or their attorneys.

Because he had very few questions before asking how we get

started, it seems that Peter Jones was predisposed toward retaining me as a mediator. Perhaps he had already obtained enough information from his colleague and only wanted to find out my methodology and what I charge. Some potential clients take more time and want additional information (my Curriculum Vitae, references, etc.) before deciding to mediate.

Regardless of the type of dispute, I usually halt, at the phone consultation stage, any conversation about the substance of a situation.

Occasionally a caller insists on telling me something "important." And in several of these instances, I have acquiesced. However, I listen guardedly and politely interrupt when I sense they are about to say too much.

Attorneys typically want to send me statements or briefs on behalf of their client. However, I uniformly decline their offer, explaining that my accepting and then reading this information would cause me to develop certain opinions or preconceived notions about the matter. This is admittedly unusual and many attorneys don't fully understand it—that is, until they are actually in session and experience the situational approach to mediation.

I insist on complete confidentiality and will not report on the mediation to anyone unless the participants decide otherwise. Confidentiality encourages the honesty and openness that my reporting to a third person would dampen. Indeed, my having to report to a third person would most likely result in one or more of the participants refusing to mediate. Finally, if I were to report to a third person I might find it hard not to judge the participants. This would be inconsistent with the situational approach to mediation because such mediators relate to participants as equals, not as judges.

I also insist that all mediation sessions occur away from the workplace. This ensures privacy and avoids distractions (although at the beginning of the first session I frequently must ask participants to shut off their pagers and cell phones). When mediating in cities other than Phoenix, I ask that the client arrange for the use of a hotel conference room.

Suggesting that potential participants visit Out-of-Court Solutions' Website helps in three ways: (1) they find out a little about me by reading my biography and looking at my picture; (2) they learn about the mediation process by reading the information and articles pertaining to workplace disputes; and (3) they become more comfortable about the prospect of participating in mediation.

At this pre-mediation stage, I usually have my assistant deal with participants if they want more information or have particular concerns. She is trained to answer the most frequently asked questions about workplace mediation. She is also trained to defer answering any unusual questions until she has checked with me. On rare occasions, I have talked directly with a participant prior to the commencement of mediation. However, I limit the conversation to an elaboration on the mediation process and to clearing up misunderstandings. Under no circumstances will I listen to or discuss any of the particulars involved in the dispute. I have also, on occasion, provided participants with our *Rules and Procedures* for workplace mediation (Appendix, page 287). My experience is that many participants feel less anxious about mediation after reading them.

The contract I use is brief but covers the essentials of Out-of-Court Solutions' relationship with the client. It defines the scope of the work as "mediation services" and my role as an "independent contractor." It also provides for the confidentiality of anything said or written during the mediation as well as payment terms and various expenditures (travel, etc.). As with the contract I sent Peter Jones, I usually obtain authorization to provide up to 15 hours of mediation services (with a proviso for additional time should everyone involved concur that it is warranted).

There are two more comments I want to make about the consultation with Peter Jones. First, I establish a first name basis with clients from the very beginning, as I did with Peter. This kind of familiarity is consonant with the humility intrinsic to the situational approach to mediation and most seem to welcome it. Second, some of those who are involved in workplace disputes don't have a choice as to whether they will or will not participate in mediation. They are told they must (or sense that they must) participate. I heard this when Peter said, "They know that I'm concerned." And this was confirmed when he said, "They know that something must be done."

However, this lack of choice need not detract from the mediation. On the contrary, it is all the more reason to use the situational approach. Sooner or later during mediation a participant will in some way let it be known that his or her job would have been in jeopardy had they refused to mediate. In the public sector, where it is more difficult to terminate an employee, it is likely that they would have been subjected to poor performance evaluations, decreased opportunities for promotion, and other negative consequences. Situational mediators respond empathically to this lack of choice by acknowledging the feelings of frustration and anger that mediation typically engenders. Situational mediators also respond compassionately when they help participants understand that they nevertheless have many choices, including the ultimate choice of what decisions are made during mediation.

Chapter 9:
The Journey Begins (*Taking Off*)

Kent Stone and Cynthia Sanders arrive at my office for their first mediation session. After each completed a brief intake form, they were escorted to a conference room, offered refreshments, and told that I would join them shortly.

A review of their intake forms revealed that Kent Stone had been with MDI for 12 years, whereas Cynthia Sanders had been there for less than one year. I also learned that neither Kent nor Cynthia had retained legal counsel in this dispute.

Kent and Cynthia were about to begin their journey in mediation, which as with airline travel entails rules and procedures aimed at ensuring safety and reducing anxiety. Passengers on an airplane are instructed as to policies such as those regarding seatbelts and emergency exits. Participants in mediation are informed about the use of legal counsel, private sessions, etc.

I enter the conference room, introduce myself, and shake hands. We all sit down, and I begin the session.

DIALOGUE
"Did either of you have a chance to visit our Website?"

Kent and Cynthia simultaneously answer, "Yes."

"Good. So you both know that my background is in law, business, and psychology, and that I've been a full-time mediator for the last seven years?"

"Yes," Cynthia responds.

Kent merely nods his head, indicating his understanding.

"Okay then. I have an agenda in mind to start off today's session, and with your permission I'll put it up here on the flipchart."

Standing up and moving to the flipchart, I write *Tentative Agenda* at the top the page. I then continue: "I'm going to call this a Tentative Agenda because if it works for you we'll use it. If it doesn't, we'll figure out something else.

"The first thing I'd like to do is explain the *Rules and Procedures* (Appendix, page 287) that govern mediation, or at least the way that I conduct mediation. We'll invest about 10 or 15 minutes going over each of the *Rules and Procedures* in detail. However, my experience is that this drill literally saves hours because it provides a map, if you will, for the mediation. Let me put it this way. Let's say that we all jump in a car to take a trip together, say to the East Coast. Wouldn't we want a map to get us there as quickly, inexpensively, and smoothly as possible in terms of stress and strain?"

"Yes, that's true," Cynthia responds.

"Yeah," Kent answers.

"And I take it that both of you might share in the goal of getting through this mediation quickly, inexpensively, and smoothly. Is that right?"

Kent hesitates, shrugs his shoulders, and then says: "Not necessarily."

I respond, "I hear you, Kent. Would you be willing to elaborate on that?"

Kent replies: "I just want to do my job! Cynthia has caused me a lot of trouble, and I'm not at all concerned whether things go smoothly. I just want to be able to work without her always looking over my shoulder."

"Might you still want to get through the mediation quickly and inexpensively?"

"Yes, obviously. I can't do my job sitting here, and I certainly don't want to spend a lot of the company's money on this."

"Alright. What about you, Cynthia? Which of these goals do you share in?"

"All three. I want to get this accomplished quickly and inexpensively. I also want to avoid any unnecessary disruption, and I certainly want Kent to get his job done. But I'm not sure that he understands what his job is."

Kent counters: "We'll see about that!"

Both Cynthia and Kent remain silent for a few seconds, and I continue: "So what I'm hearing is that you both share in the goals of getting through this mediation quickly and inexpensively, with Kent doing his job. But you differ as to getting through this mediation smoothly. Is that right?"

"Yeah," Kent answers.

"It seems so," Cynthia replies.

"Alright then. What I want both of you to know is that I'm here to support each of you in achieving these and whatever other goals you have in this situation. And part of being supportive is to tell you that it is common for emotions to surface during mediation: frustration, anger, even sadness. In fact, mediation is like taking an airplane ride in that you can be up there flying along smoothly and then all of a sudden, out of nowhere you hit turbulence, it gets bumpy, and then you're bouncing all over the sky. Here in mediation we may be going along smoothly with both of you discussing and sorting things out, and then all of a sudden one or both of you gets triggered by something that's said or done, and it gets bumpy in here.

"This kind of emotional turbulence is to be expected. But part of my job as your mediator is to help you weather it, that is, to help each of you deal with your emotions in ways that further your goals, including getting through this mediation quickly and inexpensively, with Kent being able to do his job. Is that clear?"

"It is to me," Kent replies.

"Yes, it's clear to me too," Cynthia answers.

"Then I'm going to make a promise to both of you. It's the only promise I ever make in mediation: If you stay with this process, in other words, if you stay seated even when it gets bumpy, you will land safely. Research shows that mediation is effective in over 80% of the cases submitted, and my success rate is even higher. So the odds are with you. Okay?"

"Yeah," Kent responds.

"Okay," Cynthia replies.

Standing up and moving to the flipchart, I begin to talk while writing the next agenda item:

"The next thing I'd like each of you to do is what I call *Getting Current*."[11]

While sitting down, I continue: "At this point I'm going to ask each of you to tell me about your situation from your own perspective. My experience is that we all see things a little differently. We all have different points of view. What I would like each of you to do is to share with me, from your own perspective, what's going on here.

"You should know that I didn't discuss this situation with Peter Jones. In fact, I made it clear to him that I wouldn't discuss anything substantive about your situation with him or anyone else. So anything that's said here will remain confidential unless and until both of you decide otherwise."

Cynthia states: "Yes, Peter told me about that."

Kent adds: "Yeah, he told me that, too."

"Good. Since I don't know anything about your situation it would be helpful if each of you were to tell me about it from your own point of view. I would like to know what's gone on in the past, and what you identify as the issues that presently need to be resolved. I'd also like to know about any concerns you may have. My experience is that most people come into situations like this with real concerns, if not worries and fears. So I would like to hear what you're concerned about, or perhaps fearful of. Finally, I'd like to know about your goals: what you would like to see come out of this mediation for yourselves, for your company, or any other goals you have? So I'm asking each of you to share with me everything and anything you can to get me up to speed or 'current' with you. Okay?"

"Fine," Kent responds.

---

[11] I learned this term during a mediation training conducted by James C. Melamed, Esq., founder of the Mediation Center in Eugene, Oregon, and a world-class mediator.

"Yes," Cynthia replies.

"Thank you. And I have one more request: Would you let each other talk without interruption? I know that this can be hard. I remember situations when I was personally involved in a conflict, and someone said something that I experienced as hurtful or painful, or just not true. Before I knew it my old lawyer-self came back and I jumped right in, interrupting, wanting to 'set the record straight.' I'm asking you to do your best not to interrupt each other. Okay?"

"That's fine," Kent answers.

"Certainly," Cynthia says.

"Yet knowing that we're all human and can slip, may I have your permission to remind you of this if I hear either of you interrupting the other?"

"That's not a problem," Cynthia replies.

"Yeah, okay," Kent answers.

"Thank you again."

Standing up and moving to the flipchart, I write *Issues* and continue: "After the *Getting Current* portion we will probably — and I emphasize the word probably — start talking about the *Issues*. We will define them, clarify, and discuss them."

Placing my hand over the word *Issues*, I continue:

"I say probably because the truth is that after the *Getting Current* portion I really never know where mediation is headed. Each mediation seems to take on a life of its own, and you will be the ones who decide what we discuss next. It will be your decision to make, not mine. In fact, as I will explain in detail in just a few moments when we review the *Rules and Procedures*, you will be making all of the decisions in this matter, including what we discuss after the *Getting Current* portion. Any questions about this?"

"No," Cynthia replies.

Kent merely shakes his head, indicating "no."

"Good. So here's a copy of the *Rules and Procedures* for each of you. Please take a couple of minutes to read them, and then I'll elaborate on each provision."

COMMENTARY

I begin all mediations by (1) setting forth a *Tentative Agenda*; (2) explaining that the *Rules and Procedures* will serve as a map for the mediation; and (3) describing the *Getting Current* portion. Regardless of whether the dispute is between two key executives, an employee and supervisor, business partners, or parties to a contract, starting out this way has proven highly effective. Starting out this way is essential to the situational approach to mediation.

My experience is that most participants are relieved when I get down to business quickly, promptly offering an agenda. Similar to airline passengers who appreciate the pilot announcing anticipated weather conditions, arrival times, and the like, participants in mediation are relieved to know what's in store for them. For passengers and participants alike, starting out this way reduces tension and assuages fear of the unknown. It is also empathic and compassionate and thus in conformity with the situational approach to mediation.

The airline metaphor also serves to reduce tension and fear. Many people view it as unprofessional or a sign of weakness to show their feelings, especially in business situations. I experienced Kent as angry when he said that his primary goal was to "do my job." Although unexpressed, Cynthia undoubtedly had her share of feelings about this. Explaining that emotions are common in mediation, as is bumpy weather in airline travel, normalizes the display of feelings. This metaphor also serves to instill hope that the vast majority of participants "land safely" despite the occurrence of turbulent emotions.

A flipchart is an important tool for a mediator. It can be used to organize a session (as with a *Tentative Agenda*) or focus everyone's attention on particular issues. It can also be used to intervene on emotional outbursts. Often all it takes to end an angry exchange between participants is for the mediator to stand up, move to the flipchart, and begin to write. Indeed, as I will now explain, mediators need be conscious of the strategic importance of standing and sitting.

I always make it a point to sit down when explaining the *Getting Current* portion of the first session. When asking people to share their perspectives, especially their concerns, worries, and fears, I want to be humble, demonstrating as best I can that we are all very human, subject to error and emotion. My experience is that this can best be accomplished when I sit down, physically putting myself on an equal level with everyone else.

Another way for mediators to demonstrate humility is to ask participants in advance for permission to say or do certain things. For example, having asked for permission to remind them about letting each other "talk without interruption," I can respectfully intercede later on if, for example, one person were to repeatedly interrupt the other.

I also always make it a point to help participants establish shared goals early on in the mediation. This is what I attempted with Kent and Cynthia when I asked if they shared "the goal of getting through this mediation quickly, inexpensively, and smoothly." Although Kent wasn't interested in getting through the mediation "smoothly," he did concur in the goal of getting through it "quickly and inexpensively." He and Cynthia also agreed on the goal of Kent doing his job (although they differed on what his job is). After these shared goals have been agreed upon, they can be used later on as an intervention when, for example, one or both of them becomes angry. Reminding them of one or more of these goals is often all that is needed to get them back on course.

In mediation time is money. It is for this reason that I always use the word "invest" when talking about the time it will take to explain the *Rules and Procedures*. I want participants to recognize that the money spent during this time is truly an investment in the future. Without this, the mediation is apt to stray off course and unnecessary time and expense could result.

DIALOGUE
Noticing that both Cynthia and Kent have finished reading the

Rules and Procedures, I continue the session:

"Let me start out by talking about the first and second paragraphs together, for when combined they explain what I do and what I don't do as your mediator.

"My job is broken up into several parts. One part helps you communicate and negotiate effectively. I know from personal experience that my emotions often get in the way of self-expression and hearing others clearly. Knowing this, part of my job as your mediator is to help you deal with the emotions that are likely to surface during mediation so that you communicate and negotiate as effectively as possible and stay on course toward your goals.

"Another part of my job is to offer you options and alternatives, different ways of resolving whatever issues there are between you. After all, with my background in law, business, and psychology, there are likely to be some options or alternatives I can offer for your consideration which will individually and then collectively make sense."

Pausing momentarily, I go on: "Yet another part of my job as your mediator is to provide legal and financial information. However, I want you to clearly understand that I will provide you with legal *information* but I will not give you legal *advice*. When I practiced law, I would give legal advice such as, 'I think you should do this or you shouldn't do that.' If you were to hear me say something like that as your mediator, you would know that I had slipped into the role of attorney—which is not my role. Sure, I'll provide you with a lot of legal information based on my understanding of the law in certain areas. But I won't be providing you this information for the purpose of telling you what you should or shouldn't do. Rather, I'll be providing it for the sole purpose of letting you compare it to what you think is fair. Okay? Any questions about this?"

"No," Cynthia and Kent answer, simultaneously.

Standing up and moving to the flipchart, I continue: "I can sum up everything I've just said in these two words: *Informed Decisions*. In fact, I always write these two words on the flipchart, as I've just done, and leave them in plain sight during the mediation because they will remind all of us of what my job is and isn't as your mediator. It's not my job to make any decisions for you. I am not here as an attorney or a judge. Nor am I here to say what you should or shouldn't do, who wins, who loses, who's right, or who's wrong. The essence of my job is to try as best as I can, using my head and my senses, to assist each of you in making fully informed decisions. Is that clear?"

"Yes," Cynthia responds.

"Yeah," Kent says.

COMMENTARY

I go to great lengths to clearly delineate what I do and don't do as a mediator. Many people readily understand that mediators aren't judges, deciding who's right or wrong, or who wins or loses. Indeed, this is the very reason why many people choose mediation. They don't want to turn over control to some outside authority or "roll the dice" on a decision made by a stranger. However, the distinction between mediator and attorney can be harder for some people to grasp. Many people are accustomed to relying on so-called experts to tell them what to do, and no matter how much I explain my role as mediator, sooner or later they forget and either ask me what they should do or seek legal advice from me.

I'll admit that at times it's been hard for me to resist the temptation of taking on the role of judge or attorney. Some participants appear or actually ask for help and it sometimes seems easier, even more compassionate, to just tell them what to do. It is on these occasions that the evaluative approach to mediation may be the most effective; this approach calls for the mediator to direct participants toward settlement. Yet knowing that I rarely know what's best or fair for someone else, and that it borders on arrogance to suppose that I do, I usually resist this temptation and let participants find their own way toward fully informed decisions.

Writing the words "informed decisions" on a flipchart page

and keeping it in plain sight during the mediation provides a readily accessible tool for dealing with participants who forget or confuse the mediator's role. Typically, all I need to do is point to these two words to remind that person of my role as mediator, and then begin a discussion about other options for getting additional information or advice, whether from legal counsel or some other expert.

Informed decision-making by participants is central to situational mediation and my role as mediator. If at any time during mediation I were to conclude that a person was unable or unwilling to participate in this way, I would terminate the mediation.

In this case, my impression was that both Kent and Cynthia were experienced business people, and readily grasped the distinctions between mediator and judge, and between mediator and attorney. I also experienced them as quite capable of making fully informed decisions.

DIALOGUE

I continue by elaborating on the third paragraph of the *Rules and Procedures.*

"Let me talk about the next paragraph. This paragraph deals with 'information and documents.' When I practiced law, part of my job was to make it as difficult, expensive, and time-consuming as I could for the other side to get information and documents. After all, litigation is an adversarial system; it's a fight and one way to fight is to financially wear down the other side. Here in mediation, it's the exact opposite. By cooperating with these *Rules and Procedures* you are agreeing to be open, honest, and fully disclosing of any and all information needed to make fully informed decisions. Are you both willing to do this?"

Cynthia answers: "Yes, certainly."

Kent replies: "I have my file with me and I'm perfectly willing to let her see anything that's in it."

I respond: "Good. So I take it that you are both willing to fully disclose all information necessary for each of you to make fully informed decisions?"

"Yes," Kent and Cynthia answer, simultaneously.

COMMENTARY
The willingness to provide all the information and documents needed by each participant to make fully informed decisions is an essential part of the situational approach to mediation. No one can or should be expected to make decisions without having all of the information they require to do so.

Sometimes information from a third party is required. In Kent and Cynthia's situation, it may come to pass that information is needed from others in their company, such as the Director of Human Resources or perhaps the President, Peter Jones. In other situations, say a mediation involving the dissolution of partnership, information may be needed from an accountant and/or business appraiser as to the value of the partnership's business.

On occasion, a participant has been reluctant to provide certain information or documents because of cost, time, or some other consideration (despite his prior agreement to abide by the third paragraph of the *Rules and Procedures*). However, only once in seven years have I encountered a participant who steadfastly refused to provide needed information. In this instance I had no choice but to terminate the mediation.

DIALOGUE
I next elaborate on the confidentiality afforded to mediation:

"The fourth paragraph deals with confidentiality and I'd like to explain this. Here in Arizona (as in many states) we have a statute that basically provides that anything said or written during mediation is strictly confidential, meaning that if you were not able to reach full agreement through mediation, nothing that went on here could be used later in court. So in the unlikely event that you couldn't resolve your differences here and had to retain separate lawyers, you would have the protection of confidentiality. I couldn't be brought in to say 'Kent said this,' or 'Cynthia said that,' and a judge couldn't order me to produce my notes in court."

"Good," Kent comments.

Cynthia merely nods her head, appearing to indicate her approval.

"Okay then. I would like to discuss one more aspect of confidentiality, that is, will anyone else be told about what went on here? For example, would you both want to talk to your spouses about this?"

Cynthia replies: "I'm not married."

"But is there someone you might want to talk or confer with?"

"No."

"Good enough. What about you, Kent?"

"I might want to talk to my wife. Not about everything, but some things."

"How do you feel about that, Cynthia?"

"That's fine. I would expect him to talk to his wife," Cynthia replies.

"What if either of you consults with an attorney, or perhaps a therapist? Would they be excluded from your agreement concerning confidentiality?"

"They should be," Kent asserts.

"I agree," Cynthia replies.

"Is there anyone else that either of you would exempt from the confidentiality of this mediation?"

"I don't think so," Cynthia says.

"Neither do I," Kent answers.

"So could you both agree not to divulge anything about this mediation to anyone else, including anyone at work?"

"Absolutely," Kent answers.

"Certainly," Cynthia replies.

"Do you want me to add a provision about this to the *Rules and Procedures*?"

Cynthia replies: "That's not necessary."

Kent says: "I agree."

COMMENTARY

The confidentiality of anything said by participants or written by the mediator during mediation is essential. Very few people, especially those involved in a workplace dispute, would agree to mediate without the safety afforded by confidentiality.

As the mediator I am bound to confidentiality unless both participants decide otherwise. I established this during my telephone consultation with Peter Jones, and confirmed it with Cynthia and Kent.

By reason of signing the *Rules and Procedures*, specifically Paragraph Four, as well as Arizona state law, participants are also bound to confidentiality. However, my experience is that many people want someone (their spouse, close friend, attorney, therapist, or some other trusted advisor) with whom they feel free to confide details about the mediation without violating confidentiality. Thus, I uniformly inquire about anyone who should be exempted from confidentiality. It is also my experience that most participants fully expect that married participants will talk with their spouses, as did Cynthia with Kent, and rarely require that the *Rules and Procedures* be amended to include a specific exemption.

DIALOGUE

I continue by explaining the fifth paragraph of the *Rules and Procedures*:

"The fifth paragraph talks about joint sessions and private sessions. Right now all of us are together in joint session. However, there may come a time when I ask that we break into private sessions where I'll meet with each of you individually. Let me give you an example of when this may be needed. Let's say we have been talking about a particular issue for some time but we seem to just keep circling around it without resolution. At this point, recognizing that you may not be progressing as quickly as you want, I might ask that we break into private session. I would turn to one of you, say Cynthia, and ask if you would excuse Kent and me while we talk privately. Cynthia, you would then leave the room while Kent and I talk about whatever issue or issues were under discussion. Then, Kent, when we were done, you would leave the room, and Cynthia would come back and we would meet privately to discuss the same issue or issues. Then we would get back together in joint session. Any questions so far?"

"No," Cynthia and Kent answer, simultaneously.

"Good. So I want you to know that there is absolutely nothing about private sessions that is intrinsically good or bad. It is simply a method that has proven effective to help move the mediation process forward. I've had situations where we have never met privately and others where we have met privately six, seven, even ten times.

"As to the confidentiality of anything that is said in private session, let me give you three options in this regard. One option is that I'm bound to keep anything you tell me in private session strictly confidential, meaning that I cannot disclose it to the other. My concern about this option is that it's contrary to full disclosure and puts me in a control position because I have information that one of you doesn't. But some people insist on it, and..."

Kent cuts in: "I have nothing to hide!"

I respond: "So you don't like this option?"

"No. Not at all!"

"What about you, Cynthia?"

"I don't like it either."

"Then let me explain a second option. At the other end of the spectrum is for me to be able to disclose *everything* you tell me in private session. In other words, if you tell me something that I believe is important for the other to know, I would be free to appropriately disclose it. In this way, the person who's outside the room doesn't have to wonder what I'm being told. There wouldn't be any secrets at all."

Pausing momentarily, I continue:

"A third option is a combination of the first two. That is, I would be at liberty to disclose anything you tell me privately unless you specifically tell me not to. The way this would work is that at the end of each private session I would ask whether there was anything you said that you do not want me to disclose to the other. This would give you the opportunity to tell me anything you don't want disclosed. And it would give me the opportunity to discuss it with you."

Cynthia speaks up: "That last option sounds good to me."

Kent counters: "Hey Cyndi, what's wrong with letting everything out?"

"Look, Kent," Cynthia retorts, "I'm not going to get into that with you. We're here because of you, and I might want to tell the mediator something that quite frankly is none of your business!"

"Yeah, Cyndi. That would be just like you!" Kent argues.

I break in: "So what I'm hearing is that you, Kent, want no secrets from these private sessions and you, Cynthia, want to reserve the right not to disclose certain things."

Cynthia replies: "Yes. I just want to be careful. I'm not saying that I will actually tell you not to disclose something, but right now I want the right to decide as we go along."

I respond: "I hear you, Cynthia. Perhaps what you are saying is that you feel safer reserving the right not to disclose certain things, but may never actually exercise this right."

"Yes, exactly."

Turning toward Kent, I inquire:

"What do you think now?"

"I guess we can do it her way."

"Are you sure?"

"Yes."

"Okay then. My understanding is that at the end of each private session I'll ask if there is anything you said that I shouldn't disclose to the other. Is that right?"

"Yes," Cynthia answers.

"Yeah," Kent replies.

"Good. The last thing I want to tell you is that if either of you at any time thinks that it would be helpful to break into private session, all you need do is say so; if you both agree, that's exactly what we'll do."

COMMENTARY

There has been a longstanding controversy among mediators as to the use of private sessions. For example, evaluative mediators usually adhere to a structure in which participants routinely meet in private session and rarely in joint session, whereas transformative mediators often refuse to ever meet privately. I usually spend most of my time in joint session, but don't hesitate to meet privately with participants whenever I sense that doing so would provide greater opportunities for understanding and empowerment, or would otherwise help participants reach agreement.

Here are some of the situations in which I am apt to ask for private sessions. As in the example I gave Kent and Cynthia, I may ask to meet privately with participants when I sense that they are stuck on a particular issue. Perhaps they have spent hours discussing the issue; I've provided information as well as different options and alternatives, but one or both participants are stuck and unable to make further progress. My experience is that more often than not the reason for this problem is that one participant hasn't fully disclosed all of the information needed for the other to make a fully informed decision.

In one situation, for example, two partners in an architectural firm were involved in a dispute that on the surface appeared to concern professional standards. During the first several hours of mediation they argued back and forth about who was "right" about these standards. Then, after a particularly angry exchange, I asked to meet privately. It was then that I learned that until recently these men had a close personal friendship that existed before they became partners and extended to their wives and children. I also learned that an incident at work involving several other architects had caused a complete breakdown in their friendship. In joint session, both partners denied any desire to restore their friendship. It wasn't until we met in private session that one partner admitted he valued the friendship but was too embarrassed to say so in front of the other partner. He then asked me to assist him in expressing this desire, which I did, and when we returned to joint session both partners openly discussed the incident and thought of ways to restore their friendship.

Another instance in which I am likely to suggest private sessions is when I sense that one party may be attempting to intimidate or dominate the other. This dynamic commonly occurs in workplace mediations where one participant is subordinate to the other. It also frequently occurs as a result of differing conflict resolution styles: when faced with conflict, some people are by nature dominating, while others are avoidant, compromising, or obliging.

Yet another instance in which I am likely to use private sessions is when there are repeated or extreme outbursts of anger and other emotions. Sometimes one or both participants simply need a "time out." Other times, private sessions provide the opportunity to give participants information about their particular conflict resolution style or teach them anger management tools (which are discussed at length in Chapters 13 and 14). Private sessions allow intimate and frank discussions without causing either participant undue embarrassment or discomfort.

You may have noticed that although I told Kent and Cynthia about three options concerning the confidentiality of anything said in private sessions, I was clearly discouraging selection of the first option (where everything they told me in private session would remain strictly confidential). I usually choose to be evaluative and directive about these options. This is because I have yet to encounter a situation that requires, or in which the participants have benefited from, this degree of nondisclosure. Moreover, this degree of nondisclosure contradicts the provisions of Paragraph Three of the *Rules and Procedures* (concerning full disclosure of all information and documents).

DIALOGUE

I continue to explain the sixth paragraph of the *Rules and Procedures*.

"Paragraph Six addresses an attitude that I am going to request that both of you strive to maintain during mediation. I call it one of 'mutual respect.' So could we make it a rule that each of you will let the other talk without interruption?"

"Yes," Cynthia replies.

"Fine," Kent says.

"Well, sometimes that's easier said than done, at least for me. As I've said before, emotions are normal in mediation. Remember it's like an airplane ride, and knowing that you are likely to experience at least some bumpy weather, and that we're all human and slip and make mistakes, may I have your permission to remind you about letting each other talk without interruption if I hear either of you forgetting about this?"

"Yes," Cynthia answers.

"Alright," Kent replies.

"Thank you. Could we also have it that any threats, intimidation, or any other kind of verbal aggressiveness is against the rules?"

"Certainly," Cynthia responds.

"Yeah," Kent says.

"I have one more request in terms of maintaining an attitude of mutual respect. Would you be willing to do your best to call each other by your first names? Instead of using pronouns, such as 'he, she, and you' or the like, would you use each other's first names when talking about each other? I know this can be a little awkward at first, but my experience is that it helps maintain an atmosphere of mutual respect. And since I've already taken the liberty of calling you by your first names, I'm wondering if you would call me Oliver? Okay?"

"Yeah, okay," Kent replies, looking impatient.

"I'm fine with that, but as long as we're speaking of mutual respect, my name is Cynthia, not Cyndi, and Kent knows that!"

I respond: "Is it your request that Kent call you Cynthia, not Cyndi?"

"Yes, that's my name."

"How do you feel when he calls you 'Cyndi'?"

"Angry. It's disrespectful."

Turning to Kent, I add: "What about it, Kent? Would you be willing to honor Cynthia's request?"

"I don't see the big deal, but whatever."

"Thank you. And if I hear you slipping on this, may I have your permission to remind you about it?"

"Yeah. No problem."

"And if I were to hear either of you forgetting that we are going to be on a first name basis, may I remind you of it?"

"Certainly," Cynthia answers.

Looking even more impatient, Kent merely nods his head.

COMMENTARY

Never wanting to presume authority, situational mediators ask permission to remind participants of a rule or procedure. This is one of the ways in which situational mediators express humility. Furthermore, having obtained permission, the mediator can respectfully intervene if, for example, someone were to later on threaten, become verbally abusive, or repeatedly interrupt. Thus, knowing the importance of getting this permission, I simply ignored Kent's apparent impatience.

As to referring to each other by first names, use of pronouns such as "he" or "she" is generally innocuous in ordinary conversation. However, in situations of conflict, these pronouns are frequently used to indirectly communicate negative, hostile, or antagonistic messages. Participants may be unaware that they are sending these indirect messages, but they definitely detract from an attitude of mutual respect. In this case, it seemed to me that Kent knowingly used the name Cyndi as an indirect and hostile form of communication. Cynthia let it be known that she experienced this as disrespectful, and with my assistance requested that Kent call her by her given name. Finally, asking that participants also refer to the mediator by first name gives voice to the situational mediator's desire to approach participants humanisticly; empathy, humility, and compassion are most likely to occur when people are together as equals.

DIALOGUE

I continue by explaining the seventh and eighth paragraphs of the

Rules and Procedures:

"Paragraph Seven deals with the use of attorneys during mediation. I saw from your intake forms that neither of you is represented by counsel in this matter. Yet I want you to know that if either of you wants to consult with an attorney, I encourage you to do so. It's perfectly okay, at any time during this process. As I said, I encourage it. Okay?"

Kent replies: "Yeah, I know a lot of lawyers, but we'll see how it goes."

I respond: "That's fine, Kent. It often helps to get additional information from an attorney."

"We'll see," he says.

Turning to Cynthia, I ask: "What about you, Cynthia?"

"I don't think that will be necessary."

"Okay. But I want to make sure that you are aware of this option."

"I'm aware of it," she replies.

Pausing momentarily, I continue: "I call the last paragraph of the *Rules and Procedures* (Paragraph Eight) my 'escape clause' because if someone were to continually violate one or more of the rules, I reserve the right to either suspend or terminate the mediation. Okay?"

"Fine," Kent replies.

"Okay," Cynthia answers.

COMMENTARY

Many participants in key personnel mediation never consult with or retain an attorney. They simply don't see the necessity for legal counsel, as was the case with Kent and Cynthia.

My experience is that many participants opt not to consult with or retain attorneys because in their minds the dispute has not progressed to the point where they feel a need for legal advice. However, sometimes I get the feeling that a participant has intentionally withheld information about having previously consulted with an attorney. I suspect there are many reasons for withholding this information, including a lack of trust and fear of negative consequences should anyone, particularly their employer, find out about it. Another reason could be to gain strategic advantage.

Indeed, this is the sense I got when Kent said: "I know a lot of lawyers, but we'll see how it goes." My impression was that this was his way of letting Cynthia know that he had an attorney waiting in the wings. In any event, my obligation as mediator is to make sure that participants fully understand their right to consult with and retain legal counsel at any time during the mediation. It is up to them to decide whether and to what extent to involve an attorney.

In other types of workplace disputes, for example, claims of discrimination in the workplace, most if not all participants have retained legal counsel and often include them as participants in the mediation. My experience is that most attorneys are very helpful in these situations. They provide the legal expertise typically required for participants to make fully informed decisions.

As to Paragraph Eight, in all of my years as a mediator I have never had to invoke this paragraph when mediating a workplace dispute. Nonetheless, reserving the right to suspend or terminate the mediation is an important safeguard.

Once I finish explaining the *Rules and Procedures*, I ask both participants to sign an original. Then I sign it myself, and make a copy for each of them. This routine is intended to give the *Rules and Procedures* additional credence and importance in the minds of the participants.

Chapter 10:
Gaining Understanding *(Altitude)*

Following a short break, I continue the first mediation session with Kent and Cynthia. As is typical with airline passengers who feel a wide range of emotions, from calm when flying conditions are smooth to fear when turbulence is present, participants in mediation are likely to experience varied emotions in this, the *Getting Current* stage.

Before proceeding further, it should be noted that in this stage of mediation I begin to organize the information disclosed by participants into three categories: *What, Want,* and *Willing.*

These three categories provide a simple yet highly effective model for conducting any type of mediation. I first strive to bring out each participant's perspective as to *what* is involved — in the past as well as the present. These are the facts, circumstances, concerns, worries, fears, and issues as perceived by each participant. I have learned to take my time when eliciting this information; not doing so greatly increases the likelihood that the mediation will stall, deadlock, or otherwise run into trouble.

Next, I attempt to engage each participant in dialogue about the different things that they *want.* Having had the opportunity to disclose their perspectives about the past and present, most participants are willing to shift their attention to how they *want* things to be in the future.

Many of the things that participants *want* are obvious from the positions they take, the needs they express, and the demands they make. However, many of the other things that people *want* involve emotional needs and are harder to discern. These are the things that subconsciously influence their thinking and behavior, and include human needs for safety, security, acknowledgement, respect, honesty, fairness, trust, etc. Situational mediators endeavor to discover and then bring out these interests. This opens the way for collaborative problem solving.

Finally, I seek to elicit information about the things that participants are *willing* to do to get what they *want*. These are changes in position, modifications of demands, and adjustments of needs that each participant is *willing* to make to resolve the dispute.

DIALOGUE

Addressing both Kent and Cynthia, I introduce the next agenda item: "What we'll do now is called *Getting Current*. As you will recall, this is the time in which each of you will let the other talk without interruption, sharing with me from your own perspectives: (1) what's gone on in the past; (2) what you identify as the issues that presently need to be resolved; (3) what concerns or worries you about this situation; and (4) what you would like to see as results or outcomes of this mediation. In other words, I'd like you to tell me anything and everything that would help me get current with you. So who would like to go first?"

"I will," Kent asserts.

"Fine," Cynthia acquiesces.

I respond: "Okay, Kent. Where would you like to start?"

"How about with the fact that my whole career has gone south since she took over? She changed everything. She thinks..."

I interrupt: "Do you mean Cynthia?"

"Yeah, sorry."

"I know it can be hard to refer to each other by first name, and that emotions can get in the way, but it does help maintain an atmosphere of mutual respect."

"Okay."

"Thank you. Perhaps you could start by telling me about your educational and professional backgrounds."

"Sure. I graduated high school in 1976. Then I was in the Air Force for four years. After that, I went to work as a casualty claims adjuster and attended community college at night. I wanted to be a paramedic."

"Where was that?"

"New Jersey."

"What company did you work for?"

"National Insurance, but a year later I moved to Keystone Mutual. I wanted to get into management, and they had a great program. Then Keystone was bought out by Health America, which had a large portfolio of med-mal policies. With my paramedic and physiology classes, my boss asked me to work the med-mal claims."

"Med-mal?"

"Medical malpractice."

"Oh, I see. By the way, what year was that?"

"1985. Anyway, I've worked in med-mal ever since."

"When did you start working for MDI?"

"1988. My wife was working for them—until we had our first kid."

"How many kids do you have?"

"One while I was in the Air Force, but that marriage was over within a year. I have two more in this marriage."

"Boys or girls?"

"One boy from my first marriage, and a boy and girl from my second."

"I can relate to that. I've been married twice, and have four children, two boys from my first marriage, and a boy and girl from my second. So your second wife was involved in you going to work for MDI?"

"Uh huh. She was with MDI when we met in their New York office. I was at Health America. Then, in 1988, she was offered an administrative position in Phoenix. Her folks live here. Anyway, we were engaged at the time and Phoenix had an opening for a Claims Tech. I got the job, and we moved here."

"What does a Claims Tech do?"

"Gathers information about new claims: does a background check on the claimant; gets statements from our insured, doctors, nurses, hospital staff, and anyone else who may have been involved in the claim; and gets copies of the medical records. Then they organize and summarize all of this information and give it to a Claims Analyst."

"What happens to it after that?"

"The Claims Analyst prepares a Risk Assessment Report which includes the dollar value of the claim. This is the amount we anticipate paying out on the claim; the company is required by law to set up a reserve for that amount. After that, it's given to the Senior Claims Analyst for his approval, and if it's above $50,000, it goes up to the Claims Manager for concurrence. Any claim with a reserve of more than $100,000 goes up to the Vice President of Claims at corporate headquarters in Chicago."

"I see. How long were you a Claims Tech?"

"Two years. I worked hard, took night classes at the Insurance Institute and in 1990 was promoted to Claims Analyst."

"When did you become the Senior Claims Analyst?"

"In 1994, but there are actually two Senior Claims Analysts in each office: Chicago, New York, and Phoenix. We each have our own team: four Techs and two Analysts."

"So there were four Analysts in Phoenix at the time you were promoted to Senior?"

"Uh huh, two for each team."

"So you presently supervise six people?"

"Right."

"Okay, so when Cynthia was hired you were one of two Senior Claims Analysts in Phoenix?"

"Yeah, but for the first eight months of last year I was in charge of the whole Claims Department."

"How did that come about?"

"Bob retired in December of 1999, and they didn't hire anyone until the following September. So I was in charge from January to August."

"Who is Bob?"

"Bob Thompson. He was the Claims Manager for Phoenix. In fact, he was the one who hired me back in 1988."

"I see. So when Bob left you were put in charge of the entire

Claims Department?"

"That's right."

"As Manager?"

"Kind of, but not officially. But I was in charge until they hired Cyndi, I mean Cynthia. Sorry about that; it was an accident."

"I hear you. But with all due respect, are you open to the possibility that there are no true accidents?"

"What do you mean?"

"Are you open to the possibility that on a subconscious level we actually *intend* so-called accidents to happen?"

"I don't know anything about that."

"I hear you, Kent. But would you consider it?"

"I guess."

COMMENTARY

The *Getting Current* stage is an essential part of the situational approach to mediation. Early on it creates an environment in which participants can talk about their situation and be heard by each other. Having the opportunity to talk and be heard is curative, as Sigmund Freud knew when he initially called psychoanalysis "the talking cure."

The *Getting Current* stage is structured so that conversation occurs between one participant and the mediator, while the other participant(s) listens. This structure affords each participant the opportunity to dialogue with the mediator without interruption by the other participant(s). It also affords them the opportunity to listen to each other without having to plan a response. As with Kent and Cynthia, many co-workers never truly communicate. The *Getting Current* format provides an opportunity for this to happen.

Getting Current in this way also sets the stage for later sessions. Except for occasional private sessions, situational mediation takes place in joint sessions in which participants talk directly with one another. Thus, they are able to hear one another, experience each other's emotions, and simultaneously get the information needed to make informed decisions.

In the *Getting Current* stage situational mediators strive to create an environment in which participants begin to relax and feel comfortable. Knowing that empathic, humble, and compassionate interactions promote this environment, situational mediators look for opportunities to demonstrate these qualities. It is for this reason that I typically look for openings to ask participants about their family situations, as I did with Kent when I asked about his children. Questions of this nature provide mediators with opportunities to relate to participants with humility (in this case, as one parent to another) and to empathically disclose their own family background — all of which goes a long way toward reducing stress and creating a relaxed, comfortable environment.

In this block of dialogue, it was clear to me that Kent was continuing to act out his anger toward Cynthia, this time by referring to her as "she" and "Cyndi." Initially, I intervened by asking: "Do you mean Cynthia?" This served as a gentle reminder that we had all agreed to avoid the use of pronouns and to refer to each other by first name. Later on I intervened more assertively, making it clear that "on a subconscious level we actually *intend* for the things we call accidents to happen." As with his previous expressions of indirect hostility toward Cynthia, Kent's acting out manifested *passive-aggressive* behavior. This type of behavior is subtle and harder to detect than overtly offensive or insulting remarks, but is no less disrespectful. Thus, as I did here with Kent, situational mediators take prompt action to prevent the recurrence of this behavior and thereby restore an atmosphere of mutual respect.

Finally, it should be noted that situational mediators consistently strive to be humble and thus never presume authority. It is for this reason that I always begin the *Getting Current* stage of mediation by asking, as I did with Kent and Cynthia, "Who would like to go first?" It's also worth noting that Kent disclosed a good deal of information about the past and present circumstances involved in his dispute with Cynthia, which I recorded in my notes under the category *what*: (1) the dates and substance of significant events; (2) Kent's family history; and (3) the nature of his behavior.

DIALOGUE

I continue with Kent:

"So I take it that you expected to become Claims Manager?"

"Yeah, that's right."

"Do you have any idea why that didn't happen?"

"They blamed it on my so-called lack of 'people skills.' I guess one or two Techs and Analysts thought I was too demanding. Anyway, I never expected them to hire someone from the outside. I've got much more experience, and I certainly don't micromanage."

"Who made the decision to hire from the outside?"

"The Executive Committee, in Chicago."

"In addition to you, were there any other candidates from within the company?"

"The other Senior Analyst in Phoenix, Ron Anderson. But he has far less experience than I do. And I guess they could have promoted someone from New York or Chicago, but that wasn't likely."

"Why not?"

"Because it never happened before, and I was doing a good job."

"I hear you. So you never expected them to consider anyone else besides Ron Anderson and yourself?"

"That's right."

"So I imagine that you were upset when they hired Cynthia?"

"That's an understatement; I was blown away! I resent everything about it."

"How's that?"

"Every month or so I would call Jim Peterson in Chicago and ask whether a decision had been made. He's the Vice President of Claims and a member of the Executive Committee. He kept telling me 'no,' but then without a word they hired from the outside."

"Did you ever ask Jim Peterson whether they were considering anyone else?"

"No."

"Why was that?"

"Because I never dreamed that they would hire from the outside. I worked hard, took classes, and did everything else I could to get that job."

"And you were 'blown away' when you found out that Cynthia had been hired?"

"Yeah, but I got over it."

"You did? So you're not angry?"

"Nope, it's not a problem."

"Is there still resentment around this?"

"Nope, it's a done deal."

After pausing for a moment to make note of Kent's last few comments, I continue:

"Let me ask you about something that you said a minute ago: about Cynthia 'micromanaging.' What's that about?"

"She has all of these forms for everything; you know, like the government. And now I have to complete a daily report."

"And you experience this as being micromanaged?"

"Yeah, of course. I'm a Senior Claims Analyst and resent being treated like a child!"

"I take it that you expect to be treated as an adult?"

"Of course, wouldn't you?" Kent asserts.

"If I were acting like an adult," I reply.

"What do you mean by that?" Kent asks, antagonistically.

"I certainly didn't mean it in a disrespectful way, and I apologize if you took it that way. Okay?"

"Yeah, fine; it just took me by surprise. Anyway, what did you mean?"

"Well, I heard you mention several *expectations* that were unmet. You *expected* to become Claims Manager, but didn't; you *expected* the Executive Committee to promote someone from within the company, and they went outside; you *expected* that Cynthia would treat you as an adult, but in your view she micromanages and treats you like a child. True?"

"Yeah, so what?"

"Well, I also heard you mention several *resentments*. In regards to Cynthia being hired you said: 'I *resent* everything about it.' Regarding Cynthia's micromanagement, you said: 'I *resent* being treated like a child.' You see, Kent, I've learned that there is a direct connection between *expectations* and *resentments*?"

"Connection?" Kent inquires.

"Yes, they are connected. In fact, resentments come from unmet expectations, or, put another way, unmet expectations are the most frequent source of resentments—as well as a lot of other kinds of unhappiness, including anger. Looking back I can now see that whenever one of my expectations went unmet, I experienced some degree of unhappiness: from disappointment, frustration, anger, and resentment, to sadness and depression.

"When I was in college I always expected to get the highest grade in the class, and got pissed off when I didn't. When I was a trial lawyer I expected to win all of my cases, and got angry or sometimes depressed when I lost. When my ex-wife unexpectedly left me, I was resentful.

"So now, whenever I get angry or resentful, sooner or later I discover that these feelings are connected to an unmet expectation: I expected something to happen, but it didn't, like when you didn't get promoted to Claims Manager. Or, I didn't expect something to happen and it did, like in your situation when MDI hired from the outside. Is this beginning to make sense?"

"Kinda."

"Let's see if I can make it clearer. You see, now when I get angry or resentful, I first try to figure out what expectation was unmet: what was it that I expected, but didn't get; or, what was it that I didn't expect to happen, that happened. In other words, I try to trace my feelings back to their source. Clear so far?"

"Yeah."

"Okay then. After I discover what my expectation was, I check to see whether it was *realistic*. You know, Kent, in retrospect it's amazing to see how many of my expectations turned out to have been unrealistic. That's the trouble with expectations; that's why they cause so much unhappiness—so many of them are *unrealistic*.

"For example, in retrospect it's clear that my expectation about always getting the highest grade in every college class was pretty unrealistic. It's also clear that it was unrealistic of me to expect my ex-wife to stay in an unhappy marriage. The same when I was practicing law; it wasn't realistic for me to expect to win every case. Do you relate to that in your work?"

"Yeah. Sometimes we have to pay a lot more on a claim than we expected. I can't help what some idiot jury decides to do!" Kent replies.

"So let me ask you: in retrospect, do you think that it was *realistic* to expect that the Executive Committee wouldn't interview other people?"

"I'm not sure; maybe it wasn't. But it's not fair; I worked hard for a lot of years!"

"I hear you, Kent, and I imagine that you are very disappointed. I've never experienced quite the same thing, but I can think of certain events in my life that blew me away. In fact, one comes to mind. Could I share it with you?"

"Sure."

"When I was practicing law, one of my partners suddenly left my firm and took three other attorneys with him. I was, to say the least, disappointed. In fact, I was really blown away and angry.

"But you know what? Looking back I can see that my expectations of this partner were unrealistic. I had put him under a lot of pressure in terms of producing billable hours and satisfying clients, and he just wasn't as driven as I was. So it was unrealistic for me to expect that he would stay in the firm and work as hard as I demanded."

Appearing pensive, Kent remains silent.

"It took me a long time to figure out the connection between *expectations* and *resentments*. And then, a few years ago, I wrote an article about it. It's called *The Anatomy of Anger* (Chapter 13), and I'm wondering if you would be willing to read it before our next session?"

"I can do that," Kent replies.

"Good. I will also give Cynthia a copy. Perhaps, if she's willing, the three of us can discuss it during our next session. Would that be alright?"

"I guess."

"Thank you. And would you hold on a second, Kent, while I ask Cynthia a couple of questions?"

Kent nods his head, indicating "yes."

I turn to Cynthia and ask: "What about you, Cynthia? Would you be willing to read the article?"

"Yes."

"Good. And let me check in with you for a moment. How are you doing?"

"Fine."

"Good. I know it can be difficult to just sit and listen. So thank you for being so patient about letting Kent and I talk without interruption."

"It's fine."

"Well, thank you anyway."

COMMENTARY

Most people are unaware of the connection between *expectations* and *resentments*. They don't realize that unmet *expectations* (expectant thoughts) are the likely source of *resentments* (entrenched anger) and countless other negative emotions. As I did with Kent, situational mediators strive to educate participants about this connection in empathic ways, i.e., by disclosing instances in their own lives in which their unrealistic expectations led to anger and resentment.

Most people also don't realize the frequency with which expectations are *unrealistic*. All too often it is only in retrospect that most of us are able to see the unreality of our expectations. As I told Kent, looking back it's clear that many of my own expectations were to a large degree unrealistic.

Kent "never dreamed" that anyone outside of MDI would be hired as Claims Manager; he *expected* to get the job. However, he was aware of complaints about his people skills and one might therefore question the reality of his thinking in this regard.

One might also question the reality of Kent's expectation that Cynthia would not micromanage him. He claimed that his resentment of Cynthia was a done deal and expected that she treat him "like an adult." Yet his passive-aggressive references to Cynthia as "she" and "Cyndi" suggested a very different reality — that he was still acting out his resentment in petulant, child-like ways. The reality of the situation may have been that Cynthia had little choice but require daily reports and otherwise micromanage him.

In this block of dialogue we saw another example of assertiveness by the mediator. When Kent countered my question about his expectation of being treated as an adult with a question of his own ("Of course, wouldn't you?") I answered assertively, "If I were acting like an adult." My assertiveness was intended to break through the wall of resentment I perceived Kent had built in relation to Cynthia. It seemed to me that Kent was stuck behind this wall and unable see the part he played in the dispute with Cynthia. I hoped that my answer would provide the cognitive dissonance necessary to break through Kent's wall and show him the connection between *expectations* and *resentments*.

It should be noted that assertiveness (firmness) on the part of a mediator is not the same as aggressiveness (combativeness). As I said before, my intent in being assertive was to break through Kent's wall of resentment, not to be belligerent. However, sensing that he may have misinterpreted my intent, I promptly apologized for any offense he may have taken. In this and other instances, situational mediators are quite willing to humbly admit and apologize for any harm they may have unintentionally caused.

It should also be noted that mediators run the risk of appearing self-important or arrogant when explaining the psychological dynamics ("psychodynamics") underlying a participant's behavior. It is for this reason that situational mediators explain these matters by recounting situations from their own lives. Thus, for example, I explained the connection between expectations and resentments by recounting instances in which I became angry, resentful, and depressed as a result of my own unrealistic, unmet expectations concerning school, my law partner, and my ex-wife.

While one participant is *Getting Current*, it's important that the mediator be aware of the other participant(s). Although Cynthia was exceptionally good about not interrupting, she was likely to have been affected by what Kent said. Thus, I made it a point to check in with her.

DIALOGUE

I continue with Kent:

"So are you open to the possibility that your unmet expectation about the Executive Committee not interviewing anyone else, especially someone from outside the company, was somewhat unrealistic?"

"Yeah, I'll give you that."

"Okay, but it's not my intent to be *right*. After all, plenty of my own expectations turned out to be unrealistic. All I want to do is give you and Cynthia the opportunity to look at how your expectations may have influenced your behavior."

"I get that. But I worked hard to get that job and now I don't have a clue as to where I stand."

"You mean, where you stand with the company?"

"Yeah."

"Where do you *want* to stand?"

"I'm not sure. But you know those private meetings you mentioned?"

"Yes."

"Could we do that?"

"Sure, if Cynthia agrees."

"Well, I don't mean right away; just at some point later on?"

"I see," I turn toward Cynthia and ask: "Would that be okay with you?"

"I'm not certain," Cynthia replies.

Kent breaks in: "I don't mean right now. I mean later on!"

Cynthia responds: "I'm still not certain, Kent! Before deciding,

I want my turn to talk with Oliver."

Kent replies submissively: "Fine. Whatever."

I interject: "So what I'm hearing is that you both agree that Cynthia will have a chance to get me current before any final decision is made about meeting privately; is that right?"

"Yes," Cynthia answers.

"I guess so," Kent acquiesces.

Turning back to Kent, I continue:

"Kent, where should we go from here? Is there anything else that you can think of that might help me get current?"

"Well, yeah. Nowadays I don't know who to trust. I thought I could trust Jim Peterson, and look what happened!"

"He's the Vice President who's on the Executive Committee?"

"Yeah, he's the one who kept telling me that no decision had been made."

"Okay, I remember. Let me ask you, though: after Cynthia was hired, did you talk to Jim about what happened?"

"Yeah, I did. That's when I found out about my so-called lack of people skills."

"You had no idea before then that there was a problem in that area?"

"Well, sure, I knew there were complaints."

"How many were there?"

"Two, maybe three at the most. But nothing in writing; you know, no formal complaints were made. Bob just told me about them."

"Bob Thompson, the former Claims Manager?"

"Yeah."

"What did he say?"

"Basically, he told me to ease up. I can be somewhat of a perfectionist. He told me to relax a bit, not to be so demanding. Bob was a great guy; we were really tight. I could tell him anything and he gave me a lot of independence. I still can't believe that he said anything to Peterson."

"Did Bob report to Jim Peterson?"

"Yeah."

"And yet you never expected him to say anything about the complaints?"

"No, but I guess that was pretty unrealistic too, huh?"

"Perhaps," I concur. "But it sounds like the two of you were fairly close."

"Yeah, we were. I looked up to him, you know, like a mentor or something."

"Did you ever talk to him about any of this?"

"No, and I don't want to."

"May I ask why not?"

"I just don't."

"Okay, I hear you. Yet I imagine that you were disappointed when you found out that Jim Peterson knew about the complaints concerning your people skills?"

"Yeah, no kidding!"

"Would you say more about that?"

"No, let's just leave it alone."

"Alright. Is there anything else that you want to talk about?"

Appearing pensive, Kent pauses for a few seconds and then says: "Well, yeah, I just want to say that these days I don't know who I can count on. I trusted Bob and Jim, and got screwed. Lately, everything seems to be going downhill. I spent all those years trying to get ahead, and now I'm screwed. I'm locked in with nowhere to go."

"So what I'm hearing is that you're mistrustful, you don't know who to turn to, and you feel victimized. Is that pretty close?"

"Yeah, kinda."

"And I imagine you have some anger about all of that?"

"Anyone would! I got a screwing, and now I'm nowhere."

Nodding my head in acknowledgement, I respond: "Kent, I can only imagine how difficult all of this must be for you. And yet, it seems that whatever you've done to date hasn't made it any better. Your relationship with Cynthia, for example; your way of dealing with her hasn't improved it. Would you agree?"

"Yeah, that's obvious."

"Okay then. Let me tell you what renowned psychologist Carl Jung had to say about all of this. He said it was easy to tell when people were insane. He said that people could be considered *insane* if they expected different results while doing the same thing in the same way, over and over again.

"I don't know about you, but I can certainly relate to that. There were so many times in my life when I kept doing the same thing in the same way, all the while expecting different results; for instance, from my ex-wife and the law partner I told you about.

"Looking back there is no doubt in my mind that I was insane. I failed to tell my wife how I felt; I avoided arguments for fear that she would leave me. I did pretty much the same thing with my law partner — all the while expecting that both would change. That was pretty insane, right?"

"Yeah, I guess so," Kent replies.

"So can you also see how this might apply to your relationship with Cynthia?"

"Yeah," Kent says with a sigh, "I guess I do."

"So in the future might you want to avoid that kind of insanity, and consider doing things a little differently with Cynthia?"

"Maybe."

"Okay, I hear you. You might just want to think about it. And perhaps we can talk about it a little later on?"

"Maybe."

Noticing that Kent appears deep in thought, I pause for a few seconds and then continue: "Alright then. Is there anything else that you want to talk about?"

"No, not now."

"Okay. I haven't forgotten your request that we meet privately, and there will be plenty of time later on to talk about anything else you might think of. Alright?"

"Yeah, sure."

Mindful of the time, I address both Kent and Cynthia, asking: "How are you both doing in terms of needing a break?"

Cynthia answers: "I would like ten minutes."

"What about you, Kent?"

"Yeah, fine."

"Good, so let's do that."

COMMENTARY

When Kent said, "I'll give you that" in answer to my question about whether his expectations of the Executive Committee were realistic, I sensed that he saw himself in a debate that I had just won. Wanting to dispel this notion, and do so with humility, I went out of my way to tell Kent that "it's not my intent to be *right*" and that "plenty of my own expectations turned out to be unrealistic." Situational mediators avoid being argumentative, correcting as quickly as possible any such misimpressions.

Having elicited a good deal of information about *what* was involved in this dispute, I thought it might be time to see if Kent were willing to shift his attention away from past events and circumstances, and toward how he might *want* things to be in the future. Thus, I asked him, "Where do you *want* to stand with MDI?" However, Kent's answer ("I'm not sure"), along with his inquiry about private sessions, led me to believe that he wasn't ready to make this shift. Thus, I inquired about Cynthia's willingness to meet privately. To get more information about *what* was involved in the dispute, I asked: "Is there anything else that you can think of that might help me get current?"

Most often, mediation participants ask to meet privately with mediators for three reasons: (1) *Mistrust* of other participants. In this case, Kent didn't know "who to trust" and his mistrust was likely to extend to Cynthia; (2) *Embarrassment* about their emotional needs. Kent's protest that, "I'm a Senior Analyst and resent being treated like a child," suggested a need for acknowledgment and respect which Kent may have been too embarrassed to talk about; and (3) *Uncertainty* about whether something should be said or how to say it. In the foregoing dialogue, Kent may not have known whether or how to say something about his emotional need for autonomy (as he had had with Bob Thompson, who gave him "a lot of independence"). I made a note to discuss these emotional interests later in the mediation under the category *want*. The point is that no matter what the reason, participants (not the mediator) make all of the decisions during situational mediation, including whether to meet privately.

Cynthia conditioned any decision about meeting in private sessions on her first *Getting Current*. Initially this condition led to an exchange of words between her and Kent, but they eventually reached an accord under which Cynthia would "have a chance to get me current before any final decision is made about meeting privately." This accord was significant in two respects: (1) it was the first time in mediation that Kent and Cynthia had worked through an issue on their own (which I was quick to bring to their attention by *summarizing* it); and (2) it afforded me the opportunity to *reframe* in positive terms an occurrence that may have originally been taken as negative. Summarizing and reframing are two of the communication tools that mediators regularly use to help participants progress toward broader agreements.

In this block of dialogue Kent revealed several additional psychodynamics that appeared to be influencing his thinking and behavior: *mistrust* ("Nowadays I don't know who to trust"); *perfectionism* ("I can be somewhat of a perfectionist"); and *victimization* ("I got a screwing"). However, when Kent didn't want to discuss his reasons for not talking to Bob Thompson, I decided to simply make note of these psychodynamics under the category of *what*, and defer any discussion of them until later on in the mediation.

Sensing that Kent was nearing completion of the *Getting Current* stage, and wanting to leave him with something thought provoking to consider in regards to his behavior toward Cynthia, I told him about what Carl Jung had said about knowing when people are "insane." Using quotations from famous people, as I did in this instance with Kent, is an effective way of giving participants an opportunity to take a fresh look at *what* happened in the past. It is also an effective way to start them thinking about the future and any changes they might *want* to make in their thoughts and behaviors.

DIALOGUE

Having returned from the break, I ask Cynthia:

"Where would you like to start?"

"I'll follow the same course as Kent and start with my educational and professional backgrounds."

"Okay, good," I respond.

"I have a Bachelor of Science degree from Amherst, and a Masters in Business Administration from the University of Illinois. I have been in the insurance business since 1991. My first position was with Continental Mutual. In 1994, I accepted a position with Great Lakes Assurance and remained with them until September of 2000 when I was hired by MDI."

"What position did you have when you left Great Lakes in 1994?"

"Claims Manager."

"Were you involved with medical malpractice claims?"

"No."

"Had you ever been?"

"For a short time, while I was with Continental Mutual."

"Okay. Is there anything else that you want me to know about your educational or employment backgrounds?"

"No. I'd like to talk about my concerns."

"Please go ahead."

"Number one, I'm concerned about Kent's attitude. I realize that he very much wanted to be Claims Manager, but he has repeatedly disobeyed company policy as well as my directives. Number two, he continues to be dictatorial with his subordinates. Number three, he has done everything in his power to diminish me. He has disparaged my competency, caused a great deal of disruption in the department, and led my superiors to question my managerial abilities."

Since Cynthia appears to have completed her list, I ask her: "Would you be willing to elaborate on each of these concerns?"

"By all means. From the beginning of my tenure as manager, Kent's attitude has been hostile. One example of this is his intentional disregard of company policy concerning the approval of *extraordinary* claims. Kent told you about our approval policy for claims and that it is dependent upon the dollar value originally assigned to the claim. But he failed to mention that a Senior Analyst is required to get the concurrence of the Claims Manager on any extraordinary claims, no matter what dollar value was originally assigned. In other words, both the Senior Analyst and the Claims Manager must approve an extraordinary claim."

I interrupt to ask: "What kinds of claims are considered extraordinary?"

Cynthia replies: "Any claim that may involve intentional wrongdoing on the part of our insured, or that may generate media attention."

"I see. Please go on."

"On two different occasions Kent approved claims that were likely to result in media attention, without even mentioning them to me, much less getting my concurrence."

"And you expected him to get your concurrence?"

"Of course, it's company policy! After the first time, I spoke to Kent and made my expectations clear. But he did it again—not more than a month later. In both instances he intentionally disregarded company policy, and in the second, my explicit instructions."

"I imagine that you were pretty upset with him?"

"It's not a matter of being upset. He disregarded company policy and disobeyed my directive."

"I see. Yet I'm not clear about something and perhaps you could help me out: how is a Senior Analyst supposed to know when a claim is extraordinary?"

"Based on experience."

"Are there any written guidelines or anything like that?"

"No."

"So it's somewhat discretionary or subject to interpretation?"

"Yes, but in these two cases Kent has enough experience to have known."

"How so?"

"Because one claim involved the daughter of a professional athlete, and the other was against a physician who performs high-risk procedures with terminal patients."

"Did either of them involve intentional wrongdoing?"

"No."

"Did either actually get media attention?"

"Not, at least not yet. But that's not the point! Kent should have recognized that they were extraordinary and he should have gotten my concurrence. These matters are sensitive, and I need to know about them if I'm to do my job and keep my superiors informed."

"So what I'm hearing you say is that you are more concerned about Kent's lack of judgment than you are about the final outcome of these claims. Is that right?"

"Precisely. They are both important, but Kent should..."

Kent interrupts: "That's ridiculous! This has nothing to do with my judgment. It's about her lack of experience and micromanaging me. She..."

I break in: "Wait a minute, Kent. Remember about not interrupting each other?"

"Yeah, but it's ridiculous," Kent answers, sullenly.

"Kent, I know it can be hard to just listen, especially when you hear something that you really don't agree with. And yet, would you be willing to let Cynthia have her turn without interrupting her?"

Slouching down in his chair, Kent replies: "Fine."

"Thank you."

Turning back to Cynthia, I ask, "You were saying?"

"I was about to say that Kent should have known that these cases were extraordinary and that my concurrence was required. He intentionally disregarded company policy, and I believe this was reflective of his hostility toward me."

"That must have been difficult for you."

"It's been very disruptive to my administration of the department. It appears that Kent has his own agenda, but I am prepared to do whatever it takes to protect the best interests of the department."

"Meaning that?"

"Meaning that I won't let things continue as they are. Kent must change his attitude, or changes will be made for him!"

"Such as?"

"I'm not certain, but I can't let things continue as they are. My superiors require efficient administration of the department."

"Who are your superiors?"

"Mr. Peterson and the other members of the Executive Committee."

"Has anything already been decided, by you or by the Executive Committee?"

"Not as far as I know, but that's why we're here. Kent must change his attitude."

"Is there anything that *you* might consider changing?"

"What do you mean?" Cynthia asks.

"What I'm asking is whether there is anything you might consider changing about yourself in relation to Kent. For example, I've learned that I might be able to *influence* other people, but I can't *control* them. So are you open to the possibility that the only thing you can do is influence Kent but not control him?"

"Yes, to some extent."

"Well, let me ask if you have ever been able to control Kent?"

"No, not really."

"What I've learned is that I have no control over what anyone else says, does, or thinks; and when I mistakenly believe that I do, it sooner or later causes me grief because it's an *illusion*. It appears as if I should be able to control certain people—my wife, my teenage children, and my co-workers—but in reality I can't. All I can try to do is influence them. In fact, I've learned that the only person I have control over is myself; what I do, what I say, and what I think. But even then, my control is conditional: I only have control over myself when I'm *conscious* of what I'm doing. Am I making any sense?"

"Yes, go on."

"The problem is that all too often I'm unaware of what I do

and say. I react automatically. When someone or something doesn't live up to my expectations, I automatically repeat old thought patterns and behaviors. The solution is to become aware — to stop reacting automatically. When I'm aware, I have a choice. I can consider all of the options and alternatives that are available to me and then respond. I can take responsibility for my actions, rather than simply react."

Cynthia interjects: "Are you saying that we can only control ourselves?"

"Yes, and we can only control ourselves when we're not reacting automatically."

"Interesting," Cynthia replies.

After a brief pause in which Cynthia appears to be reflecting on the last part of our dialogue, I continue: "Cynthia, is there anything you might consider changing about what *you* say or do in your work relationship with Kent?"

"Not until he changes his attitude."

"So if Kent were to change his attitude, you might consider changes in the way you deal with him?"

"I might."

"What would that look like? In other words, presupposing that Kent was willing, what would he have to do to show you that his attitude had changed?"

"I've never thought about it in those terms. But for one thing, he would have to exercise better judgment."

"What would that look like?"

"I'm not sure."

"Might it involve Kent coming to you whenever he has any doubt about whether a claim is extraordinary? In other words, might he employ a rule I use when I'm in doubt about whether or not to do something: *When in doubt, I don't.* When I debate whether or not to say or do something, I don't do it until I have time to think about it or get advice from a trusted friend or advisor. And I'm suggesting that Kent employ the same rule whenever he has any doubt about whether he should or should not approve a claim without your concurrence. Do you think that might help him?"

"Probably."

"And might it help you too?"

"It could."

"Good. I know that Kent is listening and I'll ask him about it later."

COMMENTARY

In this block of dialogue it became apparent that Cynthia's educational and career backgrounds differed significantly from Kent's. Cynthia had much more education but far less experience with medical malpractice claims. This may have contributed to her attempts to micromanage and otherwise control Kent. It may have also deepened Kent's resentment about not being promoted to manager.

It was also apparent that Kent had lost the Claims Manager position to a considerably younger person (who was also female). Age differences alone can cause conflict between co-workers, but when combined with gender differences, as they were in this dispute, they are even more likely to produce interpersonal conflict.

Cynthia and Kent's personalities also differed. Whereas Kent manifested passive-aggressiveness, Cynthia seemed overly defensive. She repeatedly deflected any attempt on my part to be empathic. For example, when I asked, "I imagine you were pretty upset [with Kent]?" she answered, "It's not a matter of being upset." When I said, "That must have been difficult for you," she answered, "It's been very disruptive to my administration of the department." In neither instance was she willing to disclose anything about herself, especially her feelings. Thus, just as Kent had built a "wall of resentment," Cynthia seemed to have built a "wall of protection."

Situational mediators take note of these differences but are careful about *when* in the mediation they say anything about them. For example, Cynthia (and perhaps Kent) may have been embarrassed or upset had I asked questions about these differences during this joint session. This is why I decided to postpone a discussion of these differences, leaving them to private sessions.

If and when I were to bring these differences to the attention of participants, my intent would be to educate—not persuade. Under the situational approach to mediation, the participants alone decide what, if anything, they want to do with information such as this. They are free to take what they like and leave the rest. It was for this reason that I didn't press Cynthia when she answered, "Not until he changes his attitude," to my question about her willingness to change anything about herself vis-à-vis Kent. I sensed that Cynthia's mistrust of Kent was such that she wasn't willing to be the first to lower her wall. I also sensed that it would be more productive to offer her a rule (*when in doubt, don't*) and to probe for the concrete steps Kent could take (if he were willing) to garner her trust.

DIALOGUE

I continue with Cynthia, asking: "What would you like to talk about next?"

"My concerns that Kent is dictatorial with his subordinates and that he continually tries to diminish me. Kent has an authoritarian approach to management. He made light of his supervision problems, but I can assure you, and him, that the Executive Committee takes them very seriously."

"Do you know if this was the reason why Kent wasn't promoted to manager?"

"No, but I was made aware of the problem and told to do whatever I could to correct it. Employee turnover is very costly, and within the last several years an inordinate number of people from Kent's team have left the company."

Glancing at Kent to gauge his reactivity to this information, and noticing that he appears agitated, I interrupt Cynthia: "Excuse me, Cynthia. Would it be okay if I check in with Kent for a moment?"

"Certainly," Cynthia replies.

"Thank you," I respond and then ask Kent: "How are you doing?"

"I'm okay," Kent answers in a tense voice.

"Good. I know this can be hard. So please tell me if you need a break or anything else to take care of yourself."

Turning back to Cynthia, I continue: "I imagine that this is hard for you too."

"Frankly, it is," Cynthia answers. "This entire matter is very distressing! I was hired to do a job and Kent has done everything in his power to see that I fail. I can't…no, I simply *won't* let him continue to cause problems. He must change his attitude, that's all there is to it! I won't let him do this anymore, I simply won't. He must stop… He has to…"

Appearing to have realized that she is losing control and becoming emotional, Cynthia abruptly stops talking, collects herself, and then adds: "The bottom line is that Kent must change his attitude!"

Wanting to confirm that I had heard and understood her, I summarize what she said: "Alright, Cynthia, I understand that your bottom line is that Kent must follow company policy, abide by your directives, change his attitude toward you, and be more tolerant with his subordinates. Is that right?"

"Yes it is," Cynthia replies.

"So these are your requests of Kent?"

"No, he *must* do these things!"

"I see. Yet are you open to the possibility that there is a difference between a *demand*, such as I just heard you make of Kent, and a *request*?"

"What do you mean?" Cynthia asks.

"Well, most people experience a demand as an aggressive or hostile form of communication. They experience it as being told to do or not do something, without being given any choice in the matter. A request, on the other hand, is usually experienced as a respectful way of communicating. The recipient of a request is given the respect of being asked whether or not he or she is willing to do or not do something. Is that clearer?"

"Yes, but Kent *must* change his attitude!"

"I hear you, Cynthia, and yet it comes back to *control*, doesn't it? Do you have any control over what Kent ultimately decides to do?"

"No."

"So how might you best influence Kent? By making demands or by making requests?"

"Requests would probably be better."

"So making a request of Kent might be worth a try?"

"Yes."

"Might you want to try it now?"

Appearing surprised, Cynthia pauses for a few seconds, turns slowly toward Kent, and says: "Kent, I would like you to treat me as a colleague rather than an adversary, and I would like...I *request* that you be more tolerant of your team members."

Kent counters: "I want some things too!"

I interject: "I hear you, Kent, and yet at this point I'm wondering if you would tell Cynthia whether or not you are willing to honor her requests?"

"I don't know," Kent replies.

"Alright. Would you be willing to consider her requests and later on let her know what you decide?"

"Yeah, I can do that."

Turning back to Cynthia, I ask: "What about you, Cynthia. Is it okay for Kent to get back to you about your requests, perhaps when we meet next time?"

"That will have to do, won't it?" Cynthia answers.

"Yes, I guess it will. It all comes back to *control*, or should I say, a lack of it. Right?"

"Yes, it seems so."

Pausing momentarily to let this sink in, I continue with Cynthia: "Is there anything else that you want to tell me to get current?"

"No, that's all for now."

"Alright then. Let me ask about meeting privately—as Kent requested earlier."

"It's fine. We can do that."

"Alright. And are you okay with Kent being the first to meet with me privately?"

"Yes, that's fine."

Turning to both Cynthia and Kent, I say: "I'm mindful of the time and that we have been at it for almost five hours. So I'm wondering if this would be a good time to conclude today's session?"

Kent replies: "Yeah, sure."

Cynthia nods her head and says: "Certainly."

"We will start the next session with me meeting privately with you, Kent, and then with you, Cynthia. Would that be alright?"

"Yes," Kent and Cynthia answer, simultaneously.

"Would you make arrangements with my assistant for a mutually acceptable date and time for the next session?"

Kent responds by saying to Cynthia: "We can work that out, right?"

Cynthia replies: "Yes, I believe we can, Kent."

COMMENTARY

In this block of dialogue, Cynthia responded to my statement, "I imagine that this is hard for you too," by saying, "This entire matter is very distressing!" As is often the case, empathic statements facilitate the expression of emotion by participants. Three other ways in which I could have empathically made this same statement to Cynthia include: "That must have been painful for you." "I bet that was difficult for you." And, "That seems hurtful."

After disclosing her distress, Cynthia went on to talk about how Kent had done "everything in his power to see that I fail," and that she "won't let him do this anymore." However, it was at this point that she abruptly stopped talking, composed herself, and demanded that "Kent must change his attitude." It was also at this point that I sensed that Cynthia was communicating on a deeper level than her words alone conveyed. The message I heard beneath her words was that she needed *safety* and *security* in her workplace: safety from Kent continuing to try to make her fail and security in her position as Claims Manager. These are the human needs that almost always underlie participants' demands and positions; they are the unspoken things that Cynthia needed to satisfy her emotional interests.

Many people are unaware of their own needs or find it difficult to talk about them. This appeared to be the case for Cynthia as well. It was for this reason that I summarized what I heard her say, made note of these emotional interests under the category *want*, and moved on to discuss the differences between a demand and a request.

There were two additional points of interest that occurred near the close of this session. One was that although Cynthia had difficulty letting go of the illusion that she could control Kent with demands, she seemed ready to move into the willingness stage of mediation. She was willing to change her demand to a request. This was a positive step toward resolving the dispute.

The second point of interest in this dialogue occurred when Kent suggested to Cynthia, with respect to making the arrangements for the next mediation session, "We can work that out, right?" One could speculate about the meaning of this. Perhaps Kent was patronizing Cynthia, or perhaps he was responding in a positive way to her show of emotion. In any event, his suggestion was significant; it may have been the first time ever that he and Cynthia had agreed to work together toward a common goal.

Chapter 11:
Increasing Understanding and Reaching Agreement *(Cruising and Landing)*

As was the case with Kent and Cynthia, the *Getting Current* stage of workplace mediation can extend into private sessions with the participants. Whether at the request of the mediator, or a participant (in this instance, Kent), the purpose of private sessions is to increase understanding as to *what* is involved in the dispute, how each participant might *want* things to be different in the future, and the changes each participant is *willing* to make to end the dispute.

Two weeks after last meeting with Kent and Cynthia, I begin a private session with Kent:

DIALOGUE
"Hello, Kent. How are you?"

"Good as can be expected," Kent replies.

"My assistant told me that you and Cynthia agreed that she would be here in a few hours."

"Yeah. We figured there was no need for her to wait around while we met privately."

"So it seems like you are able to work together—at least on some things?"

"Yeah, I'm trying to get past this. But I'm kinda confused, you know? It seems like I'm between a rock and hard place. I actually like my job. But now I don't know what to do or who to trust. I've dug myself into a hole with Cynthia, and I'm pissed off at myself for doing it; but every time I think about it I get so damned angry!

"I kept telling myself not to let it get to me. And then, there I go again; I start thinking about it and get really mad about everything, especially that I can't trust anyone. Bob tried to call me after this all went down, but I can't bring myself to talk to him. He was like a father to me, but he told Peterson about the complaints. I can't believe he did that; I trusted him."

"So you feel betrayed?"

"Yeah, really betrayed; by Bob, by Peterson, and by the Executive Committee. And now I don't know who to trust. I'm nowhere; you know, just really screwed with no one to turn to, and…I don't know…it all seems so hopeless. Maybe I should just move on; you know, get another job. I don't know…"

"Is that an option for you?"

"No, not really. Sure, I can get another job, but I really don't want to; we would have to move back East or to Los Angeles. There aren't any other large med-mal companies with offices in Phoenix. I've just gotta figure some way out of this mess."

"Do you consider yourself a *victim*?"

"I guess; kinda."

"Really? You seem like a pretty capable guy to me, while a *victim* is somebody who views himself as helpless, somebody who feels a lot of self-pity and believes he is helpless to do anything about it. Is that you?"

"Well, no. Not really."

"Okay then. Let me ask you about all of this resentment you feel; about the Executive Committee's decision to hire Cynthia, about Jim Peterson, about Cynthia: isn't that all about being a victim and self-pity?"

"I don't know; maybe."

"Well, Kent, I've come to define *resentment* as *a hostile form of self-pity*, and whenever I find myself feeling self-piteous it helps me break out of it by reminding myself of this definition—because I really don't like thinking of myself as self-piteous. What about you?"

"I'm the same way; I've always taken care of myself. I'm not one to feel sorry for myself."

"So you don't see yourself as self-piteous in this situation with

Cynthia?"

"Well I didn't, but now I don't know; I'm not sure. I'm starting to rethink it, and you know what?"

"What?"

"I can see now that I have been feeling sorry for myself, and to tell you the truth, I don't like it very much."

"It's not a very comfortable self-image is it? At least it's not for me."

"For me neither."

"So perhaps you may want to remember this definition and bring it to mind next time you feel resentful? I'm not saying it will be easy. In fact, it takes practice and discipline—at least it did for me. But over time you might find it easier and easier, and all of sudden you may not feel any resentment at all. By changing your thoughts in this way, you can actually change how you feel."

"Oh, I get it! It's like that article you gave me; where the guy said, 'Change your thoughts and you change your world.' Right?"

"Exactly. By thinking about this definition of resentment you are actually taking responsibility for your feelings. No longer are you blaming someone else—the Executive Committee, Jim Peterson, or anyone. You are putting the responsibility for your feelings right where they belong: on your own thoughts, your unrealistic expectations that Bob wouldn't tell Jim about the complaints, that you would be automatically promoted to Claims Manager, and so on. Is this making sense?"

"Yeah, but it's hard to keep hold of."

"I know. It can be really hard to keep all of this straight, especially when we get triggered, and strong emotions come up like anger and resentment. But my experience is that the more I remembered this definition of resentment, the easier it became to change my thoughts."

"Yeah, I can see how that could work."

"It might help if you had a *tool* to help you remember to change your thoughts; to remember this definition of resentment."

"How's that?"

"Do you recall reading in *The Anatomy of Anger* article how I used a rubber band to snap out of reactivity toward my former father-in-law?"

"Kinda."

"Well, you could try wearing a rubber band to help you snap out of resentment. Every time you feel yourself slip into resentful thoughts, say about Cynthia, you can give yourself a snap of the rubber band to remind you that those thoughts are 'a hostile form of self pity.'

"Here's a rubber band. Do you want to try it?"

"Why not," Kent remarks while putting the rubber band on his wrist.

COMMENTARY

In this block of dialogue we saw another example of assertiveness by the mediator. When Kent reiterated, "I'm nowhere... I'm screwed," I challenged him by asking, "Do you consider yourself a *victim*?"

Many people unwittingly fall into the role of victim, and as a result wind up resenting other people and tough situations. As a victim they feel helpless and self-piteous, as if they were without any choice in the matter. But the truth is that we all have choices. As explained at length in Chapter 13, when we take responsibility for our thoughts and behaviors, we have the ability to respond rather than merely react as helpless victims and thereby have a choice in our course of action.

In this instance I wanted to empathically disabuse Kent of the notion that he was a victim. Thus, I shared my perception that he seemed "like a pretty capable guy," defined resentment as a hostile form of self-pity, and asked if he thought of himself as self-piteous. Similar to most people, Kent didn't realize that self-pity is implicit in the victim role. Defining resentment as a hostile form of self-pity helps people become aware of this.

I also wanted to give Kent a practical way to begin to deal with his resentment. Thus, I suggested the use of a rubber band as a tool he could use to remind himself of the self-pity involved in resentment.

Finally, I wanted to be compassionate in helping Kent become aware of his victim role. Mindful of the pain involved in this role, and wanting to alleviate his suffering, I made it a point to remark, "It's not a very comfortable self-image is it? At least it's not for me."

DIALOGUE
I continue with Kent:

"Alright then. There's another thing I'd like to check out with you. It strikes me that you have encountered a lot of *losses* in this situation: loss of your close relationship with Bob Thompson; loss of trust with Jim Peterson; loss of the Claims Manager position. Would you agree?"

"Yeah."

"Well, research shows that there is usually a *grief process* that follows these kinds of losses. You see, whenever we lose a relationship with someone or something we value, we usually go through certain stages of grief, including denial, anger, sadness, and other emotions. Most of us eventually reach the *acceptance* stage of grief but that can, and usually does, take time.

"Research also shows that the most traumatic losses of relationships occur by reason of death or divorce. But unless we choose to self-medicate — with alcohol, drugs, TV, sex, work, etc. — we go through these same stages of grief when we lose relationships for other reasons as you have with Bob and Jim. Does that make sense to you?"

"Kinda."

"So I'm wondering if the emotions that you've been feeling aren't part of a grief process? By that I mean that perhaps you're feeling anger and resentment because you're grieving the loss of key relationships."

"Maybe."

"I don't know for certain either, Kent. Yet I want you to know that it's normal to go through these stages; it's a natural part of the grief process to want to deny painful losses and to feel angry, frustrated, bitter, and even resentful. Would you at least consider this?"

"Yeah, sure."

"Good enough."

"So it may be that your current feelings of confusion and hopelessness are also part of your grief process around these losses. What do you think?"

"Sometimes I do get really down about all of this."

"Sad?"

"Uh huh."

"So might it be that your sadness is causing you to feel somewhat depressed?"

"Maybe."

"That would be pretty normal. Depression is another stage in the grief process."

Appearing pensive, Kent remains quiet.

After a few moments I continue: "There's one more thing I want you to know about the grief process. It's very common to swing back and forth between anger and sadness, depression and resentment — and even, at times, back into denial. I know that happened to me during my divorce. One day I was mad as hell, the next day I was crying."

"Yeah! Now that you mentioned it, that's how it was for me too. Wow, that was quite a ride!"

"Yes, it was for me too. But you finally came to *accept* it, didn't you?"

"Yeah, it all worked out."

"So perhaps where you stand with the company and your relationship with Cynthia will also work out?"

"I hope so."

COMMENTARY

The *grief process* can be and often is an integral part of workplace disputes. As sentient beings we all are subject to the emotions that stem from the loss of a valued relationship. Thus, as I did with Kent, situational mediators help participants understand the grief process and how it applies to their situation. They also help participants transit through the various stages of grief.

There have been numerous studies done on the emotions involved in suffering a loss. Sigmund Freud began with the concept of having to do "grief work." Later, others came up with their own versions of this process. In 1982, J.W. Worden wrote of the "four tasks of mourning."[12] These include accepting the reality of the loss, experiencing the pain, adjusting to a life without your loved one, and finally being able to invest your emotional energy into a new life.

Perhaps the best-known theory on the grief process is Elisabeth Kübler-Ross's "Five Stages of Grief." Kübler-Ross[13] defined these stages as Denial, Anger, Bargaining, Depression, and Acceptance. In the first stage, Denial, people tend to refute that the loss has taken place and may withdraw from their usual social contacts. This stage may last a few moments, hours, days, or even longer. Anger is the second stage. Here the grieving person may become furious at the person who inflicted the hurt, or at the world for letting it happen, or he may be angry with himself for letting the event take place.

The third stage is Bargaining. Here the grieving person may make a bargain with herself or perhaps a Higher Power. Such as, "If I do this, will you take away the loss?" In the fourth stage people feel numb, although anger and sadness remain underneath. This is called Depression and is experienced to greater and lesser degrees. The final stage of the grief process is Acceptance. This is when the anger, sadness, and mourning have tapered off and the grieving person comes to terms with the reality of the loss.

Most researchers, including Worden and Kübler-Ross, agree that there are no absolute beginnings and endings in the grief

---

[12] Worden, J.W. (1982) *Grief Counseling and Grief Therapy: A Handbook for the Mental Health Practitioner*. Springer Publishing Co., New York.

[13] Kübler-Ross, Elisabeth. (1997) *On Death & Dying: What the Dying Have to Teach Doctors, Nurses, Clergy, and Their Own Families*. Simon Shuster, New York.

process and that each person will experience his or her grief differently. While one person may spend a great deal of time and energy in depression, another may move quickly to acceptance. Also, these stages can overlap and recur. A person may have gotten over most of the anger that was involved in his or her loss and then out of nowhere something can occur that will send him or her right back into the throes of the rage he or she first experienced. Most often, a person feels several of these emotions at the same time, perhaps in different degrees. The only certainty is that the grief process must take place for healing to occur.

In this dispute, Kent was intermittingly in denial, anger, and depression. In the first mediation session, Kent talked about being "blown away" when Cynthia was hired, and in private session, he talked about Bob Thompson trying to phone him and Kent's inability "to bring myself to talk to him." Both of these statements may have been expressions of Kent's recurrent denial about the losses he had suffered, i.e., the loss of trust with Jim Peterson and the loss of relationship with Bob Thompson.

Kent's anger toward Bob, Jim Peterson, the Executive Committee, and Cynthia was plain. However, in this private session he also admitted to being "pissed off at myself." Anger turned inward often leads to depression, and this, in addition to his admissions about sometimes being "really down" and "sad," left little doubt that he was recurrently in and out of the depression stage of the grief process.

Kent also appeared to have been at one point in the bargaining stage of the grief process. Near the beginning of this private session he said, "I kept telling myself not to let it get to me," which I took to mean that he had made a bargain with himself — albeit one he wasn't able to keep.

Kent also seemed to be edging toward the acceptance stage. Earlier in this private session he expressed the desire to "figure some way out of this mess." In the preceding dialogue he answered affirmatively, "I hope so" when I asked him whether he thought things would work out. I interpreted these statements to mean that Kent was ready to move out of the past and into the acceptance stage.

As pointed out in the preceding paragraphs, all of Kent's emotions were normal and endemic to the grief process. Thus, situational mediators make it a point to acquaint participants with the grief process, as I did with Kent. They also make it a point to normalize this process and to aid participants in transitioning through their emotions. It was for these reasons that I shared how in my divorce I had swung back and forth between denial, anger, and depression; I was angry one day while crying the next. Finally, however, I came to accept it.

Taking the time to fully explain, normalize, and help participants progress through the grief process has two additional benefits: (1) it provides participants with a context for their recurrent, shifting, and often intense emotions; and (2) it instills hope. As Kent learned from his divorce, the grief process can be a turbulent ride, but eventually most people come to accept their losses and get on with their lives.

DIALOGUE
After a 15-minute break, Kent and I continue in private session:

Kent begins: "I really want things to work out, but it's hard because I really don't know who to trust."

I respond: "Yes, you've mentioned that several times. Do you want to talk about it?"

"Yeah, this is a real bitch for me."

"You're not alone, Kent. Mistrust occurs frequently in these kinds of disputes, especially when one person feels betrayed by someone he was close to, as you were with Bob. So I'm not at all surprised that you don't know who to trust. How could you trust Bob when you believe that he betrayed you? And how could you trust Cynthia in light of your brief history together? It would be natural for you *not* to trust these people, wouldn't it?"

"I guess so."

"Okay, but having said all of that, I also know that it's impossible to undo the past, and so it seems to me that the real concerns are whether you want to restore trust with Bob, and whether you want to build trust with Cynthia."

"I'm not sure I follow."

"Let me ask you this: Have you ever been able to un-ring a bell?"

Kent appears puzzled, so I answer my own question: "I haven't because it's impossible, isn't it?"

"Yeah."

"Well, it's the same when it comes to undoing the past; it's impossible. The only thing that can change is the present; what's happening right now. Would you agree?"

"Yeah, but how's that done? I've made such a mess of things — with Bob, and with Cynthia."

"Perhaps it would help if we take them one at a time, okay?"

"Sure."

"Do you want to start with Bob?"

"Sure."

"Might it be possible for you to simply phone him?"

"I don't know. I wouldn't know what to say."

"How about, 'Hi. How are you?' "

"Yeah, but what do I say about not returning his calls?"

"Perhaps a simple apology would work; something like 'I'm sorry for not getting back to you sooner; a lot of things have been going on for me.' You know, Kent, I've found that apologizing in this way is very powerful. Let me explain it this way: Do you remember when President Nixon got in trouble with the Watergate scandal?"

"Yeah."

"He handled it by taking the position that the best defense is a good offense. He kept making excuses and blaming everyone else. He never apologized. And what happened to him? He had to resign, right?"

"Uh huh."

"Okay then. Compare that to how President Reagan handled the situation in Lebanon when 40 or so Marines got blown up in a terrorist attack. He took to the television that night and said something like, 'My fellow Americans, I'm sorry, I made a mistake.' He took responsibility and apologized. And what did we do? We basically said, 'Okay,' and went on with our business. So sincerely saying 'I'm sorry' is very powerful."

Kent nods his head, and then says: "Yeah. I guess I could call Bob and see what happens."

"Alright. Could I check in with you about this at our next session?"

"Sure."

"Thanks. Do you want to talk about Cynthia?"

"Okay."

"From listening to each of you it seems to me that you have both built walls. Remember when we talked about your 'wall of resentment'?"

"Yeah, I can see that real clear now."

"My impression is that Cynthia has built a wall of her own. I call it a 'wall of protection' because it appears to me that it was built to protect herself against people whom she perceives as dangerous; people who have attacked her in the past and are apt to attack her in the future."

"You mean like me?"

"What do you think?"

"Yeah, I can see that."

"Cynthia may have built this wall a long time ago, way before she ever met you. But you might consider whether there is anything you want to do about it?"

"Like what?"

"I'm not sure. One option might be to take the same approach that you are going to use with Bob."

"You mean, apologize?"

"Perhaps. Is that an option for you?"

"I don't know; she has her part in this too!"

"I hear you, Kent. Yet recognizing that you believe Cynthia had her part in this, I imagine that one of you must be the first to lower your wall. Would you agree?"

"Yeah, but she's probably been this way forever; you know, having all these rules and forms, and micromanaging people."

"Maybe so. But that's the past, and you can't change it, right? All I'm suggesting is that you consider what you can—and more importantly what you are *willing*—to change in your relationship with Cynthia."

"I'll have to think about it."

"Fair enough. Could I ask you about it at a later time?"

"Sure."

COMMENTARY

Trust is one of the most frequently encountered issues in mediation. Indeed, conflict breeds mistrust and, when severe, it may be the deciding factor in mediation. Thus, as I did with Kent, it is the role of the mediator to first determine what, if anything, participants *want* to do to restore or build trust so that their situation will be different in the future.

It was clear that Kent wanted to restore trust in his relationship with Bob, and to build trust in his relationship with Cynthia, but he claimed not to know how it could be done. The role of the mediator includes offering participants different ways to resolve issues, including options such as apologizing. Thus, I suggested that Kent might apologize to Bob, and also to Cynthia—thereby determining if this was something Kent was *willing* to do.

In writing about the role of apology in mediation,[14] Deborah L. Levi recognized that "apologies may facilitate satisfying conflict resolution in certain cases," but cautioned against "generalizations about the power of a simple *I'm sorry*." However, she also said that "well timed gestures and sensitive intervention, [and] a climate that permits honest, vulnerable communication" are among the factors that contribute to a "happy-ending apology." With its emphasis on empathy, humility, and compassion, the situational approach to mediation fosters the intervention, communication, and climate that maximize the potential for "happy-ending" apologies.

---

[14] Levi, Deborah L. (1977) *The Role of Apology in Mediation*. New York University Law Review 72 N.Y.U.L, Rev. 1165

Kent was willing to apologize to Bob, but wanted to think about whether he would be willing to apologize to Cynthia. Apologies involve risks such as exposing oneself to possible rejection should the intended recipient of the apology not accept it. My sense was that Kent foresaw that Bob would accept his apology, whereas Cynthia would not. The element of embarrassment may also have influenced Kent's thinking; he may have felt that it would be too embarrassing to apologize to her. Finally, having proclaimed that "She has her part in this too!" any apology on Kent's part may have been less than sincere. It was for these reasons that I sensed that Kent was reluctant to be the first to lower his wall, and left it up to him to think about anything that he might be *willing* to do to build trust in his relationship with Cynthia.

Finally, in this block of dialogue we saw another example of the mediator asking permission rather than assuming authority. When Kent said, "Yeah, I guess I could call Bob and see what happens," I asked, "Could I check in with you about this at our next session?" And when Kent said that he would have to think about whether he would be willing to apologize to Cynthia, I asked, "Could I ask you about it at a later time?" Obviously I wanted to know about the outcome of Kent's conversation with Bob and decision concerning Cynthia; asking permission to follow up allowed me to do so without appearing authoritative.

DIALOGUE
I continue with Kent:

"Okay, is there anything else that you want to talk about?"

"No, I think that's about it."

"Well, there is one other thing that you said in our first session that I'd like to discuss. Do you remember saying that you can be 'somewhat of a perfectionist' when managing your team?"

"Yeah, I can be kinda demanding."

"Would it surprise you to learn that perfectionism is a set up for failure?"

"Why is that?"

"Because to expect myself or anyone else to be perfect is an illusion, a misconception of the mind; it's not possible. To my knowledge there is only one 'Entity' that's perfect; we human beings are far from perfect. Would you agree?"

"Yeah, that's for sure."

"So the expectation that we can be perfect is a set up for failure—and also an excuse to blame our failures on someone else. Again, it all comes back to *expectations* and *control*. When my expectations about being perfect are unmet I am apt to slip into the illusion of control, mistakenly thinking that other people can be perfect, getting angry, and blaming them when they're not. Make sense?"

"Uh huh."

"So what's the only thing that you can change in this equation?"

"I know, *me*. I can change my expectations of my team members."

"Right, you can change your attitude. Is that something you want to do?"

"I think that I'd better."

Pausing momentarily, I continue: "Alright then, one last thing. Remember my rule, *when in doubt, don't*, and my discussion about it with Cynthia?"

"Yeah."

"Well, what do you think? Might it be a way for you to start to build Cynthia's trust in you? So that whenever you have the slightest doubt about whether a claim is extraordinary, you get Cynthia's concurrence?"

"That's not a bad idea."

"So I take it that you'll try it?"

"Yeah, I'll give it a try."

COMMENTARY

As with the concepts and psychodynamics discussed in Chapter 10, and those that will be discussed in the upcoming private session with Cynthia, victimization, mistrust, resentment, grief, and perfectionism are frequently encountered when mediating disputes between co-workers. Often they are integral to *what* is going on in a dispute, as they were with Kent, and situational mediators help participants become aware of them.

Once participants are aware of these concepts and psychodynamics, they have a choice whether or not they *want* to do anything about them. Before then, they are without choice; they are locked into subconscious repetition of old patterns of *insane* behavior, "doing the same thing in the same way, but expecting different results."

When a participant wants to change his or her attitude or behavior, it is also the role of the mediator to probe and determine what they are *willing* to do. Mediators offer participants different tools; for example, use of a rubber band to stop reactivity and anger, and a sincere apology to build or restore trust. They also encourage participants to think of other things they might be *willing* to do to change their situation.

DIALOGUE
I resume with Kent:

"Remember when I said that part of the *Getting Current* stage is to identify goals, i.e., the results or outcomes you would like to see come out of this mediation?"

"Uh huh."

"Well I'm mindful that we're approaching the noon hour and I'm wondering if you might be willing to discuss your goals?"

"I told you; I want Cynthia to stop micromanaging me."

I stand up, move to the flipchart, and write at the top of a page:

Kent's Goals
• *Change in Cynthia's management style*

I then ask: "Could you be more specific about what 'micromanaging' means?"

"No daily reports," Kent responds.

I append the first bullet point as follows:

<u>Kent's Goals</u>
• *Change in Cynthia's management style*
  i.e., daily reports

"Does that sum it up?" I inquire.

"Yeah, that does it," Kent answers.

"Okay. What else might you want to see come out of this mediation?"

"Oh, I see what you want. Okay, getting rid of some forms. I have to admit that some of them are good. But we can get rid of a bunch and streamline others."

I add a second bullet to *Kent's Goals*:

• *Reviewing Claims Department forms*
  (streamlining and condensing)

"How's that?" I ask.

"It will do," Kent replies.

"Are there any other goals you have for this mediation?"

"Yeah, I want to know where I stand with the company. I don't think the Executive Committee gives a damn about what I think, or for that matter whether or not I stay."

"So you would like to know whether the members of the Executive Committee value your opinions and want you to stay with the company?"

"That's right."

I add a third bullet point to the list of *Kent's Goals*:

• *Information from Executive Committee:*
  Value of Kent's opinions?
  Value of Kent's continued employment?

"Does that cover it?" I ask.

"Yeah, that's good," Kent answers.

"Alright. Is there anything else that you've identified as a goal?"

After pausing for a few seconds, Kent answers: "No, that's it."

I move back to the conference table, sit down, and continue by asking: "I'm wondering if you might have overlooked a couple of goals?"

"How's that?"

"Well, I sense that underneath your demand that Cynthia manage you differently, and your complaint about the forms she requires, is an underlying need for *respect*?"

Bolting forward in his chair, Kent exclaims: "Oh man; that's absolutely right! I want respect. That's what I really want! I've got so much more experience with med-mal claims than she does; hell, I even managed the department for a while. And she's treating me like some kid. Having to complete those daily reports is demeaning! I deserve respect!"

"Do you want me to add that to the list?"

"Absolutely!"

After adding *Respect from Cynthia* to the bullet point list of *Kent's Goals,* I continue by asking: "Could this also be about *acknowledgement*? Meaning that perhaps another one of your goals is to be acknowledged — for your knowledge and for your years of experience in handling medical malpractice claims?"

"The Executive Committee sure didn't care about that, did they? They just passed me by without a word."

"So would acknowledgement by the Executive Committee be another one of your goals?"

"Uh huh; it's only fair."

I add as the next bullet point, *Acknowledgement by Executive Committee,* and then ask: "So you want things to be fair?"

"Yeah, what's wrong with that?"

"I'm not suggesting that there is anything wrong with it. All I'm trying to do is be clear that *fairness* is one of the things that you are interested in, one of your goals. Okay?"

"Yeah, I get it; no problem."

"Alright then. Are there any other goals that you have in

mind?"

"No."

After pausing briefly to let Kent reconsider, I say: "Good enough. Is there anything else that you want to talk about privately?"

"I don't think so."

"Alright then. Is there anything that you said during this private session that you don't want me to disclose to Cynthia?"

After several seconds, Kent answers: "Nothing that I can think of."

"So I'm at liberty to disclose anything that we talked about if I feel it's important for Cynthia to make fully informed decisions, right?"

"Right."

"Good. My assistant told me that Cynthia called and will be here after lunch. So perhaps we should call it a day, and I'll see you when we all get back together in joint session."

COMMENTARY

Mindful that Kent had disclosed a good deal of information about *what* from his perspective was involved in this dispute, I sensed that it was time to inquire about his goals, that is, how he would *want* things to be different in the future. More specifically, during the joint session with Cynthia and in this private session, Kent and I had talked at length about pertinent facts and circumstances, as well as the issues as he saw them and his concerns—all of which pertained to *what* was involved in this dispute. Thus, sensing that Kent was ready, I switched the focus of the dialogue with him to how he would *want* his situation to change. This is one of the benefits of using the *what, want, willing* model for organizing my thoughts and notes. It is a mental reminder that at some point in every mediation it's important for the mediator to determine if the participants are willing to shift their attention away from the past into the present and beyond.

Kent quickly identified the goal that Cynthia "stop micro-managing" him, and it was at this time that I began a bullet point list of *Kent's Goals*. Listing goals in this way serves several purposes: (1) it assures that the mediator clearly understands the goals, and can communicate them with specificity to the other participant(s); (2) it affords the mediator the opportunity to reframe negatively termed goals (i.e., that Cynthia "stop micromanaging") into affirmative terms (i.e., "Change in Cynthia's management style"). Reframing in this way avoids the implication that one participant (in this instance, Cynthia) did anything bad or wrong; and (3) when kept in plain view, written goals provide a focal point the mediator can use to foster collaborative dialogue.

In this block of dialogue, Kent was either unaware of or unable to articulate his emotional needs for respect, acknowledgement, and fairness. This is fairly typical, especially with male participants. Thus situational mediators help participants become aware of and express their basic human needs (interests), including those involving acceptance, acknowledgement, appreciation, autonomy, closeness, emotional safety, empathy, fairness, financial security, honesty, love, self-worth, trust, and understanding. Most often, it is the awareness and expression of these needs that opens the door for humility, empathy, and compassion between participants.

DIALOGUE

After a lunch break and an exchange of greetings with Cynthia, I begin a private session with her by asking:

"Where would you like to start?"

"I'm a little unsure."

"That's okay. Do you want me to ask some questions?"

"No, it's not that. I'm unsure as to how much I should say."

"Are you concerned about confidentiality?"

"Well, in a way. I'm not worried about you telling anyone else, but I am concerned about how much you disclose to Kent."

"Okay, so what I'm hearing is that you might tell me something that you're not sure you want Kent to know?"

"Yes."

"Okay. Remember though, you and Kent agreed that at the end of each private session I would ask if there was anything that you didn't want disclosed. So perhaps you want to invoke that agreement now?"

"Yes, that's what I want to do."

"Okay, I understand that what you're about to tell me is confidential between the two of us—unless later on you direct me otherwise. Is that good enough?"

"Yes, that's fine. I'm not trying to be difficult; I want you to know that."

"I hear you. Yet I imagine that this entire situation is difficult for you."

"Yes, it's extremely difficult. I never expected it. I was re-cruited by MDI and came here from a very different work environment. Quite frankly, I've never worked at a place where there are so many things left unsaid. I realize that corporate cultures are such that people are reserved and cautious. But this situation is different; it's extreme. People are guarded; no, they are actually secretive. I'm not used to this kind of environment and to my way of thinking, it's entirely counterproductive—in fact, destructive."

I silently nod my head.

Cynthia leans forward in her chair, crosses her arms with her elbows resting on the conference table, and continues: "So this is what I want kept confidential: after we met last time I phoned Jim Peterson because I wasn't happy not knowing why the Executive Committee hired me instead of Kent. One would think that this would have helped, but it didn't. In fact, it increased my discomfort. He was evasive and secretive. He did tell me that the Board of Directors, not the Executive Committee, made the decision to hire me, and that the complaints about Kent were not the deciding factor."

While Cynthia is telling me this last bit of information, I too lean forward. When she finishes, I cross my arms, let my elbows rest on the conference table, and ask: "Did that information surprise you?"

Cynthia replies: "Yes it did. Here I am telling Kent that he must change and thinking that I have the Executive Committee's backing, and now I'm not at all sure of that. How am I to get Kent's respect when I can't get a straight answer from anyone—most of all the person to whom I directly report, Jim Peterson?"

"So you want Kent's respect, right?"

"Yes, certainly."

"How do you intend to get it?"

"At this point I'm not sure."

"Do you think that you will succeed by continuing to do what you've done in the past?"

"No, not really."

"Well, Kent said that you micromanage him; what do you think about that?"

"I had to know what he was doing; especially with the extraordinary claims. How else could I do it?"

"I'm not certain; anyway, hindsight is always 20-20. Yet it seems to me that micromanagement involves controlling others, being dictatorial. What do you think?"

"Yes, but how else could I get him to give me the information I needed to do my job? I still need this information, but now I can tell that Jim Peterson isn't happy about this situation."

"How can you tell?"

"I just can."

"Did he say that?"

"No, not directly; that's the problem around here. But the message was that my management abilities were being questioned."

"Sounds frustrating."

"Very!"

"It also sounds like you are concerned about your job."

"I am, on several levels. I'm concerned about the secretive environment at MDI, and Jim's indirect message."

"What are your options?"

"I have to think about that. But I'm not ready to make another change; this was a good career move for me, and to leave now would look bad."

"Would it be an option for you to adjust your management style?"

"How?"

"Again, I'm not exactly certain, and ultimately that will be up to you. However, it strikes me that both you and Kent view each other as dictatorial.

"Do you remember saying in our first session that one of your concerns about Kent is that he is dictatorial with his subordinates?"

"Yes."

"So are you open to the possibility that both of you have been dictatorial in certain ways: Kent with his team members; you by micromanaging Kent?"

After pausing momentarily, Cynthia responds: "Perhaps, but that wasn't my intent."

"I understand. Yet I wonder if this way of reacting to conflict has become automatic for you; that without intending it, you habitually react this way?"

"I don't know."

Standing up and moving to the flipchart, I write:

React

Continuing to stand at the flipchart, I explain: "To react is to automatically repeat old behavior. Most of us do it in certain circumstances; no matter what the situation or who is involved in a confrontation or dispute, we habitually and subconsciously react in the same way. We try to control, or perhaps in your case, micromanage, without intending to; we go on automatic and unwittingly repeat old behavior. So it seems to me that the question is whether you want to keep reacting to Kent, that is, doing the same things in the same way over and over again, all the while expecting him to change?"

While sitting down, I continue: "Perhaps it would be helpful if I shared with you the same information that I did with Kent. It's about what a world famous psychiatrist, Carl Jung, once said about 'insanity.' Would that be okay?"

"Yes."

"Alright then. Jung, who at one time was a colleague of Freud's, said that he could tell when people were insane. He said that when people kept doing the same thing in the same way over and over again, expecting different results, they were insane. Looking back in my own life, I realize that I was insane at times. It was crazy for me to keep doing the same thing in the same way over and over again with, for example, my first wife, all the while expecting her to change. So it seems to me that the question you might want to ask yourself is whether you want to keep doing the same things with Kent; do you want to keep trying to get Kent's respect by being dictatorial, micromanaging, or otherwise trying to control him?"

Appearing pensive, Cynthia remains silent and I follow suit. After a few moments, she responds: "Something has to change."

COMMENTARY

When Cynthia invoked confidentiality about her conversation with Jim Peterson, I confirmed that "what you're about to tell me is confidential between the two of us — unless, later on, you decide otherwise." In this way I was able to abide by the decision that she and Kent had made about the confidentiality of information disclosed during private sessions, while at the same time preserving the possibility that Cynthia might change her mind. This was directive on my part; however, the situational approach to mediation is eclectic and experience has shown that full disclosure of information is frequently the deciding factor as to whether or not participants resolve disputes. Thus, I intentionally preserved the possibility that later on Cynthia would be willing to disclose the information she was about to share with me.

In this block of dialogue, Cynthia seemed less protective; she admitted that this situation was extremely difficult for her, and that she was feeling very frustrated by her conversation with Jim Peterson. My impression was that Cynthia was beginning to lower her wall. This may have been a result of the discomfort she felt after her conversation with him. On the other hand, it may have resulted from the added comfort she, as do most participants, experienced when meeting privately with the mediator.

When I asked Cynthia whether she was "open to the possibility that both of you have been dictatorial" and then explained Carl Jung's definition of insanity, my intent was to raise *doubt* in her mind about the way she had managed Kent. Then, when I asked her whether she wanted to keep trying to get Kent's respect by "micromanaging or otherwise trying to control him," my intent was to create *dissonance* in her mind. Situational mediators ask questions that create doubt and dissonance to help participants free themselves from the insanity involved in "reaction." This is one of the ways that situational mediators help create the potential for change.

Finally, I want to comment on the use of *nonverbal communication* by mediators — such as when I silently nodded my head and when I leaned forward with my arms crossed and elbows resting on the conference table. By nodding my head, I silently let Cynthia know that she was being heard. By leaning forward and otherwise matching Cynthia's body posture, I was able to nonverbally build additional rapport with her. Body language and facial expressions are highly effective ways of communicating. They also greatly enhance the mediator's ability to demonstrate and promote humility, empathy, and compassion. As such, benevolent nonverbal communication is integral to the situational approach to mediation.

DIALOGUE
Standing again, and moving to the flipchart, I write:

Response

"Cynthia, if you say, 'something has to change,' the question becomes, what might that change look like?"

"I hate to admit it, but the answer is my response," she replies.

"Yes, that's been my experience. When I stop reacting, then I can change my response. And instead of repeatedly doing the same thing in the same way, I can take responsibility for my behavior. In other words (I say while writing on the flipchart) I have the *ability* to choose my response:

Response-ability

Sitting down, I continue: "Once we are free of automatic reaction, we are able to see the many options that are usually available to us and respond accordingly. Might this apply to your situation with Kent?"

"Yes, I guess we've both been reacting to each other."

"Perhaps so. Perhaps you've both been trying to control one another, each of you being dictatorial to greater or lesser extents. However, that's the past isn't it? And you can't un-ring those bells, can you?"

"No, we can't go back."

"So the only thing you can do is stop reacting now and in the future, and instead choose your response; that is, take responsibility for your behavior."

After pausing momentarily to let this sink in, I ask: "Would it be helpful if we were to think of ways in which you might be able choose your response rather than react to Kent?"

"Yes, I would say so."

"Alright then. Perhaps a starting place for this would be to talk about what you *want* in your work relationship with Kent; in other words, your *goals*?"

"Certainly."

COMMENTARY

When Cynthia answered my question about what might change in her situation with Kent by saying, "I hate to admit it, but the answer is my response," my sense was that she was ready to move out of *what* was involved in the dispute and into how she would *want* things to be in the future. One could speculate about the reasons for her readiness; however, from my point of view, it's unimportant. Whether it came about as a result of her conversation with Jim Peterson, her new awareness about expectations, control, and insanity, by Divine Grace, or any other reason, the important thing is that she was able to escape from reaction and was indicating her desire to *choose* her responses. As the Zen proverb says, "If you understand, things are as they are; if you don't understand, things are as they are."

I then asked Cynthia if she were willing to talk about her *goals*. As with Kent in his private session, my intent in shifting Cynthia's attention to goals was to facilitate her transition out of the past, into the present and beyond.

DIALOGUE
Cynthia continues by saying:

"As I've told you, one of my goals is for Kent to respect me as the manager of the Claims Department; to follow my directives and keep me informed, especially about extraordinary claims."

I stand up, move to the flipchart, and write:

Cynthia's Goals
•*Respect from Kent re: Claims Dept. directives and extraordinary claims*

"Does that capture it?"
"Yes."
While returning to my seat, I say: "Good. I'm wondering though, how would you intend to get Kent's respect?"
"I'm not certain."
"Do you think that it might have something to do with building *trust*?"
"Yes. Kent needs to trust that I know what I'm doing; he needs to realize that I have the credentials and, yes, the experience to manage the department."
"Okay, but what about you? Do you need to start trusting Kent as well?"
"Probably, to some degree."

"How would you go about doing that?"

"We could talk about it here with you."

"Yes, that's certainly an option. However, I sense that it's going take the willingness on both your parts to change—at least to some extent. Could I explain that a little more?"

"By all means."

"Do you remember when I talked to Kent about the 'wall of resentment' I perceived he had built in his relationship with you?"

"I certainly do. And I agree with you."

"Okay then. Are you open to the possibility that you too have built a wall; one that I call a 'wall of protection'?"

"I have every right to defend myself against him; he's done all that he can to see that I don't succeed. He has been downright mean, and I tried my best to..."

Cynthia stops abruptly, crosses her arms in front of her chest, and in a strained voice finishes her sentence: "deal with his petulant behavior."

"I hear you, Cynthia. And as you said before, this situation with Kent has been extremely difficult for you; in fact, I imagine that it's been very stressful and caused a lot of emotion?"

"I can handle it."

"I'm not saying that you can't. But I get the sense that it's not okay for you to feel emotional about it?"

"I'm a professional; my emotions are unimportant."

"So it would be unprofessional for you to feel angry or sad, or any other emotions concerning your work?"

"In a way, yes."

"And it would be counterproductive in terms of your relationship with Kent?"

"Yes, it would make me appear weak!"

"Vulnerable?"

"Yes."

"And it's bad to be vulnerable; especially with someone you need to protect yourself from?" I inquire.

"Yes. So you can see why I needed to defend myself, build what you called a 'wall of protection.' What else could I do?"

"Perhaps that was true in the past; however, remember the difference between reaction and response. What about the possibility of choosing a new response rather than reacting as you have in the past?"

Like a balloon that had lost much of its air, Cynthia slumps down in her chair and in a quiet voice says: "Yes, as I said, something has to change. So I guess it needs to be me. I need to figure out an appropriate response."

I nod my head and say: "Perhaps both of you need to do some changing; what do you think?"

"That would be nice; but I won't hold my breath."

"Fair enough. Yet you might be interested to know that I sense that Kent is willing to consider some changes too; in fact, at one point he said, 'I need to find a way out of this mess.' I don't know for sure what he has in mind, yet he seemed to indicate a willingness to change. So the question I have is: Might it be that Kent would be more likely to change if you and he established some degree of trust for one another?"

"Perhaps."

"And would you consider the possibility that Kent and you might begin to trust each other if you related to one another on a human level—each with your own feelings and emotions?"

"But what if he used my feelings to attack me?"

"I guess there is some possibility of that; however, would you be surprised to know that Kent said that he wants the same thing that you want from him? He wants respect from you—for his years of experience, for his position as a Senior Claims Manager—just as you want respect from him for being a well-educated, professional manager. So it seems to me that one of you might consider being the first to lower your wall, to take a risk and trust the other. Is that an option for you?"

Cynthia pauses momentarily before answering: "I'm not certain."

"That's fine. Can you think about it?"

"Yes, I will. Thank you."

"You're welcome. Do you have any other goals?"

"Respect is the most important one because it also includes the way Kent treats his subordinates. I want Kent to respect the people on his team, to develop a collegial working relationship with them. This will help greatly to lower the turnover rate on his team, and reflect well with the Executive Committee."

Standing up and moving to the flipchart, I write as Cynthia's next goal:

• *Respect for / collegial attitude toward team members*

"Is that what you had in mind?" I ask.

"Yes, it will do."

"How would you think Kent might be able to do that?"

"He would have to learn."

"Who would teach him?"

"I know where you're going with this; you're going to say that I could teach him."

"Yes, you read my mind. Is that an option for you?"

Appearing to brighten a bit, Cynthia answers: "Yes, I think so."

I continue: "In fact, it might provide a good way for you and Kent to relate to each other, don't you think? He could learn how to develop better relationships with his team members and I imagine that you might learn from him as well. He does seem to have a lot of experience with medical malpractice claims and you might ask him to share that with you in return for teaching him better management skills. That way you both benefit, and neither of you would feel inferior. Does that make sense?"

"I see what you mean."

"Good. Any other goals?"

"I would like him to consider me a colleague. That goes along with what you just said about learning from each other. I would like to feel that we could develop a cooperative working relationship such that we can both succeed."

"Are you willing to share this with Kent?"

"I'm not sure; I'll have to see how it goes when we all get back together."

"Alright, but should I add it to your list of goals?"

"Why don't you just say 'better working relationship with Kent' and let's see what happens."

I add this to the list of *Cynthia's Goals*, and ask: "Are there any other goals that you want to include in the list?"

"No. That's sufficient."

"Okay then. Is there anything else that you would like to discuss?"

"No, except I want to make certain you remember our agreement that you won't tell Kent about my phone conversation with Jim Peterson; you know, that the Board of Directors, not the Executive Committee, made the decision to hire me, and that the complaints about Kent were not the deciding factor."

"Yes, Cynthia, I understand that information is to remain confidential between the two of us, unless you change your mind later on. Is there anything else that we discussed that you want kept confidential?"

Cynthia looks at the list of her *Goals* for a few moments, and then responds: "No, everything else is fine."

"Good enough. So I'll see you when we all three meet again, right?"

"Yes," Cynthia answers, hesitates briefly, and then continues: "One more thing. After what you said about control at our first session and reading your article about the anatomy of anger, I'm beginning to see that I can't control anyone else, Kent included. But I can influence them and perhaps that's what I need to do with him — at least that's my hope."

I respond: "And remember when I quoted Norman Vincent Peale's adage, 'Change your thoughts and you change your world?' It may very well be that since your thoughts seem to be changing, it would follow that your world — in terms of Kent — will also change."

CLOSING COMMENTARY

In this block of dialogue we saw Cynthia surrender, albeit haltingly, to the realization that "something must change." She appeared to have crossed a threshold, to have finally come to accept that she couldn't control Kent, but that she could influence him should she decide to risk lowering her wall and trusting that he wouldn't attack her. Wanting to encourage her willingness to consider this risk, I didn't press her when she said, "I'm not certain," in answer to my question whether it was an option for her. Pressing or otherwise trying to get her to answer affirmatively would have been less than compassionate, and any agreement she made would have been less than volitional. It was for these reasons that I backed off, assuring her, "That's fine; just think about it. Okay?"

In further recognition of her willingness to consider changes in the way she related to Kent, I offered Cynthia the hope that, "Perhaps both of you need to do some changing," and I also shared my sense that Kent was indeed willing to consider it. Having compassion for the difficulties involved in many of the decisions made by participants, situational mediators look for opportunities (such as this) to instill hope.

As you saw, Cynthia began to think about lowering her wall of protection, but she certainly wasn't ready to take it completely down. For example, she made it clear that she wanted "to see how it goes when we all get back together," before deciding whether to share with Kent her goal that he treat her as a "colleague." As you may recall, this was also true for Kent; he was willing to make some changes in his behavior toward Cynthia, but wasn't ready to actually lower his wall of resentment and apologize to Cynthia.

Under the situational approach to mediation, participants alone decide what, if anything, they are willing to do to resolve their dispute. Had Kent and/or Cynthia decided to end the mediation after their private sessions, I would have respected their decision, trusted that they knew what was best for them, and had faith that this was meant to be. It is very dangerous for a mediator to become emotionally invested in the outcome of mediation; it is a sure sign that the mediator has his or her own agenda, which is antithetical to the situational approach.

However, the mediation between Kent and Cynthia did not end after their private session. One week later it continued with another joint session in which both Kent and Cynthia went on to lower their walls (at least to some extent). Kent actually apologized to Cynthia and she reciprocated by admitting that it was wrong to force him to complete daily reports. They discussed their respective goals, particularly the respect they wanted from one another, and what each of them would be willing to do to further these goals. As is typical, during much of this session Kent and Cynthia took the lead in discussing and considering various options for resolving their differences; I became an observer and facilitator of their process.

By no means did Kent and Cynthia fully let go of the past or resolve all of their differences. Cynthia remained guarded and never did disclose the information she obtained from Jim Peterson, while Kent's resentment reappeared when he and Cynthia disagreed about certain forms and the extent to which he would be autonomous in his position as a Senior Claims Analyst. I didn't expect them to settle all of their issues; such an expectation would have been unrealistic. Most disputes between co-workers end with incremental progress having been made, not full agreement. Indeed, situational mediators strive for progress, not perfection and understand that perfection is not possible.

Part B: Contract Disputes

Chapter 12:
Disputes Between Parties to Contracts

There are an infinite number of personal and business contracts. Some pertain to the manufacture, purchase, or sale of property. Others relate to the provision of services. However, the situational approach to mediation can be used to resolve any type of contractual dispute.

There is one type of contract that is frequently the subject of mediation: real estate contracts for the sale of residential property. It has become commonplace (due to the time and cost effectiveness of mediation) for standard form residential real estate contracts to include provisions that require mediation prior to arbitration or litigation.

The following represents an example of mediation involving residential real estate:

On June 21, 2001, Bradley and Bonnie Bentley entered into a Residential Resale Real Estate Purchase Contract to buy a home in Scottsdale, Arizona from Steven and Selma Sandstone.

The Contract included provisions for: (1) the payment of an Earnest Money Deposit of $15,000 that was subject to forfeiture should the Buyers breach the Contract; (2) the closing of escrow on August 21, 2001; (3) the obtaining by the Buyers of an inspection and the admonishment that they should inquire about the premises with all "governmental agencies, lenders, insurance agents, architects, and other appropriate persons and entities"; (4) the requirement that the Buyers and Sellers "mediate any dispute or claim arising out of or relating to the Contract before resorting to court action"; and (5) to equally share all costs.

Prior to entering into this Contract, the Buyers and the Sellers authorized Lynne Lindsey, a licensed real estate broker, to represent both of them under the terms of a Limited Dual Representation Agreement.

This Agreement included the following provisions: (1) the Broker will "exercise reasonable skill and care" in the performance of her duties; (2) the Broker will be obligated to "deal honestly and fairly with all parties"; (3) "the duties of the Broker do not relieve the Seller or the Buyer from the responsibility to protect their own interests"; and (4) "the Seller and Buyer agree to indemnify and hold the Broker harmless against any and all claims, damages, losses, expenses or liabilities arising from the Broker's role of limited dual representation."

On August 19, 2001, two days before the scheduled closing date, the Buyers caused their attorney to send a letter to the Sellers in which they cancelled the Contract and demanded an immediate refund of the $15,000 Ernest Money Deposit. The Sellers refused to cancel the Contract or refund the Earnest Money.

On September 10, 2001, the Buyers contacted my office. Here are the steps that were taken during the mediation of this dispute:

Step One: *Pre-mediation Consultation (Pre-flight)*

Most pre-mediation consultations involving contract disputes occur in two stages. The first stage begins when one party, such as the Buyers in this case, contacts my office to initiate mediation in accordance with their contractual obligation to do so. The second stage occurs as a consequence of the first, and begins with my office corresponding with the other party(s) to determine if they are willing to mediate.

Most of the time my assistant is able to help people (in this instance, the Bentleys) initiate mediation. She explains the mediation process, the time it usually takes to resolve these types of disputes (four to six hours), and the hourly fee. She also suggests that they visit Out-of-Court Solutions' Website. This helps in two ways: (1) they find out a little about me by reading my biography and looking at my photo; and (2) they learn more about mediation by reading the information and articles pertaining to real estate and other contractual disputes.

COMMENTARY
Occasionally an attorney for the buyer and/or seller will contact my office to initiate mediation on their client's behalf, and asks to talk directly with me. Sometimes the buyers or sellers themselves insist on telling me something "important" about their situation. In either event, I listen guardedly and politely interrupt when I sense they are about to say too much. I explain that a likely result of my hearing about the details of the dispute would be that I would form preconceived notions about it, and that this would not be helpful in terms of my role as an impartial mediator. Virtually everyone that I've explained this to has readily agreed, and limited their pre-mediation disclosures accordingly.

Often, attorneys want to send me statements or briefs on behalf of their clients. However, I uniformly decline their offers, explaining that this information would cause me to develop certain opinions about the matter. This response is admittedly unusual and many attorneys don't fully understand it—that is, until they are actually in session and experience the situational approach to mediation.

The second stage of pre-mediation consultation typically begins with my assistant sending a letter to the other party(s), the Sandstones in this case, inviting them to participate. Most of the time recipients of these letters respond by calling my office and asking for more information. Once again, my assistant is usually able to answer all of their questions and assuage their concerns on her own. However, consistent with compassion and other humanistic aspects of situational mediation, I am willing to talk to them personally and take as much time as is necessary to help them make fully informed decisions about mediation.

Step Two: *The Journey Begins (Taking Off)*
When all of the parties (except for Bonnie Bentley who was ill) and the broker, Lynne Lindsey, arrived at my office, they were welcomed and then escorted to a conference room.

Upon entering, I introduced myself by briefly recounting my educational and professional backgrounds, including my experience with adversarial litigation as both a trial lawyer and a client (in my own divorce). I explained that the adversarial system is a fight, and as such is likely to increase hostility and tension, whereas mediation is intended to reduce antagonism and stress — not to mention costs. I also explained how mediation is similar to airplane travel; one can expect bumpy or turbulent times.

Next, I offered an agenda, labeling it *Tentative Agenda* to make it clear that the participants (not the mediator) would have the final say as to whether or not to follow it. This *Agenda* included the following items:

(1) *Rules and Procedures.* I proposed that we invest 15 minutes or so in my explaining each of the rules and each of the procedures that pertain to real estate mediation. I also explained that this investment of time was likely to save many hours because the *Rules and Procedures* serve as a "map" for the mediation and thus help participants reach their goals quickly, inexpensively, and smoothly.

(2) *Getting Current.* I explained that the *Getting Current* stage gives each participant an opportunity to talk, and the mediator to learn, about the issues involved in the dispute as well as each participant's concerns and goals. I also explained that this stage of the mediation lets everyone involved *hear* each other's perspectives and *experience* each other first hand.

(3) *Immediate Concerns.* I explained that this agenda item is intended to give priority to, say, time-sensitive matters. I also told them that it was difficult for me to concentrate on other matters unless and until my immediate concerns were addressed, and that my experience showed that most people would agree.

(4) *Issues.* I suggested that it's often helpful to define and clarify whatever issues are raised in the *Getting Current* and *Immediate Concerns* stages before attempting to resolve them. I also explained that I never really know the direction the mediation will take after the first three stages, as the participants will decide this for themselves.

COMMENTARY

Contrary to other types of disputes, for example those involving key personnel (Chapters 8–11), I do not ask participants in contract mediation to complete an intake form. This is because the party who first calls my office is asked to complete a "Request to Initiate Mediation" form (Appendix, page 289), and thus provides the names, addresses, and telephone numbers of everyone else he or she wants to include in the mediation.

The *Tentative Agenda* in contract mediation is identical to that used in the mediation of key personnel and other workplace disputes (Chapter 9). So too with the "airplane" metaphor; regardless of the nature of the dispute, it serves to give participants a visceral picture of what's in store for them.

Next, I give each participant a written copy of the *Rules and Procedures* (Appendix, page 287) and then proceed to elaborate on each. Except for one additional paragraph pertaining to the mediator's fee (Paragraph Eight), the *Rules and Procedures* for real estate mediation are the same as those used to mediate key personnel disputes (I refer you to Chapter 9 for in-depth dialogue and commentary about them).

In contract mediations I usually elaborate further about the role of the mediator (*Rules and Procedures*, Paragraph Two). After making it clear that I will not function as a judge or as an attorney, I go on to explain that while the purpose of a court trial is to determine what happened in the past, the purpose of mediation is to determine how participants want things to be different in the present and future; thus, the legal system is past-oriented while mediation is present- and future-oriented. I then ask if each participant would be willing at some point in the mediation to shift their focus away from the past into the present; that is, if they would be willing to talk about how they would want the dispute to be resolved.

Making this distinction between a court trial's focus on the *past* and mediation's focus on the *present* serves to: (1) emphasize the point that the mediator neither has nor desires any authority to decide anything for the participants — they alone will make all of the decisions necessary to resolve the dispute; (2) set the stage for intervention later on should a participant get bogged down in the past by, for example, continually attempting to assign blame or fault for past events. Once having agreed to shift focus, the mediator can remind a participant of this and thus help the participant shift his or her focus away from the past into the present; and (3) facilitate the initiation of future-oriented, problem-solving dialogue, thereby saving the participants' time and money.

One more comment before proceeding further. The mediation of contractual disputes necessarily involves the interpretation of agreements and the evaluation of legal positions relating to them. Furthermore, the parties to contracts often have no desire or reason for a continuing relationship, as was the case in this real estate dispute between the Bentleys and Sandstones. Accordingly, situational mediators are apt to make much more use of the evaluative approach (as opposed to, for example, the transformative approach) when mediating contractual disputes.

Step Three: *Gaining Understanding (Altitude)*

This step involves the *Getting Current* stage of situational mediation. In the dispute between the Bentleys and Sandstones, I began by reminding everyone that this was the time in which each of them would have an opportunity to talk without interruption and tell me from their own perspective: (1) the facts and circumstances involved in the dispute; (2) the issues in need of resolution; (3) their concerns, worries, and fears; and (4) their goals and objectives for the mediation.

(The *Getting Current* stage is an integral part of the situational approach to mediation, and Chapter 10 features extensive dialogue and commentary about it. I encourage you read—or re-read—this material before proceeding further in this chapter).

After asking who would like to go first, everyone agreed that Bradley Bentley would. From him I learned that: (1) Bradley and Bonnie Bentley had two high school age children, and that a key factor in their buying the Sandstone's house was so their children could attend Chaparral (Scottsdale's top academic and much sought after high school); (2) at the time they entered into the Contract with the Sandstones, the Bentleys were still living in Los Angeles; (3) on July 7, 2001, the Scottsdale School Board changed the boundaries for Chaparral such that the Sandstone's house was no longer within Chaparral's district, and the Bentley children would have to attend a different high school; (4) the Bentleys didn't learn about this change in Chaparral's district until July 24, and had tried without success to get an exception for their children; (5) as a result of this district change, the Bentleys felt that they had no choice but to cancel the Contract; and (6) on August 11, the Bentleys hurriedly leased another house that was located within the revised district for Chaparral High School.

In accordance with the *"what, want, willing"* model for organizing information (see Chapter 10), I made note of all of this information under the category of *what*, and then asked Bradley Bentley how he would *want* the dispute to be resolved.

DIALOGUE

Bradley responds: "We feel awfully bad about this whole thing and really liked that house, but we were living in Los Angeles and couldn't have been expected to know what the school board here was doing. This whole thing was very upsetting, especially for my wife. She's not a well person and moving was stressful. But then finding out about the school situation and rushing around trying to get an exception was very hard on her!"

"I hear you. It sounds like it was very hard for you, too."

"Yeah, it really was. Steven knew how important it is that our kids attend Chaparral; he and I hit it off from the start and had several conversations when we looked through the house."

"How did that come about?"

"I was there three different times, and one time he and I were out by the pool talking about things, and we talked about Chaparral. His kids had gone there, and he knew how hard it was to get in unless you lived in the district. So anyway, they were in a much better position to know about the change. After all, there must have been some notice or hearing — or something like that."

"When you say 'they,' do you mean the Sandstones?"

"Yeah."

"So let me see if I've got this right: your perspective is that since the Sandstones were here in Scottsdale and you were in Los Angeles, they were in a better position to know about the redistricting of Chaparral's boundaries; is that it?"

"Yeah, that's right."

"Is there anything else that you want to say about what went on in the past concerning this situation?"

"No, I think that covers it."

"I'm wondering if this might be the time for you to shift your focus away from the *past* and into the *present*, and for you to talk about how you might want this matter resolved?"

"Yeah, sure. I think that in light of everything we should get our deposit back."

"The full amount?"

"Yeah, all of it."

"And that's based on?"

"The change in Chaparral's district. They were in the best position to know about it, and with all due respect to them, we actually think that they *did* know about it."

"What leads you to believe that?"

"We talked to some other people who have kids at Chaparral and they all knew about it. They say it was common knowledge."

"So what I hear you saying is that from your perspective it was likely that the Sandstones knew about the redistricting; is that right?"

"Yeah, that's right. They had to know!"

"Okay, I hear you. Is there anything else that you want to talk about at this point?"

"No, that's it."

"Alright, thank you."

COMMENTARY

In this block of dialogue, I actively listened while Bradley was *Getting Current*. I let him know that he was heard ("I hear you"); *asked* clarifying questions ("When you say 'they,' do you mean the Sandstones?"); *summarized* what I heard him say ("So let me see if I've got this right: your perspective is..."); and *reflected* back the emotions underlying his words ("It sounds like it was very hard for you, too.") Active listening fosters greater disclosure of information and understanding.

I also asked Bradley if he were willing to shift perspectives out of the past into the present, and tell me how he would *want* to resolve the dispute. This is when he said, "I think that in light of everything we should get our deposit back."

One could speculate about Bradley's intention when he suggested that the dispute could be resolved if the Sandstones refunded the full amount of his deposit. He may have sincerely felt entitled to a full refund. Or he may have been engaged in *positional* negotiation, starting out the negotiation at one extreme. In any event, as a former trial attorney, I realized that it would be difficult, time-consuming, and expensive for the Bentleys to try to prove that the Sandstones actually knew about the school's redistricting. I also realized that the contractual provisions in this matter concerning forfeiture and responsibility to "inquire about the premises with all governmental agencies," were problematic for them. Nevertheless, I didn't confront or in any way criticize Bradley's suggestion as to how to resolve the dispute. On the contrary, I asked clarifying questions: "The full amount?" "And that's based on?" "So what I hear you saying is that from your perspective it was likely that the Sandstones knew about the redistricting; is that right?"

It was in this way that I began to create, in a compassionate way, *doubt* and *dissonance* in Bradley's mind. Steadfastly mindful of the efficacy of empathy, humility, and compassion, situational mediators don't cross-examine or aggressively confront participants; rather, they ask questions to help participants see that their thinking may be distorted or unrealistic, thus creating openings for settlements that involve less than the full amount.

The participants agreed that Steven Sandstone would be next to *Get Current*.

DIALOGUE
I start off by asking:

"Alright, Steven, where would you like to begin?"

"I would like to say that Bradley is a nice guy and everything, but he's treating this like we're friends. As far as I'm concerned this is a business transaction. It has nothing to do with friendship, and I want to stick to the Contract that clearly states on page 1 that, 'Buyer agrees that, if Buyer breaches this Contract, any earnest money is subject to forfeiture.' The house passed inspection, after we made the repairs they requested, and they qualified for a loan. It's clear to me that they lose the deposit!"

"The full amount?"

"Yes."

"I hear you, yet I'm wondering if you give any weight to the phrase, *is subject to?*"

"What do you mean?"

"I'm sorry, let me explain. The provision you just quoted states that the deposit *is subject to* forfeiture, not that it is *forfeited*. So there seems to be some discretion built into the provision. Do you see what I mean?"

"I guess so."

"As I told you when we went over the *Rules and Procedures*, part of my job as your mediator is to provide legal information and I'm wondering if I could tell you about my understanding of provisions such as this?"

"Fine. Go ahead."

"The legal information I want to give you is something that I learned early on in my legal career; in fact, I first learned it in law school. It's a legal maxim, a truism, and goes like this: *the law abhors forfeitures*. Courts usually go out of their way to avoid forfeitures because they consider them punitive as opposed to compensatory. Thus, they are reluctant to order any automatic loss of a right or property.

"So I'm not at all certain that you can count on a court awarding you the entire deposit, that is, without first considering all of the facts and circumstances. I'm not saying that there isn't any chance that you won't get the whole $15,000; I'm saying that since 'the law abhors forfeitures,' a court is likely to want justification for whatever amount it awards you. So in light of this legal information, perhaps it would be helpful if you were to tell me about any losses or expenses you incurred as a result of the Bentley's canceling the Contract?"

"I still think that we're entitled to the whole $15,000."

"I hear you. And I'm not saying that you are or you're not. Remember, I'm not here as a judge. All I'm suggesting is that it might be helpful if everyone knew about any losses or expenses you suffered as a result of the cancellation."

"Fine—they're more than $15,000 anyway."

COMMENTARY

This block of dialogue illustrates another way in which mediators, by providing legal information, create *doubt* and *dissonance* in a participant's mind. As with Bradley, I didn't cross-examine or aggressively confront Steven. Rather, I asked questions to help him consider the possibility that it may be unrealistic for him to expect that a court would award him all of the $15,000 deposit.

I was, however, more evaluative as well as assertive with Steven than I had been with Bradley. This is because I sensed that Steven was more strident in his position than Bradley had been, and that it would take greater degrees of evaluation and assertiveness on my part to break through his stridency. Thus I immediately provided Steven with legal information about forfeitures rather than waiting until later on, as I did with Bradley. There is no right or wrong when making tactical decisions such as these; it is simply a matter of the mediator trusting his or her own judgment.

Steven went on in *Getting Current* to claim the following losses and expenses: (1) the total amount of the mortgage payments he made on the Scottsdale house during the two-month escrow, $3,600; (2) the total amount he paid for utilities (electric, gas, and water) during the two-month escrow, $420; (3) the total cost of repairs to the Scottsdale house after the Bentley's inspection, $2,250; (4) the amount it cost to move his furniture, appliances, and other household items to his new residence in Hawaii, $8,700; (5) estimated loss of value to the Scottsdale house as a result of it having to be resold while vacant, $12,000; and (6) the total attorneys' fees he had paid for legal advice, $2,000. These claims totaled $28,970.

As with Bradley, one could speculate that Steven was engaged in *positional* negotiation; that he intentionally went to an extreme, claiming any and all losses and expenses he could think of so as to make a high opening demand. This approach to negotiation (also known as the "competitive" approach) is fairly common. However, as will be illustrated later in this chapter, situational mediators strive to create opportunities for *interest-based* rather than *positional* negotiation.

Lynne Lindsey, the real estate broker who represented both parties, was next to *Get Current*. Before discussing the substance of what she said, it should be noted that the Contract in this matter (as with most standard form real estate contracts) did not provide for the mandatory participation in mediation by anyone other than the Buyers and Sellers. However, as with many real estate professionals, Lynne felt duty-bound to her clients, and thus voluntarily agreed to participate.

The substance of what Lynne disclosed while *Getting Current* was that: (1) as a professional real estate broker, she regretted not knowing about the change in Chaparral's district; (2) she wanted to help the parties resolve their differences; (3) she found a house for the Bentleys to lease after canceling the Contract; and (4) all of the parties had released her from any liability when they signed the "Limited Dual Representation Agreement."

Step Four: *Increasing Communication and Collaboration (Altitude and Acceleration)*
Here situational mediators strive to help participants define, clarify, prioritize, and otherwise sort out their disagreements, concerns, and goals. They also strive to foster effective communication and facilitate interest-based negotiations.

After everyone in the Bentley and Sandstone mediation completed *Getting Current* and took a short break, we resumed in joint session. However, the parties stuck to their positions and argued back and forth for the next 20 minutes or so. It was then that I commented that they seemed to have hit "bumpy weather" and suggested the idea of private sessions. This idea was readily accepted and everyone agreed that Bradley Bentley would be first.

DIALOGUE
I begin a private session with Bradley:

"Bradley, I've heard your position about wanting all of your deposit back, yet I keep wondering what's really motivating you here?"

"Motivating me?"

"Yes, in addition to getting all of your money back, what are your *interests* here?"

"I don't know exactly, but this whole thing isn't fair. Somebody should have found out about the redistricting! It seems to me that we're the only ones who have suffered any loss. Everybody else will come out great; the Sandstones will get free money. Lynne will get her share of that, plus the $1,800 commission we paid her to lease a house. It seems lopsided; unfair."

"So you're interested in *fairness*; a settlement that would be fair to everyone, including you and Mrs. Bentley?"

"Yes, that's right. My wife is not well; she has recurring bouts of depression and this situation was pretty rough on her. We should get something for that alone."

"So part of fairness for you is getting something to compensate for the additional problems your wife experienced. Is that right?"

"Yeah. It's hard to put a value on it; but I would have paid a lot to avoid having her be so upset — you know, depressed. When she's in that condition, it's a big toll on the whole family."

"I hear you, Bradley, and on a personal level, I'm sorry."

After pausing momentarily, I continue:

"Do you have any amount in mind that might compensate for this toll?"

"No, not really."

"Perhaps you could think about it while we talk about some other things; would that be alright?"

"Yeah, sure. What other things?"

"The Contract, for one."

"What about it?"

"Well, there are a couple of provisions that I'd like to give you some legal information about. Okay?"

"Yeah, okay."

COMMENTARY

Situational mediators recognize the importance of participants being heard and private sessions are apt to facilitate this. Often, participants feel more comfortable, safe, and secure when alone with the mediator, and this helps to create an atmosphere in which participants are better able to identify and articulate their emotional interests in acknowledgement, honesty, respect, trust, etc. As you saw in the previous dialogue, this was the case for Bradley, who was eventually able to express his need for *fairness*.

I also used this private session with Bradley to provide him legal information about his Contract with the Sandstones. As to the provision concerning forfeiture, I pointed out that even though *the law abhors forfeitures*, no respectable lawyer would guarantee against a given court ruling in favor of the Sandstones and awarding them the entire $15,000. As to the provision requiring both parties to inquire about the premises with all "governmental agencies…and other appropriate persons and entities," I pointed out that a court might rule against him because he had failed to inquire of the Scottsdale School Board about any change in Chaparral's district. Once again, my intent in giving this information was to create *doubt* and *dissonance* in Bradley's mind so that he would reconsider his position.

It should be noted that private sessions usually afford mediators with additional opportunities to demonstrate empathy and compassion, as did this private session with Bradley. When Bradley talked about his wife being upset and depressed, and the toll it took on his family, I commiserated with him and said, "On a personal level, I'm sorry." I was genuinely moved by his situation, and wanted him to know that. Furthermore, as a situational mediator, I knew that my demonstration of these qualities would increase the chance of Bradley following suit in his negotiations with the Sandstones.

At the close of this private session, Bradley authorized me to convey an offer of settlement in the amount of $2,200. More specifically, in exchange for a release of the remainder of the deposit to him, Bradley agreed to reimburse the Sandstones for one-half of the total amount of the mortgage payments they made on the Scottsdale house during the two-month escrow ($1,800) plus all of the money they paid for utilities during that time ($420).

DIALOGUE

I next meet in private session with Steven and Selma Sandstone:

"Where would you folks like to start?"

"You asked for these private sessions, so you start," Steven replies, curtly.

"Alright, could we talk about the losses and expenses you listed?"

"That's fine with me," Steven answers.

Noticing that Steven is answering my questions, I turn to Selma and ask: "Is that alright with you, too?"

"Oh yes. Steven can speak for both of us," Selma responds.

"Good enough," I say and turn back to Steven.

"Let me first ask you about the mortgage payments you made. As I remember, they totaled $3,600?"

"That's right."

"And I take it that part was for interest, and another part was for principle?"

"That's right."

"Could you break it down for me?"

"About $1,200 was for interest; the rest was for principle."

"So about $2,400 in total was for interest, and that's tax deductible, right?"

"Yes."

"And in your bracket, how much of a deduction would that give you?"

"I don't think that's relevant here!"

"Please excuse me, Steven. I don't mean to pry. Yet you are claiming the mortgage payments as a loss, and it seems that if this matter doesn't settle through mediation and you have to use separate lawyers to litigate it, a court would want to know your out-of-pocket or after-tax loss. Does that make sense to you?"

"I'm not sure, and quite frankly, I don't care. Let's just say that after taxes my loss was about $1,500."

"Alright, thank you. And I take it that the rest, the part that went toward principle, reduced the balance on your mortgage?"

"Obviously!"

"So would that really be a loss to you? Won't you recover that when you re-sell the property?"

"Yes, but I've lost the use of the money."

"So what I hear you saying is that you're entitled to interest on the money you paid toward principle, and on the money you paid toward interest. Is that right?"

"Absolutely."

"At what rate of return?"

"This is getting ridiculous!"

"Please forgive me, Steven, I'm not trying to be annoying or disrespectful. Yet these are the things you would have to know and prove if you go to court."

COMMENTARY

Mindful of Steven's stridency, I wanted to create additional *doubt* and *dissonance* by asking specific questions about his alleged losses and expenses. In addition to those included in the previous block of dialogue, I also asked Steven specific questions about (1) the repairs he had made, and whether he would have had to make them no matter who purchased the property; (2) the $8,700 he spent to move furniture and furnishings to Hawaii, and whether he thought a court would likely reimburse him for the full cost of an overseas move; and (3) the $12,000 alleged "loss of value" due to the house being vacant, and whether he could substantiate this loss through expert testimony (as would be required should he take this matter to court).

Mediators ask these types of questions to help participants see their positions from a different perspective. Reference to what a court might do, or what a party would have to prove if they were to go to court can be particularly effective in accomplishing this; most people want to avoid the time, expense, and hostility involved in court battles. Nevertheless, as I did in this instance, situational mediators go out of their way to be humble and compassionate when asking such questions.

My private session with Steven and Selma also included dialogue that led to their identifying a number of interests, including their needs for: (1) *acknowledgement* in terms of their having done everything required of them, for instance, making repairs to the house and moving their furniture and furnishings so as to close escrow on schedule; (2) *respect* for one's word as embodied in the Contract; and (3) *fairness* in terms of being fully compensated for the losses and expenses they incurred as a result of Bradley's cancellation of the Contract.

Near the close of my private session with the Sandstones, I conveyed Bradley's offer of $2,220. Initially Steven reacted with a good deal of anger, exclaiming that he was insulted by Bradley's offer. However, after acknowledging and normalizing his anger, and reminding him of his goal of getting through the mediation quickly and inexpensively, Steven was able to redirect his attention to his goals in the negotiations at hand. Moreover, Selma spoke up at this point, and insisted that Steven "get this over with." It was then that Steven said that he was willing to give up his right to $28,970, and settle for $15,000.

As things turned out, I also met privately with Lynne Lindsey. She told me she felt guilty for not having known about the change in Chaparral's district. She explained that she was a long-time resident of Scottsdale, and took pride in keeping abreast of civic matters (especially those related to schools). She also told me that she had re-listed the Sandstones' house at a reduced commission rate.

Near the end of our private session, Lynne expressed great concern about her professional reputation, explaining that she had worked "long and hard to develop an excellent reputation," and that under the circumstances she would be willing to contribute "a reasonable amount" to a settlement.

I want to end this block of commentary by discussing the *confidentiality* of what was said during these private sessions. Earlier on in the mediation, when we reviewed the *Rules and Procedures*, the participants decided to keep what was said confidential (i.e., undisclosed to the other participants). Thus, at the end of each private session, I asked if there was anything that was said that should be kept confidential. Bradley, Steven, and Selma didn't request confidentiality; however Lynne invoked confidentiality as to her offer to "contribute a reasonable amount to a settlement."

DIALOGUE

I resume the mediation in joint session: "Well, let me begin by reporting that certain settlement discussions occurred while we were in private session. It seems that Bradley is willing to settle this matter by releasing the sum of $2,220 to Steven and Selma in exchange for their release to him of the balance of the $15,000 deposit. And it seems that Steven and Selma are willing to forgo the $28,970 of losses and expenses they were claiming and settle for a release to them of the $15,000 deposit. Is that accurate?" I ask Bradley, Steven, and Selma collectively.

They all nod their heads and I continue: "So it strikes me that you've actually made some progress toward resolving this matter. Instead of being apart by $28,970, you're now apart by $12,800 (the difference between $15,000 and $2,200)."

All of the participants remain silent, don't make eye contact with each other or me, and appear tense. So I continue: "Another thing I'd like to report is that you all seem to have some of the same interests."

Bradley speaks up in a sharp tone of voice: "Like what?"

"For one, it seems that all of you want fairness; you are all interested in a settlement that's fair."

Steven interjects: "I have other interests too; it's not just about fairness!"

Bradley counters: "So do I, but the bottom line is that you're trying to get a windfall by keeping my $15,000 — and that's not fair! I was living in L.A., and you were here. And now we're stuck in a leased house that's way too small, making my wife even worse. You should have known about Chaparral; I find it really hard to believe you didn't!"

Steven argues back: "I'm going to say this for the last time: we didn't know about it! And, anyway, you cost me a lot of money!"

Bradley angrily asserts: "That's a lot of bull! My attorney says that you'll never get a lot of the things you're claiming, like those ridiculous moving expenses to Hawaii. So let's cut the bullshit, okay?"

Steven defiantly counters: "I don't give a damn what your

lawyer said! You talk about not being fair! We do everything possible to see that the house will close on time—make all those repairs, move our furniture—and then two days before the closing, you cancel the Contract. The least you could have done is called us yourself. But no, you didn't have the courtesy to do that! You just had your lawyer send us a letter and demand your money back, like nothing ever happened. You signed a Contract; doesn't your word mean anything to you?"

Bradley doesn't respond, and for the next few seconds he and Steven stare angrily at each other. After a few more seconds, I remark: "So it sounds to me like each of you have another interest in common; it seems that each of you want the other to *acknowledge* the hardships you suffered in this situation.

"It seems like you, Bradley, want Steven and Selma to acknowledge the stress this situation has caused your wife and yourself—having to scramble around at the last minute trying to get an exception, and having to live in a leased house that's too small for your family and adversely affects your wife's health.

"And it seems like you, Steven and Selma, want Bradley to acknowledge that you did everything that was required of you under the Contract. For example, you made all of the repairs that were requested, and then received an impersonal cancellation letter from an attorney.

"So it seems to me that all of you are interested in *acknowledgement*; each of you wants the other to recognize that you suffered several hardships as a result of this situation. Would you agree?"

Bradley slumps down in his chair, casts his eyes downward, appears pensive, and remains silent.

Steven and Selma glance at each other, appearing to silently communicate. After a few seconds, Selma says in a low voice: "Let's get this over with, Steven."

Steven nods his head, slowly turns to Bradley, and asks: "Do you want to find a way that we both can come out of this with something that's fair?"

Bradley responds: "Yeah, we can try."

COMMENTARY

This block of dialogue is illustrative of the transformation that can occur when participants are able to express their needs. Often, as with Bradley and Steven, anger acts as the catalyst that enables participants to say what's really motivating them, that is, to disclose their emotional interests in fairness and acknowledgement.

Situational mediators view expressions of anger by participants as expressions of emotional needs, and thus respond to them compassionately. At the same time, situational mediators know how to manage anger and otherwise safeguard participants from disrespectful or abusive communication.

As I did with Bradley and Steven, situational mediators listen for underlying emotional interests and help articulate them. This is one of the chief ways by which situational mediators "facilitate communication and negotiations" (Paragraph One of the *Rules and Procedures*, Appendix, page 287) and help participants move off their positions to negotiate settlements.

Step Five: *Continuing Onward (Cruising)*

This step typically involves the mediator helping participants discuss, negotiate, and make fully informed decisions about their situation. Having established *what* is involved in their situation and how they *want* things to be in the future, it is at this point that participants begin to discuss, negotiate, and decide the things they are *willing* to do to get what they want.

In the Bentley and Sandstone mediation, I helped the participants discuss, negotiate, and make decisions about their respective rights under the Contract, the practicalities and costs involved in pursuing those rights, and their differing views concerning fairness. As things turned out, all of the participants, including Lynne, contributed to a settlement that none of them were happy about, but as is usual, all of them could live with.

Step Six: *Finalizing Settlement (Landing)*

Most contract mediations end with the participants entering into a "Mediated Settlement Agreement." Here is the one that I prepared in the Bentley and Sandstone mediation.

MEDIATED SETTLEMENT AGREEMENT

This Agreement dated September 21, 2001 is between Bradley and Bonnie Bentley (collectively "Buyer"), Steven and Selma Sandstone (collectively "Seller"), Lynne Lindsey of Lindsey Select Reality ("Lindsey"), and concerns a real estate dispute mediated by Oliver Ross of Out-of-Court Solutions.

Recitals:

A. On or about June 21, 2001, Buyer entered into a Residential Resale Real Estate Purchase Contract and Receipt for Deposit ("the Contract") with Seller with respect to certain residential real property located at 10211 Frontier Street, Phoenix, Arizona 85262 ("the property").

B. Lindsey represented both Buyer and Seller pursuant to the terms of a Limited Dual Representation Agreement, dated June 2, 2001.

C. Pursuant to the Contract, Seller and Buyer opened an escrow at North Scottsdale Title Insurance Company, escrow #01-01504 ("the escrow").

D. Subsequent to the Contract, a dispute arose between Seller and Buyer as to the earnest money deposited in the escrow and certain damages claimed by Seller as a result of Buyer's cancellation of the Contract ("the dispute").

Having mediated all of the issues involved in the dispute, THE PARTIES AGREE:

1. $5,020.00 of the earnest money held in the escrow shall be released to Seller.

2. $9,980.00 of the earnest money held in the escrow shall be released to Buyer.

3. On or before June 21, 2001, Lindsey will pay Buyer the sum of $320.00.

4. On or before August 21, 2001, Lindsey will pay Seller the sum of $1,180.00 (or credit said sum to Seller in any subsequent escrow that may be opened for the sale of the property).

5. Immediately upon its receipt of this Agreement, the escrow shall, and is hereby instructed, to pay the sums stated in paragraphs 1 and 2, above.

6. Upon full performance by the escrow and Lindsey in accordance with paragraphs 1 through 4, above, the parties hereby release and discharge each other from any and all claims, liabilities, causes of action, demands for reimbursement, requests for payment, and/or claims for relief, of any sort or description whatsoever, known or unknown, contingent or liquidated, past, present, or future, related in any way to the property or the Contract.

7. Neither this Agreement nor any of its terms shall in any way be considered or construed as an admission of fault and/or liability on the part of any party.

8. Each party represents and declares that in

signing this Agreement it has relied solely upon its own judgment, belief, and knowledge, and upon the advice of any independently selected counsel concerning the nature, extent, and duration of their rights and claims.

9. This Agreement constitutes the full agreement among the parties relating to the dispute, property, and Contract, and the parties acknowledge that there are no other agreements among them, written or oral, relating to the subject matter of this Agreement.

10. This Agreement shall be construed according to Arizona law and, if any action is brought to enforce this Agreement, the prevailing party shall be entitled to an award of reasonable attorney's fees, legal expenses, and court costs.

11. The parties agree that the terms stated in this Agreement are contractual and not mere recitals.

12. This Agreement is to be effective upon its execution.

Having read and fully understood the terms of this Agreement, the parties have signed below.

_____   _____
Bradley Bentley   Date

_____   _____
Bonnie Bentley   Date

_____   _____
Steven Sandstone   Date

_____   _____
Selma Sandstone   Date

_____   _____
Lynne Lindsey   Date

CLOSING COMMENTARY

It should be noted that the six numbered Steps presented in this chapter are intended only as guidelines; they are not meant as a set formula or sequentially ordered measures. Thus, for example, in situations where participants are having difficulty in discussing, negotiating, or making decisions about certain issues (Step Five), it is often helpful to transition back to the *Getting Current* stage (Step Three) so as to ferret out the additional information. Or, when anger surfaces in the later stages of mediation, it's often necessary to spend additional time enhancing communication and understanding between the participants (Step Four) before involving them in additional problem solving (Step Five).

The practice of mediation is an art as opposed to a science, and the process of mediation is more circular than linear in nature. It is for these reasons that situational mediators steadfastly respond to the vicissitudes of human behavior with humility, empathy, and compassion, and selectively use the most effective aspects of the evaluative, facilitative, transformative, and humanistic approaches to mediation.

Section III: The Management of Anger and Other Emotions

Chapter 13:
The Anatomy of Anger

My exploration of the anatomy of anger began as a self-study and continued for many years. During this time I came across various quotations that profoundly influenced my ability to manage my anger and other emotions. I share them with you in the hope that they help demonstrate how anger develops.

When angry, count to ten before you speak;
If very angry, a hundred.
Thomas Jefferson

Sounds easy, doesn't it? Then why is it difficult to remain composed when we're aggravated, frustrated, exasperated, or just plain old pissed-off? Why do we sometimes lose control, reacting in hostile, counterproductive, or childlike ways toward our spouse, child(ren), parents, friends, and coworkers? Certain people and things just make us angry. We can't help it! It just happens. And what can we do about it? Do we have a choice whether to be angry? Can we opt not to feel upset, furious, or resentful? Based on my own experiences, as well as helping others deal with anger in my role as a professional mediator, I have come to know that the answer to both of these questions is unequivocally yes! Here's why:

Simply put, we get angry when people, situations, and other stimuli don't meet our expectations—our thoughts about the future, what we look forward to or wait for.

Our expectations can motivate us toward achievement and attainment of goals. However, when entangled with early childhood thinking, they are likely to cause anger and other feelings of unhappiness.

Early in life, we feel omnipotent, all-powerful, and in control. We expect to control mom, dad, and others, getting them to fulfill our needs and desires. We also expect to be able to control situations and outcomes of events. As we mature, we realize that our expectations may be unrealistic—that we may not have any real external control, that we may only *influence* people and situations. But we cannot actually control them, or necessarily determine what will happen in the future. To expect otherwise is to fall prey to the "illusion of control."

When our standards of good and bad, right and wrong go unmet, we may subconsciously revert to early childhood thinking. It is then that we slip into the illusion of control, unrealistically expecting all people to behave and all situations to turn out as we think they should. Thus, we unwittingly set ourselves up for unhappiness, disappointment, anger, resentment, rage, and the like.

Personally, I am now able to see the connection between my control-based expectations and negative feelings. In my prior marriage, I expected my wife to help and comfort me when I was upset or frightened. If she was indifferent or could not meet my needs, I became angry and, over time, resentful. In college and law school, I expected good grades. When my expectations were unmet, I was angry and unhappy. While building a law firm, I expected my associates and partners to be workaholic, as was I. When they weren't, I became filled with anger and rage. In these instances I slipped into the illusion of control.

Today, in my mediation practice, I work with divorcing couples, co-workers who aren't getting along, and other people in conflict. Time and again I watch them become frustrated, angry, and hostile when they slip into control-based expectations of one another. Helping them recognize these control-based expectations is essential to real movement toward agreement.

Anger co-opts our energy by diverting
it toward punitive action.

Marshall B. Rosenberg, Ph.D.

When we slip into the illusion of control and revert to early childhood thinking and behavior, we are set up for errors in thinking. Feeling angry and unhappy for not realizing our expectations, we often incorrectly assign blame to others, making them responsible for our feelings. We rationalize: "she *made* me angry." We are unable to see that no other person or situation can make us angry. It is our own thoughts and expectations that are to blame for our anger. We mistake the stimulus (in the form of a person, a thing, or an event) for the cause. Blind to reality, we are unable to see that we have slipped into the omnipotent thinking of early childhood — erroneously expecting to be in control.

Perhaps subconsciously, we are likely to deny responsibility for our thoughts in other ego-defensive ways. We are apt to judge people, situations, and other stimuli as bad, sick, crazy, and evil. Or, we may characterize the outcome of a situation or event as ridiculous, stupid, unfair, or unjust. In this way, we once again mistake the stimulus for the cause, shifting responsibility for our unhappiness to someone, or something, else. We are also likely to act upon these erroneous thoughts, behaving in counterproductive, frequently adolescent ways toward the blameless stimulus.

Looking back, I can see how this fall into blame and judgment occurred with my brother. The slightest involvement with him would trigger anger and resentment on my part. Today, I realize that I repeatedly resented him because my own expectations of him went unfulfilled. Thus, he was the *stimulus*, not the *cause* of my anger.

As a mediator, I consistently witness this fall into blame. People in conflict typically have numerous unmet expectations of one another that are likely to function as catalysts for outbursts of anger, hostility, and resentment. A significant part of my job, as I will explain later, is to help disputants recognize their control-based expectations, and then replace them with realistic expectations and goals.

In summary, it is our unmet expectations which usually cause anger—not other people or events. Falling prey to the illusion of control, we mistake the stimulus for the cause of our anger, and then blame, judge, label, and otherwise shift responsibility away from the true cause of our unhappiness: our control-based expectations.

A tamed mind brings happiness.
                                                The Buddha

Most of us are powerless to prevent certain thoughts from coming to mind. These thoughts come and go, seemingly at random, entering our heads without invitation, at times becoming obsessive. We may be powerless over the feelings generated by our thoughts; however, we are not helpless. We can stop reacting to the feelings generated by unmet expectations and, instead, start responding.

Reacting is the reliving of a subconscious pattern; it's habitual, automatic, something you don't think about. *Responding*, on the other hand, involves choice, conscious awareness that we can choose our thoughts and thereby redirect our feelings and behavior.

Thus, we can tame our mind to stop reacting and start responding. Indeed, this is the first step toward happiness. Rather than reacting as we have in the past, we can take responsibility for our thoughts. We can decide; we can make up our minds to be happy.

Most folks are as happy as they make their minds up to be.
                                                Abraham Lincoln

If we are to have any chance at all of choosing whether or not to be angry, we must first master our reactions—the feelings and behavior generated by old, habitual, subconscious, childlike thoughts. In my experience this requires active intervention, some contrary action that provides the time and space needed to break out of reactivity. Here are some of the actions I took, and suggest you consider.

Sometimes I followed Thomas Jefferson's advice, counting to 10 or 20. In other situations where I anticipated problems, I placed a rubber band around my wrist, snapping it to shock myself into consciousness. Today, I most often use affirmations or a favorite prayer, calling on a Power Greater than myself to break the chain of reactivity.

No matter what the method, the task is to stop reacting. Until we change our pattern of reactivity, we remain enslaved to environmental stimuli, unaware of the thoughts that generate our anger and blind to their inaccuracy. Any action that stops our fall into the illusion of control will do. If nothing more, simply bite your tongue. The important thing is to build an arsenal of mental practices — tools — that are instantly accessible to create a moment in time in which you can choose to change your thoughts.

Change your thoughts and you change your world.
Norman Vincent Peale

Once out of reaction and into response, once out of unawareness and into consciousness, there is the opportunity to trace anger or other feelings back to their source. We can then reexamine our expectations, determining if they are control-based and, if so, change our thoughts accordingly.

For example, I used to be triggered by my former father-in-law, frequently getting angry and acting out at him with hostility. This is when I learned about using a rubber band to snap out of reactivity. Now I realize that the use of a rubber band in this way (or the use of any of the other tools I've mentioned) provides the moment in time needed to ferret out the expectations causing my anger. That gave me the opportunity to look at the situation realistically, perhaps remembering that I have no control over anyone else — what they say, do, or think — and that my own control-based expectations caused my anger.

Another, perhaps more advanced, way to discover the expectations causing our anger is to use the word ANGER as an acronym. First, concentrate on "A"cknowledging the anger and "N"ormalizing it as very common and human. Next, think about your "G"oals in relation to the other person or situation. For example, when angered by my wife, I'm apt to think about my goal to have a loving and caring relationship with her. Since goals are necessarily future oriented, focusing on them helps to redirect our thoughts away from the past, away from reaction, to the present.

The next step is to think about the accuracy your "E"xpectations. Are they grounded in reality? Are they appropriate to the people or circumstances with which you are presently involved? If so, anger may be an appropriate response. On the other hand, your expectations may be so entangled with early childhood thinking that you fall prey to the illusion of control, getting angry because you mistook the stimulus for the cause. The task here is to trace your feelings back to their origin — your expectations.

By tracing our feelings and behavior back to their source, we free ourselves of enslavement to reactivity. Moreover, we afford ourselves the opportunity to "R"espond, selecting our thoughts and thereby generating feelings and behavior that are in furtherance of our goals.

Initial use of this acronym may be difficult and awkward. With practice, however, it can become a readily available mental tool for responding rather than reacting. Indeed, it has become very helpful in my mediation practice. When anger surfaces, I use this acronym to redirect it. First, I acknowledge and normalize the anger, commenting in a divorce situation, for example, that anger is a necessary stage in the grief process and central to the loss of any significant relationship.

Next, I remind the angry person of the goals they established at the beginning of the mediation (e.g., getting their issues resolved quickly, inexpensively, and smoothly). Finally, I ask the angry person if it's realistic to expect that the other will suddenly change, and then discuss what response (rather than reaction) would best help them accomplish their goals.

Again, the important thing is to develop a readily available method for escaping the dark and narrow place of reactivity so that you may reach, if you will, the Promised Land where you are free to choose your thoughts. This method, or tool, will allow for the shift of consciousness (awareness) necessary to return from the past to the present, selecting the many options or alternatives that are usually available and best suit the situation. Then, when someone does or says something that doesn't live up to your expectations, you will have the freedom to see the situation clearly. Instead of subconsciously reverting to childhood thinking, you will have the opportunity to examine your expectations, change your thoughts, and decide upon the best course of action.

Keep adding little by little and you
will soon have a big hoard.
                    Latin Proverb

My journey from reaction to response has unfolded over the course of many years — and it continues. In changing my thoughts and behaviors, I have learned to be gentle with myself, striving for progress, not perfection. And it has all been wonderfully worthwhile. No longer am I helplessly blown by the winds of subconscious, control-based expectations. With continued practice and discipline, I am increasingly able to respond rather than react.

Furthermore, and much to my surprise and delight, I am now developing the ability to replace control-based expectations with benevolence-based thoughts that are grounded in my desire to be good to myself and others. This, for me, is the greatest miracle of all. It has led to an abundance of serenity and joy, as well as growing compassion, enabling me to respond to situations with humility, relating to other people as one human being, one soul, to another.

Chapter 14:
Management of Anger and Other Emotions

Situational mediators employ an assortment of methods to manage the anger and other emotions that participants commonly experience during mediation. In the material that follows I will describe a number of these methods. However, the efficacy of any given method depends on the degree to which the mediator has developed the capacity to *respond* rather than *react* to his or her mediation participants.

It would be unrealistic to think that mediators don't experience a variety of feelings during the course of mediation. I myself regularly experience emotions ranging from disappointment to sadness, frustration to anger, happiness to awe, etc. For example, here's what happened to my emotions during a recent divorce mediation.

A couple with one adult daughter was divorcing after 25 years of marriage. The wife initiated divorce mediation to, in her words, "end my co-dependent relationship with my husband and his gambling addiction." During the *Getting Current* process, I learned that: (1) the wife had always been the primary wage earner for the family; (2) the husband worked as a car salesman, but rarely made more than $20,000 per year; (3) the husband admitted to having a gambling addiction but refused to attend "any of those soppy recovery meetings"; and (4) the couple's marital assets were limited to their home equity and her retirement account. Their debt included substantial credit card balances.

During the first two sessions, I experienced moments of sadness around this couple's situation. Knowing the perniciousness of addictions (no matter what the type), I felt sad for both of them. He admitted his gambling addiction, but was convinced that Gamblers Anonymous was beneath him. She took more than 25 years to realize the addictive nature of her co-dependency and how it had negatively affected her marriage.

The third session dealt with division of assets and allocation of debts. Normally, sessions involving limited assets, such as this one, usually take no more than two or three hours. In this situation, however, it took more than nine hours (four additional sessions) to resolve these issues!

During these additional sessions, I experienced the husband as alternately obsessive-compulsive and petulant, while the wife was both bitter and coddling. In fact, they seemed to play off one another, as if in a well-rehearsed dance. For example, when the husband became obsessive-compulsive, she would coddle and otherwise baby him; when she became bitter, he would sulk or throw a tantrum.

I also experienced a change in my own emotions during these additional sessions — sadness occasionally tinged with frustration. Nonetheless, I was able to respond compassionately; that is, until the second to the last session when my frustration boiled over. It was then that I *reacted* and chastised the husband for being stubborn and inflexible.

He reacted to my strong words with the same type of sullen-ness I saw when his wife became bitter. Recognizing this, I became aware of my own reactivity and promptly apologized for it.

The point I want to make here is that situational mediators must develop the capability to be aware of and promptly deal with their own emotions before they can effectively help participants manage theirs. They must have done sufficient internal work to *respond* rather than *react* to participants; they must recognize their own reactivity and promptly take responsibility for it (in this instance, by apologizing).

This point made, I will now describe a number of the methods employed by situational mediators to help participants manage their anger and other emotions:

1. *Providing Information*

One way in which situational mediators help participants manage their emotions is by providing information. For example, in Chapter 1, I provided legal information to temper an angry exchange between divorcing couple John and Mary:

"I don't want a divorce! She should try harder! I can't believe she thinks divorce is good for our kids!" John insists, raising his voice.

"I hear you. So you want Mary to try harder to stay in the marriage?"

"Yeah!" John snaps back.

"And what about you, Mary?"

After a moment's contemplation, Mary responds: "I tried for a long time. He wouldn't go to counseling and now he says I'm the one who hasn't worked on it. I can't live with him anymore — with his drinking and all. I never know when he's going to yell at me or the kids."

"Oh sure, Mary. What about your boyfriend?" John asks, angrily.

"He's not my boyfriend. He's just a friend," Mary counters.

At this point I intervene, saying: "Hold on folks. Since part of my job as a mediator is to provide information, perhaps it would be helpful for you to know that I neither encourage nor discourage divorce. This is your decision alone, and you can take whatever time you need to make it."

"No, I need to do this now!" Mary insists.

"I hear you. So perhaps I could mention that here in Arizona, as in most other states, if one person wants a divorce there's literally nothing the other person can do to stop it. But the other person does have a choice as to how it's carried out. They can enter the legal system with separate lawyers or they can mediate — unless of course they use a paralegal service or do it themselves."

Later on in this divorce mediation (Chapter 4) I helped the husband manage his sadness by providing information about the grief process:

John turns away from me and begins to cry. I wait silently, going within to seek Guidance while giving John time and space. Minutes pass. John reaches for a tissue, wipes his eyes and nose, and turns back toward me.

I ask: "Is it okay for you to be emotional like that?"

"Not really. But I'm not myself lately."

"Remember John that this is part of the grief process. When I was going through my divorce, one day I felt fine but the next I was totally depressed and crying. It was really hard."

"It sure is, especially with Mary thinking she's so high and mighty."

"I hear you. But I can tell you that it turned out to be a really good thing for me. I got to work through all kinds of emotional stuff including a lot of pent-up anger. And as I already told you, many blessings came from it."

"Yeah, I guess."

Situational mediators also provide personal information to help participants manage their emotions, as I did in Chapter 7:

Visibly shaken and appearing pale, Patrick lowered his head to the table and began to sob.

Everyone remained silent until several moments later when I said: "You know, Patrick, I find that my tears can be cleansing. How about you?"

Without lifting his head, Patrick replied: "I'm not sure. I'm not sure of anything any more. She's right, though. I was a lousy father."

Providing psychological information also effectively helps participants manage their emotions. Here is an example from

Chapter 11 in which I helped an executive, Kent, manage his feelings of betrayal and hopelessness:

"So you feel betrayed?"

"Yeah, really betrayed; by Bob, by Peterson, and by the Executive Committee. And now I don't know who to trust. I'm nowhere; you know, just really screwed with no one to turn to, and…I don't know…it all seems so hopeless. Maybe I should just move on; you know, get another job. I don't know…"

"Is that an option for you?"

"No, not really. Sure, I can get another job, but I really don't want to; we would have to move back East or to Los Angeles. There aren't any other large med-mal companies with offices in Phoenix. I've just gotta figure some way out of this mess."

"Do you consider yourself a *victim*?"

"I guess; kinda."

"Really? You seem like a pretty capable guy to me, while a *victim* is somebody who views himself as helpless; somebody who feels a lot of self-pity and believes he is helpless to do anything about it. Is that you?"

"Well, no. Not really."

"Okay then. Let me ask you about all of this resentment you feel; about the Executive Committee's decision to hire Cynthia, about Jim Peterson, about Cynthia: isn't that all about being a victim and self-pity?"

"I don't know; maybe."

"Well, Kent, I've come to define *resentment* as *a hostile form of self-pity*, and whenever I find myself feeling self-piteous it helps me break out of it by reminding myself of this definition — because I really don't like thinking of myself as self-piteous. What about you?"

"I'm the same way; I've always taken care of myself. I'm not one to feel sorry for myself."

"So you don't see yourself as self-piteous in this situation with Cynthia?"

"Well I didn't, but now I don't know; I'm not sure. I'm starting to rethink it."

As with all of the other methods employed by situational mediators to help participants manage their emotions, the provision of information is aimed at helping them disengage from reaction (the repeating of old, subconscious behavior patterns) so they can focus their thinking on the issues at hand. Only then can participants recognize the various options and alternatives available to them and make conscious decisions (*respond*) about their dispute.

2. *Reminding Participants about the Mutual Respect Rule*
All of the *Mediation Rules and Procedures* set forth in the Appendix include the following Rule:

> "An atmosphere of mutual respect should prevail during the mediation. The parties should address each other by name and refrain from interrupting, criticizing, intimidating, or otherwise detracting from this atmosphere."

Another way situational mediators help participants with their emotions is by reminding them of this Rule and securing their agreement to abide by it. Indeed, situational mediators introduce this intervention early on in the mediation, while explaining the *Rules and Procedures*. They make it a point to ask for permission from the participants to remind them about this Rule should they interrupt, criticize, or argue back and forth later on.

For example, in Chapter 1, I intervened when a husband interrupted his wife during their divorce mediation:

"Have you and John talked about the timing of when you might go back to work?"
"We tried."

John then interrupts loudly: "What do you expect? You lay this on me, and want me to act like nothing happened. I can't believe you. You…"

I intervene: "Excuse me, John. I understand that some of these things can be really difficult to hear, and that anger is very normal in these circumstances. I know it was hard for me in my own divorce. But remember, you agreed to let Mary talk without interruption. Right?"

"Yeah, but she acts so high and mighty!"

"I hear you. But would you try not to interrupt? It's important in terms of maintaining an atmosphere of mutual respect. Okay?"

"Yeah, I guess," John says, dejectedly.

And in Chapter 10, I interceded in workplace mediation between two executives, Kent and Cynthia:

Kent interrupts: "That's ridiculous! This has nothing to do with my judgment. It's about her lack of experience and micromanaging me. She…"

I break in: "Wait a minute, Kent. Remember about not interrupting each other?"

"Yeah, but it's ridiculous," Kent answers, sullenly.

"Kent, I know it can be hard to just listen, especially when you hear something that you really don't agree with. And yet, would you be willing to let Cynthia have her turn without interrupting her?"

Slouching down in his chair, Kent replies: "Fine."

"Thank you."

3. *Focusing on Goals*

As explained in Chapter 13, goals are future-oriented whereas emotions are based in the past (unmet expectations). Focusing on goals is another way in which situational mediators: (1) help participants detach from the past and the emotional reactions that stem from it; and (2) begin to focus on the present and how they might respond so that things will be different in the future.

For example, in Chapter 3, I helped a divorcing couple, Mary and John, deal with their anger by focusing on a shared goal:

Mary interrupts: "That's not true! He's only been there twice. I needed a ride to the gym. If you had fixed my car on time, I wouldn't have had to ask him!"

John argues back: "Oh yeah, right, Mary!"

Mary counters: "You don't know anything. And anyway, you never cared before. You…"

John shouts: "What about you!"

I intervene assertively: "Just a minute, folks. I can see how angry you both are, and as I said before, that's very common and normal in mediation. But remember your goal of getting through this quickly and inexpensively? Do you think this is helping?"

Mary replies, close to tears: "I don't like it when he says that. He's just a friend, and I resent that kind of accusation. At least he listens to me."

"I hear you, Mary. But I wonder if arguing like this is helpful. You do share in the goal of getting through this quickly, inexpensively, and with as little emotional stress and strain as possible, right?"

"Yes…"

It should be noted that helping participants focus on goals is central to the *ANGER* acronym explained in Chapter 13. Thus, in the forgoing dialogue I made it a point to: (1) Acknowledge John and Mary's anger; (2) Normalize it as commonplace during mediation; and (3) remind them of their shared Goal to get "through this quickly and inexpensively."

Later on in this divorce mediation (Chapter 5), I helped John focus on another one of his goals — for Mary to become financially independent:

"And I take it that you want Mary to become financially independent as quickly as possible, right?"

"Yeah."

"And she needs computer training to get a better paying job, right?"

"I guess so."

"So wouldn't you benefit by paying Mary support, at least during the time it takes her to complete this training?"

"Yeah, I guess it would. But she expects me to support her in grand style."

"When did she say that?"

"Well, she didn't say that exactly. I don't know what she really wants. We can't seem to talk without arguing."

"Okay, perhaps when she and I meet privately I could ask what she's looking for in terms of support. Would that be okay?"

"Yeah, that would be good."

4. Presenting Metaphors

Situational mediators present participants with metaphors to help them deal with their emotions. A familiar mental image often provides an efficient and effective way for the mediator to intervene on anger and other intense emotions.

For example, early in mediation situational mediators present the "airplane ride" metaphor (Chapter 1). This is because they know that this metaphor is apt to be helpful later on; often all that's needed for participants to put their emotions aside is for the mediator to acknowledge that they hit "bumpy weather."

Here's another example from Chapter 1 in which I used a metaphor about having been "down this road" to help John and Mary deal with their emotions:

Looking angrily at John, Mary says: "You don't want to talk about anything, do you John! You just want to work on those cars of yours. You never want to…"

John cuts in: "What do you mean? What's there to talk about? You've already made up your mind about everything!"

"Right, John. You're always right, aren't you! You're perfect, aren't you! You never do anything wrong, do you!" Mary lashes out.

John angrily replies: "Well let me tell you something! This whole thing is your idea; so don't make it seem like I don't care about my kids. I want to be with them as much as you do!"

Mary begins to cry. John remains silent, glaring at her.

After a couple of seconds, I say: "I imagine this is very difficult and frustrating for both of you, and I also imagine that you have been down this road many times before, arguing with each other like this. Is that right?"

"Many times," Mary says.

"That's an understatement!" John exclaims.

"Well, then let me ask if it's gotten you where you want to be?"

"No." Mary responds.

John merely shakes his head from side to side, indicating "no."

"Well, I guess that's why you are here. So let me ask you another question: After all these years of being together, do you really expect that either of you is going to all of a sudden change?"

"No," Mary answers.

John doesn't respond, so I ask him: "What about you, John? At this point in time, do you expect Mary to change?"

"No, not really."

"Okay, so would both of you agree that the only thing that can change is yourselves; that is, how you behave toward each other?"

"Yes," Mary says.

John merely nods his head, indicating "yes."

"Okay then, Mary. Knowing this, do you think it's helpful to lash out at John when he says or does something that aggravates you?"

"No. But I can still get angry!"

"Absolutely, and I'm not suggesting that you shouldn't. All I'm asking is whether you want to keep reacting as you have in the past?"

"Oh, I see. No. Certainly not. I want to live my own life."

"And what about you, John?"

"I'm done with her! I just want to get this over with," he

replies.

"Okay. So if I were to see either of you slipping back, going down that old road again, could I bring that to your attention?"

"Yep," John answers.

"Okay," Mary replies.

It should be noted that the foregoing dialogue is also illustrative of how situational mediators use the last two letters of the *ANGER* acronym to help participants with their emotions. I first asked John and Mary about their Expectations ("After all these years of being together, do you really expect that either of you is going to all of a sudden change?"), and then asked about their Response ("Okay, so would both of you agree that the only thing that can change is your response; that is, how you behave toward each other?") Thus, as you have just seen, the *ANGER* acronym is useful in whole or in part to help participants manage their emotions.

Later on in the divorce mediation with John and Mary (Chapter 4), I offered them another metaphor about "heat and light" in combination with the "bumpy weather" portion of the airplane metaphor:

"Looks like Mary's comps show that your home is worth $195,000, right?"

Mary asserts: "Yes! That's a lot more than John said it was worth!"

John argues: "That's not what my comps show! We don't have a pool and our street..."

Mary protests: "You said you weren't going to get comps!"

John counters: "Well I did! So what?"

I intercede: "I'm wondering if this exchange isn't adding more heat than light. In other words, is it generating more anger than shedding light on the value of your home? The comps show what they show, right? Remember that nothing is final in mediation until you sign a settlement agreement. It may turn out that both of you will change your minds several times during the course of the mediation, as it seems John did in this instance. Right?"

John replies: "Yep."

Mary complains: "That's just like him!"

I respond to Mary: "So what I'm hearing is that when John changes his mind you become frustrated."

"Yes, I can't trust him. He always says he will do one thing and then does another!"

"Alright, I hear you. My experience is that trust is a very common issue in mediation, especially during divorce. And a certain amount of mistrust can help you remain alert when making decisions. But would you agree that John should get whatever information he needs to be fully informed about the home?"

"Yes, but he doesn't have to lie!"

"Well, are you open to the possibility that he didn't lie? That he just changed his mind?"

"Yes, but I doubt it."

"Okay, fair enough. And are you also open to the possibility that arguing back and forth may be hindering your goal of agreement on the value of the home?"

"Yes. I'm sorry."

"No need to be sorry. We just hit some bumpy weather, that's all."

5. *Providing Behavioral Tools*

Situational mediators also offer tools that participants can use to manage their emotions. These tools are particularly useful in situations involving participants who are in the early stages of the grief process, as was the case in Chapter 4 when I offered to help the husband in divorce mediation by means of a "hand signal":

John angrily cuts in: "Damn it! I don't have to sit here and listen to this. I have a few beers, that's all!"

I intercede, leaning toward John and saying: "Okay, John, we can talk about that. But one of your goals is to get through this quickly and inexpensively. Right?"

"Yeah."

"Well, does interrupting help you reach that goal?"

"No, but I don't want to hear that crap about drinking!" John counters.

"I hear you, John. But remember, you don't expect Mary to all of a sudden change, do you?"

"No."

"And you want to get through this quickly and inexpensively, right?"

"Yeah."

"So what if I were to remind you of this goal by, say, holding my hand up a little? That would be our signal that you are getting off track in terms of this? Do you think that would help?"

"Fine," John answers.

Another behavioral tool is a "time out." Sometimes, all a participant needs is a time out, a break, to compose himself or herself and thereby avoid another angry outburst. Finally, as explained in Chapter 13, situational mediators also offer the use of a rubber band as a behavior tool; they describe how participants can place a rubber band around their wrist and then snap it whenever they feel themselves slipping into reactivity.

6. *Suggesting Private Sessions*
In Chapter 5, I suggested private sessions with John and Mary to help them deal with their anger:

Appearing agitated, John blurts out: "Damn it! This isn't my idea! She's the one who wants a divorce, and now I have to pay."

Mary counters: "I was the one who stayed home with the children! You paid more attention to those cars than anything else!"

"There you go again! If I was such a lousy husband, why didn't you leave a long time ago? I'll tell you why, because it's not true. What about all those times I wanted to be with you? You always had an excuse…"

Mary interrupts: "I had good reason and I don't see how that…"

John cuts in: "Well now you have your boyfriend. I'm sick and tired of you making it seem like this is entirely my fault. You never wanted to be alone with me. You started sleeping in the other room right after we had Charlie. And after Sarah, you wouldn't do anything but bitch and complain. Now it's all my fault and you want me to pay, and…"

John's face becomes flushed and his voice constricted. Lowering his head, he appears to be on the verge of tears.

I wait a moment or two and then intercede by asking:

"Remember when I told both of you that sometimes it's helpful to meet in private sessions? This is where I'd like to be alone with each of you."

"Yes," Mary answers.

Without looking up, John nods his head.

I continue: "Well, I'm wondering if we could do that now, perhaps starting with John?"

"That's fine," Mary responds.

John remains silent.

"Good. Mary, would you excuse John and me for a while? I'll come get you when we're done."

Private sessions are particularly useful when participants are highly reactive and repeatedly argue back and forth. Or perhaps they're aggressive, and try to intimidate or dominate one another. The seclusion provided by meeting privately with each participant affords the mediator the opportunity to discuss these matters humanisticly. This seclusion also goes a long way toward avoiding any embarrassment they may feel if these matters were discussed in joint session (with everyone present).

7. *Reminding Participants about the Rule concerning Suspension or Termination of Mediation*

The *Mediation Rules and Procedures* set forth in the Appendix include the following Rule:

"The mediator may suspend or terminate the process upon concluding that a party is unable or unwilling to participate meaningfully or that agreement is unlikely."

Reminding participants of this Rule is usually a last resort, a final attempt by the mediator to intercede on persistent reactivity, disrespect, or aggressiveness. I typically find it best to make a statement like the following before resorting to this Rule: "You know, folks, based on what's been going on here, it seems to me that mediation may not be appropriate for you, and that you may be better off hiring separate lawyers." Time and again I have seen this kind of statement produce a paradoxical result; instead of continuing to argue or otherwise act out, participants suddenly redirect their efforts toward getting the mediator to give them another chance to continue with mediation.

8. *Seeking Spiritual Guidance*

There are times when I simply don't know what to say or do to help participants with their emotions. For example, say a participant suddenly begins to cry and I'm not sure how to compassionately help manage his or her emotions. This is a time when I find it best to seek spiritual Guidance; to go within to that deep and eternal place that resides within all of us; to ask for direction from the Source of all empathy, humility, and compassion.

That is what occurred in Chapter 4 when during divorce mediation John suddenly began to cry:

"How are you doing?"
"Okay, I guess."
"It's really hard sometimes, isn't it?"
"Yeah. It's just that…"

John turns away from me and begins to cry. I wait silently, going within to seek Guidance while giving John time and space. Minutes pass. John reaches for a tissue, wipes his eyes and nose, and turns back toward me.

I ask: "Is it okay for you to be emotional like that?"

"Not really. But I'm not myself lately."

"Remember John that this is part of the grief process. When I was going through my divorce, one day I felt fine but the next I was totally depressed and crying. It was really hard."

"It sure is, especially with Mary thinking she's so high and mighty."

"I hear you. But I can tell you that it turned out to be a really good thing for me. I got to work through all kinds of emotional stuff including a lot of pent-up anger. And, as I already told you, many blessings came from it."

I wanted to respond compassionately to John's grief; however, uncertain of how to accomplish this, I went within to seek Guidance. It was then that I was graced with the ability to respond to John's grief with empathy, humility, and compassion.

Another example of situations in which I regularly seek spiritual Guidance is when participants become extremely angry at one another; for example, they argue nonstop and it's impossible for me to get a word in. This is another time that I find it best to seek spiritual Guidance—and it's uncanny how quickly I receive the direction I need to respond humanisticly.

I could go on to give other examples of instances in which I have sought such Guidance; however, suffice it to say that I regularly do so before the start of each mediation session and at any other time that I want or need to call on a Higher Power. No matter what's going on or who is involved, I have come to trust that seeking spiritual Guidance produces beneficent outcomes. They may not be the outcomes that I wanted, and occasionally involve termination of mediation, but I trust that they are the ones that were needed by everyone involved.

Seeking Guidance in this way has become a spiritual practice for me, not only in my role as mediator, but in all my affairs. Based on results, it is this above all that empowers me to be instrumental in helping participants resolve conflicts.

Appendix

This appendix contains samples of forms that may be used in different situations when mediation is appropriate. The forms are included in this book to provide you with examples that have worked in other practices. You will want to modify these forms to best suit the needs of your practice.

This appendix contains the following forms:

Confidential Client Intake Information (Divorce)

	Date:
Name (First, Middle, Last):	
Street Address: (include apartment number, if appropriate)	
City, State, and Zip:	
Home Telephone:	Work Telephone:
Email Address:	Cell Telephone:
Date of Birth:	SS #:
Employer/Occupation:	
Date of Marriage:	Location of Marriage:
Separated: ☐ Yes ☐ No	If Yes, Date:
Initiator: ☐ Self ☐ Spouse	Interest in Reconciliation: ☐ Yes ☐ No
Attorney:	Attorney's Telephone:
Counselor:	Counselor's Telephone:
Court Actions that have been filed: ☐ Restraining Order ☐ Order of Protection ☐ Separation ☐ Divorce	
Is there a physical safety issue? ☐ Yes ☐ No	

Information about your child(ren) from this marriage

Complete Name	Date of Birth	SS #	Primary Residence
			☐ Father ☐ Mother
			☐ Father ☐ Mother
			☐ Father ☐ Mother
			☐ Father ☐ Mother

Child(ren) told about separation or divorce	☐ Yes	☐ No
Is wife currently pregnant?	☐ Yes ☐ No	
Have you been married previously?	☐ Yes ☐ No	

If yes, provide information about your children from previous marriage(s).

Complete Name	Date of Birth	Primary Residence
		☐ Father ☐ Mother
		☐ Father ☐ Mother
		☐ Father ☐ Mother

How did you find out about Out-of-Court Solutions?

Agreement to Mediate (Divorce)

This agreement is made between the undersigned parties and a Mediator with Out-of-Court Solutions, an Arizona corporation. The parties acknowledge that they desire to reach agreement in a fair and cooperative manner, using mediation, a voluntary process. The issues to be discussed may include separation, divorce, custody of minor children, child support, spousal maintenance, division of property, and costs of mediation. This signifies that the parties will:

1. Attend scheduled sessions at mutually agreed upon times. Failure to provide 24 hours notice for appointment cancellation will result in a two-hour charge.

2. Compensate Out-of-Court Solutions at the rate of $220 per hour for time spent with the parties and for time required to study documents, research issues, correspond, telephone call, prepare memoranda and agreements, and do such other things as may be reasonably necessary to facilitate the parties' reaching agreement. The parties further understand that they are obligated to reimburse Out-of-Court Solutions for copying, postage, long distance phone calls, and other reasonable out-of-pocket expenses incurred during the mediation. A deposit of payment of $440 toward hourly fees and expenses shall be paid to Out-of-Court Solutions along with signing of this Agreement. Any unearned amount of this deposit will be refunded.

3. Assume joint and several liability for Out-of-Court Solutions' fees and charges, with the understanding that the parties may agree to divide the payment of the fees and charges between themselves as they deem appropriate.

4. Uphold the confidentiality of the mediation process, agreeing that: Out-of-Court Solutions need not retain any notes or other records of the mediation; not to subpoena any records or representatives of Out-of-Court Solutions in any pending or future legal action or proceeding.

_____   _____
Party   Date

_____   _____
Party   Date

_____   _____
Out-of-Court Solutions, by Oliver Ross, Mediator   Date

Mediation Rules & Procedures (Divorce)

1. The mediator facilitates communications and negotiations, enabling each of the parties to discuss options and make informed decisions. The mediator does not function as a judge, attorney, or therapist. The parties are encouraged to seek independent legal advice before execution of a mediated agreement or at any time during the mediation process.

2. The parties begin by meeting in joint session with the mediator. Excluding administrative matters such as scheduling of appointments, all communications are made in the presence of all parties with the exception that the mediator may from time to time consider it helpful to meet briefly (caucus) with each of the parties separately.

3. An atmosphere of mutual respect should prevail during the mediation. The parties should address each other by name and refrain from interrupting, criticizing, intimidating, or otherwise detracting from this atmosphere.

4. The parties agree that the best interest of minor children is of primary importance.

5. The mediator may encourage the parties to obtain expert advice concerning taxes, appraisals, financial planning, and mental health.

6. The parties agree to gather and disclose all the information and documents required for the mediator to understand the issues presented, and all parties to make fully informed decisions. The parties agree to provide copies of financial documents and statements, including mortgage, living expense, tax, pension plan, and other financial items.

7. Unless agreed otherwise, pending completion of mediation the parties shall not: transfer, encumber, or otherwise dispose of any assets; make any loans or extraordinary charges under any credit card; commence or take any further action, including entry of default, in a legal proceeding for dissolution of marriage or legal separation.

8. The mediator may suspend or terminate the process upon concluding that a party is unable or unwilling to participate meaningfully, or that agreement is unlikely.

Party	Date
Party	Date
Out-of-Court Solutions, by Oliver Ross, Mediator	Date

Assets & Liabilities (Divorce)

Client _____ Date _____

I. Bank Accounts (Checking, Savings, Credit Unions, Certificates of Deposit, etc.)

Bank Name	Account Number	Balance	Name on Account
		subtotal	

II. Non-Retirement Investment Accounts

Brokerage Firm	Account Number	Balance	Name on Account
		subtotal	

Please continue on next page.

III. Stocks & Bonds

Company Name/# Shares	Value/Share	Value as of	Name on Account

subtotal

IV. Stock Options

Company Name	# Shares	Exercise Date	Price	Value	as of	Name on Account

subtotal

Please continue on next page.

V. IRA, 401(k), Defined Benefit Pension Plan, Annuities, etc.

Description/ Plan Name	Acct #	Value	as of	Name on Account

subtotal

VI. Real Estate (Homes, Land, Buildings, Vacation Homes, etc.)

Property #1	
Address	
Date of Purchase	
Present Value	
First Mortgage Company	Loan Number
Name(s) on First Mortgage	Balance Due
Second Mortgage Company	Loan Number
Name(s) on Second Mortgage	Balance Due

Please continue on next page.

Property #2	
Address	
Date of Purchase	
Present Value	
First Mortgage Company	Loan Number
Name(s) on First Mortgage	Balance Due
Second Mortgage Company	Loan Number
Name(s) on Second Mortgage	Balance Due

VII. Business Interests (Corporations, Partnerships, Joint Ventures, Proprietorships, etc.)

Name of Business	
Location	
☐ Corporation ☐ Partnership ☐ Sole Proprietorship	Percentage of Ownership
	Federal Tax ID No.

Name of Business	
Location	
☐ Corporation ☐ Partnership ☐ Sole Proprietorship	Percentage of Ownership
	Federal Tax ID No.

Please continue on next page.

VIII. Vehicles (Cars, Boats, Trailers, Motorcycles, Motor Homes, etc.)

Description	License Plate	Value	Loan With	Loan #	Bal. Due

subtotal

IX. Life Insurance with Cash Surrender Value

Company	Policy #	Value	Owner(s)

subtotal

X. Accounts Receivable (Notes, Loans to Others, Mortgages Receivable, Contracts, etc.)

Due From	Balance	To Whom Due

subtotal

Please continue on next page.

XI. Income Tax Refunds or Amounts Due

Federal or State	Year	Refund	Tax Due
		subtotal	

XII. Other Property (Furnishings, Tools, Equipment, Antiques, Collections, Jewelry, Art, etc.)

Description	Value
	subtotal

Income & Expense Statements (Divorce)

Client_____   **Date** _____

Income (per month)

I. Salary

	Present	Projected	Comments
Gross Salary			
Deductions			
A. Federal Income Tax			
B. State Income Tax			
C. FICA (SS/Medicare)			
D. Health Insurance			
E. Life Insurance			
F. Union Dues			
G. 401(k)			
H. Pension			
I. Other			
Net Salary			

II. Other Income

	Present	Projected	Comments
A. Bonus			
B. Auto Allowance			
C. Rental			
D. Interest/Dividend			
E. Trust			
F. Other			
Total Other Income			

Please continue to next page.

Client_____   **Date**_____

Expense Summary (per month)

Please budget the following expenses on a monthly basis over the next 12 months.

I. Home	Self	Children	Comments
A. Mortgage (Principle, Interest, Tax)			
B. Apartment Rental			
C. Insurance			
D. Electricity			
E. Gas			
F. Telephone			
G. Water/Trash/Sewer			
H. Yard Maintenance			
I. Pool Service			
J. Association Fees			
K. Maintenance/Repairs			
L. Other			
Subtotal Home			

II. Transportation	Self	Children	Comments
A. Car Payment			
B. Insurance			
C. Maintenance/Repairs			
D. Gasoline			
E. License/Tax			
F. Public Transportation			
G. Other			
Subtotal Transportation			

Please continue to next page.

III. Insurance	Self	Children	Comments
A. Life			
B. Health			
C. Accident			
D. Disability			
E. Other			
Subtotal Insurance			

IV. Uninsured Medical	Self	Children	Comments
A. Doctors			
B. Dentist			
C. Orthodontist			
D. Vision			
E. Medicine			
F. Other			
Subtotal Uninsured Medical			

V. Household	Self	Children	Comments
A. Food/Groceries			
B. Food/Restaurant			
C. Food/Lunches			
D. Laundry/Dry Cleaning			
E. Cable TV			
F. Housekeeping			
G. Newspaper Magazine			
H. Other			
Subtotal Household			

VI. Children	Self	Children	Comments
A. Daycare/Sitter			
B. Preschool			
C. School Supplies/Tutoring			
D. Allowance			
E. Recreation			
F. Summer/Camp			
G. Other			
Subtotal Children			

Please continue to next page.

VII. Personal	Self	Children	Comments
A. Entertainment			
B. Education			
C. Hair Care/Grooming			
D. Clothing			
E. Personal Items			
F. Dues/Subscriptions			
G. Other			
Subtotal Personal			

VIII. Debt Service	Self	Children	Comments
A. Credit Card			
B. Credit Card			
C. Credit Card			
D. Credit Card			
E. Other			
F. Other			
Subtotal Debt Service			

IX. Miscellaneous	Self	Children	Comments
A. Child Support			
B. Other Taxes			
C. Vacation			
D. Gifts			
E. Donations			
F. Pets			
G. Other			
Subtotal Miscellaneous			

Confidential Client Intake Information (Families)

Name (First, Middle, Last):	Date:
Street Address:	Apt. #:
City, State, ZIP:	
Home Telephone:	Work Telephone:
Email Address:	Cell Telephone:
Date of Birth:	SS #:
Employer/Occupation:	
Is there a physical safety issue?	☐ Yes ☐ No
Attorney:	Attorney's Telephone:
Counselor:	Counselor's Telephone:
How did you find out about Out-of-Court Solutions?	

Agreement To Mediate (Families)

We, the undersigned, agree to voluntarily attempt to resolve our differences through mediation. We understand that mediation is a voluntary, non-judicial process. Accordingly, we agree that:

1. Anything said or prepared in writing for or during mediation is private and confidential to the undersigned persons.

2. We will not subpoena or otherwise involve the mediator in any court proceedings, lawsuits, or other legal actions.

3. We understand that it is not necessary to have a lawyer present for mediation, but if any of us choose to have a lawyer present we understand he/she will be asked to follow certain rules and procedures as explained by the mediator.

_____   _____
Party   Date

_____   _____
Party   Date

_____   _____
Out-of-Court Solutions, by Oliver Ross, Mediator   Date

Mediation Rules & Procedures (Workplace)

1. The Mediator facilitates communications and negotiations, enabling each of the parties to discuss options and make informed decisions. Formal rules of evidence do not apply.

2. The Mediator does not function as an attorney or as a judge. The parties understand that the mediator cannot impose any agreement on them that they do not find acceptable.

3. The parties agree to provide all information and documents required for the Mediator to understand the issues presented.

4. Anything said or any documents prepared for mediation are strictly confidential. The parties agree to maintain this confidentiality during mediation and also not to subpoena the records or representatives of Out-of-Court Solutions in any pending or future legal action or proceeding.

5. The parties begin by meeting in joint session with the Mediator. Thereafter, the mediator may from time to time consider it helpful to meet briefly (caucus) with each of the parties separately.

6. An atmosphere of mutual respect should prevail during the mediation. The parties should address each other by name, and refrain from interrupting, criticizing, intimidating, or otherwise detracting from this atmosphere.

7. The Mediator may discuss the parties' mediation process with any attorney retained by any party as individual legal counsel or any labor organization. The Mediator will provide copies of correspondence, draft agreements, and written documentation to either of these representatives at the parties' request.

8. The Mediator may suspend or terminate the process upon concluding that a party is unable or unwilling to participate meaningfully, or that agreement is unlikely.

_____   _____
Party   Date

_____   _____
Party   Date

_____   _____
Out-of-Court Solutions, by Oliver Ross, Mediator   Date

Request To Initiate Contract Mediation (Real Estate)

Date _____

1. **Party Requesting Mediation** *Please Provide Your:*

Name _____

Phone _____ *Fax* _____

Address _____

_____

You are the:

□ *Buyer* □ *Seller* □ *Broker* □ *Sales Agent* □ *Builder/Contractor*

□ *Other* _____

If this party has legal or other counsel in this matter, provide name, address, and telephone number:

_____

_____

2. **Other Party(ies) to be Included in Mediation** *(Include any party whose attendance at the mediation would be necessary or helpful in resolving the dispute)*:

Name _____

Phone _____ *Fax* _____

Address _____

_____

This party is the:

□ *Buyer* □ *Seller* □ *Broker* □ *Sales Agent* □ *Builder/Contractor*

□ *Other* _____

If this party has legal or other counsel in this matter, provide name, address, and telephone number:

_____

_____

Please continue to next page.

Name _____

Phone _____ *Fax* _____

Address _____

_____

This party is the:

☐ *Buyer* ☐ *Seller* ☐ *Broker* ☐ *Sales Agent* ☐ *Builder/Contractor*

☐ *Other* _____

If this party has legal or other counsel in this matter, provide name, address, and telephone number:

_____

_____

- -

Name _____

Phone _____ *Fax* _____

Address _____

_____

This party is the:

☐ *Buyer* ☐ *Seller* ☐ *Broker* ☐ *Sales Agent* ☐ *Builder/Contractor*

☐ *Other* _____

If this party has legal or other counsel in this matter, provide name, address, and telephone number:

_____

_____

3. Brief Description of Claim

_____

_____

_____

Use a separate page to provide additional description of claim.

4. **Amount of Money Involved** $ _____

5. **Court Proceedings**

If any formal court proceedings have been filed in this matter, provide:

Name of party who commenced court proceedings_____;

Court case #_____;

Name, address, and telephone number of legal counsel, if any

Name _____

Phone _____ *Fax* _____

Address _____

_____

Suspension or Termination of Mediation

Situational mediators are interested in the outcome of mediation, but it isn't their primary focus. They are fully aware that it is beyond their control whether participants resolve disputes through mediation. Situational mediators realize that some people are unwilling, unable, or incapable of completing the mediation process, and they are open to the possibility that these people might be better served by another form of dispute resolution, arbitration, or litigation.

Here are the most common situations that give rise to suspension or termination of mediation by mediators:

Violation of Rules and Procedures

At the outset of mediation, situational mediators ensure that participants fully understand and agree to specific Rules and Procedures (included in this Appendix). These Rules and Procedures include provisions for the participants' maintenance of an "atmosphere of mutual respect," full disclosure of all relevant "information and documents," and the mediator's right to "suspend or terminate mediation." Nevertheless, participants are apt to forget about one of more rule or procedure—especially when overtaken by anger or other emotions.

Situational mediators respond to occasional violations of a rule or a procedure by empathically and compassionately reminding participants of these provisions and of their agreement to abide by them. They may also warn participants that any further violation would result in suspension or termination of mediation. However, should any egregious violation (e.g., physical abuse) or repeated violations (e.g., recurrent threats) occur, situational mediators terminate mediation.

Inability to Make Informed Decisions

The ability to make informed decisions is central to mediation. Thus, situational mediators suspend mediation whenever they sense that a participant is unable to make informed decisions due to depression, addiction, or another perceived disability. They make it clear that the mediation will not proceed unless and until the participant employs an attorney, financial consultant, or someone else who is qualified to help make decisions. Should a participant refuse to obtain such help, situational mediators terminate mediation.

Potential Harm to Self or Others

As mediation progresses conditions may come to light that cause the mediator concern about a participant doing harm to him- or herself or to others (particularly children in divorce and family situations). Previous suicide attempts may be disclosed. Involvement with pornography may be revealed. Recurrent use of alcohol or other drugs may be divulged.

When conditions such as these come to light, situational mediators recognize their limits and compassionately insist on written clearance from a psychologist or other mental health professional before proceeding further with mediation. Situational mediators are unwilling to put anyone at risk of harm as a result of participation in mediation.

Index